W9-BRX-279

The Catholic Church in the Land of the Holy Cross:

A History of the Diocese of Portland, Maine

Vincent A. Lapomarda

Publisher:
Editions du Signe
B.P. 94 – 67038 Strasbourg, Cedex 2, France

Design and Layout:
OM Design

Photography:
Patrice Thébault

Publishing Director:
Christian Riehl

Director of Publication:
Dr. Claude –Bernard Costecalde

Publishing Assistant:
Joëlle Bernhard

ISBN: 2-7468-1211-8
Printed in Italy by Arti Grafiche s.r.l. Pomezia (Rome)

Contents

Acknowledgements

When one is involved in writing a history, it is necessary to find the sources, evaluate them, and to write one's own history. That officials of the Diocese of Portland and of the *Editions du Signe* placed confidence in the author to write this history merits a word of thanks. Yet, the pursuit of the research for the same was made easier by the help of others whose names, in the case of some, have already been mentioned in the course of this history. In that regard, the author acknowledges the extraordinary help of Msgr. Marc B. Caron, the co-chancellor, who invited him to undertake the project and who, more than anyone, was exceptional in providing his cooperation for the development of this history.

And, there are others. These include the archivists of the Diocese of Portland (Sister Therese Pelletier, S.C.I.M.), the Archdiocese of Boston (Robert Johnson-Lally), the Archdiocese of Hartford (Maria Medina), the College of the Holy Cross (Mark W. Savolis), not to mention the Sisters of Mercy (Sister M. Shaun Sevigny) and the personnel in those archives. At the same time, the author, like many of the those who had used the Archives of the Diocese of Portland, is indebted to the late Msgr. Philippe E. Desjardins whose notebooks are priceless sources of information about the history of Catholicism in Maine.

Also, there are persons who were helpful among the clergy of New England such as Monsignors J. Joseph Ford, Michael J. Henchal, Charles M. Murphy, Thomas J. Sullivan, and Vincent A. Tatarczuk; Fathers Stephen F. Concannon, Coleman P. O'Toole, and William Wolkovich; Jesuits like William A. Clark, Terrence W. Curry, Leo J. O'Donovan, Charles R. Gallagher, François Gick, John W. Keegan, Anthony J. Kuzniewski, Robert J. Levens, John P. McIntyre, Michael C. McFarland, Bruce T. Morrill, Paul J. Nelligan, William J. O'Halloran, Joseph B. Pomeroy, Lawrence C. Smith, and Paul M. Sullivan; Sister Rita-Mae Bissonnette, R.S.R., as well as Sisters Mary Eunice Boyd, Maria Cabrini Pulsoni, and Mary Quinn of the Sisters of Mercy, in addition to Sister Renata Camendzind of Casco; and lay persons like Stephen C. Ainley, Concetta Aliberti, Joëlle Bernhard, Jo-Anne Carr, Nicolino Ciccomancini, Carol A. Connolly, Jennifer Gilmore, Peter Gribbin, Althea Jackson, Gaye B. Lapomarda, Antonino LoNardo, Theresa M. McBride, Owen J. Murphy, Marc R. Mutty, Carol Phelps, James Robbins, Kenneth A. Scott, Josephine Sgroi, and Patrice Thébault have been helpful.

Likewise, one cannot overlook the Newspaper Catalog in the Portland Room of the Portland Public Library, in addition to the web archive of *The Portland Press Herald*, not to mention the sources available on the worldwide web, the standard studies of the Archdiocese of Boston, the Diocese of Portland, and the Sisters of Mercy, and the sources mentioned in the pertinent sections of the author's bibliographical essay in his work, *The Jesuit Heritage in New England* (1977).

Lastly, if someone has been overlooked, the author offers his apologies.

Vincent A. Lapomarda
College of the Holy Cross
Worcester, Massachusetts
July 29, 2003

Foreword

July 29, 2003

Dear friend:

It is a great joy for me to mark the 150th anniversary of the founding of the Diocese of Portland in 1853 and the 400th anniversary of the establishment of the first Catholic community in the State of Maine in 1604. From its humble and precarious beginnings on Ste. Croix Island to our present community of parishes and institutions, the Catholic Church in Maine has striven to be a living Gospel for all people to hear and a clear sign of the holiness of God. Inspired by the sacrifice of Jesus on the wood of the Cross, countless members of the lay faithful, religious, and clergy have lived the same sacrifice of love for their families and their communities. These anniversaries should cause our hearts to give thanks to God for this marvelous witness of faith. Te Deum laudamus!

I want to express the gratitude of the Diocese to Father Vincent A. Lapomarda, S.J., professor of history at the College of the Holy Cross in Worcester, Massachusetts, for his fine narrative which I offer to you. He has certainly captured the challenges and the accomplishments of so many people. I am equally grateful to Les Éditions du Signe for their dedication to excellence in publishing this work. I believe that this work will be a valuable resource to families and to parishes in making our history known and loved to future generations.

Finally, I encourage all who will examine these pages to recommit themselves during this anniversary observance to a deeper and richer life of holiness. That can be the greatest honor we can pay to those who have gone before us, and the best preparation for the future of the Catholic Church in Maine. You, your families, and your parishes have the assurance of my own prayers and my love.

Sincerely yours in Christ,

Joseph J. Gerry, O.S.B.
Tenth Bishop of Portland

Introduction

In their history of the Archdiocese of Boston, published in 1944, Robert H. Lord, John E. Sexton, and Edward T. Harrington characterize New England as "The Land of the Holy Cross." The origin of that title was due to the French who gave the name, "Ste. Croix," to their first colony in the New World. Located in the northern part of New England in what became the State of Maine in 1820, it was in this geographical area, throughout most of the colonial period, that Catholics practiced their devotion to the Holy Cross while English Protestant immigrants, mainly Puritans, established themselves in the southern part of the same region in Massachusetts Bay.

Certainly, the foremost event underscoring the heritage of the Holy Cross was the First Mass celebrated in what is now the United States. While there is evidence that the Franciscans who accompanied Ponce de Leon to Florida in 1521 probably offered the First Mass, it is certain that the Dominican Antonio de Montesinos (c. 1486-c. 1530) did so in Virginia at least by 1526. If in the writing of American religious history, the experts tend to focus on what happened in the English colonies with the Jesuit Andrew White (1579-1656) offering the First Mass on Maryland's St. Clement's Island in 1634, this history must begin with the First Mass offered in a colony of New France on the Island of the Holy Cross early in the summer of 1604. And, its significance, along with that of the First Mass recorded in New England at the entrance of the Kennebec River, on November 1, 1611, becomes very apparent when it is recalled that the first of these events took place before the settlement of Jamestown, Virginia, in 1607, and the second before the landing of the Pilgrims at Plymouth, Massachusetts, in 1620.

Before the Diocese of Portland, which is under the patronage of the Immaculate Conception, St. John the Baptist, and St. Patrick, came into being in 1853, its territory had historically been part of other dioceses so that its lines of descent can be chronologically and geographically traced back from Boston, to Baltimore, and to Quebec. While its earlier history has been more closely associated with Quebec, its later history, before the diocese came into being, has been more closely associated with Boston. As a result, both Quebec and Boston symbolize the two religious heritages which were important in shaping the subsequent history of the Diocese of Portland, namely, the Catholicism of the French and the Catholicism of the Irish. Yet, at the same time, one cannot forget the contribution of the Native Americans in the earlier part of that history and of the immigrants, from Europe and other parts of the world, in the later part of the same history.

And those forces in themselves call to mind what is important in any history of Roman Catholicism, that is, the explicit emphasis given by the Second Vatican Council to the People of God, including both clergy and laity. Although bishops and priests are essential for carrying on the ministry of the Catholic Church, the faithful men and women of the church should not be forgotten since, with bishops and priests, they constitute those who are the People of God. Without them, there really would not be a diocese. While the conceptual framework of this history focuses on the leadership of the Diocese of Portland, it cannot do so without also including a relationship to all who have helped to build the Catholic Church in the State of Maine, as is evident in the many parishes and the schools mentioned in this history.

Today when the Catholic Church has entered its third millennium, it faces many issues which forces it to become a countercultural force advocating the culture of life as opposed to the culture of death so characteristic of a contemporary world devoid of the values of morality and religion. In the

Panoramic view of God's creation in Maine

pursuit of that objective, Catholic leaders have engaged, at times, in an ecumenical endeavor with leaders of other faiths to bring about the improvement of society as the leaven in the loaf on the local or grassroots level as well as on the regional, national, and international levels.

While one might explore the relevant sources, reflect a knowledge of the major viewpoints, indicate a familiarity with the basic questions, one must not be surprised if questions arise about the critical analysis of the data and the validity of the interpretation whether one delves into the regional, diocesan, or parish sources of the diocese. Nevertheless, like every history, including the two previous works on the Diocese of Portland, one by Edmund J. A. Young in 1899 and the other by William L. Lucey in 1957, this one on the Catholic Church in the State of Maine is a human document subject to all the shortcomings of the same. At the same time, however, its goal is to present a narrative of what happened and to explain why it happened in the land of the Holy Cross during the past four hundred years by basing it upon the objective evidence of the available human testimony.

Chapter 1

The Planting of the Holy Cross

The history of the Catholic Church in Maine begins with the age of exploration and colonization. Of the explorers in this part of New England, there is more historical evidence about the presence of Giovanni da Verrazzano in 1524 and of Samuel de Champlain in 1604 than there is of John Cabot in 1497. While there is speculation about Cabot, there is the evidence that Verrazzano came in contact with the Abenakis in Maine and found them to be lacking in hospitality while Champlain, who explored New England from Maine to Cape Cod, actually met Chief Marchin at Prout's Neck near Portland on July 12th of 1605.

■ *Ste. Croix Island, view from the American side of the Ste. Croix River.*

Of the three explorers, Champlain stands out for the settlement on an island which he named L'Isle Ste. Croix (also known as Holy Cross Island and Dochet's Island) because the configuration of the rivers there reflected a cross. In an expedition undertaken on the authority of King Henry IV of France, Pierre Du Gua (1558-1628), Sieur de Monts, a Huguenot, founded a colony there with about eighty inhabitants. Here they built the first chapel where the First Mass was offered in the early summer of 1604.

Unfortunately, about half of the settlers at Ste. Croix, including the parish priest of Port Royal, one of the two Catholic priests on the expedition, and the Hugenot minister, did not survive beyond the harsh winter of 1604-05. The two clergymen, a Catholic and a Protestant, both victims of the scurvy, were buried in a common grave with the expectation that they would get along better in eternity than they did in this life. Nicolas Aubry, the other priest, survived and died after 1611, according to Lucien Campeau, the Jesuit historian. However, that original chapel on Ste. Croix Island was practically abandoned in the spring of 1605 after the deaths of the inhabitants.

Meanwhile, two English Catholic noblemen, Henry Wriothesley, Earl of Southampton, and Thomas Arundel, Earl of Wardour, had sponsored an expedition to the new world where, on Monhegan Island, it planted the First Holy Cross recorded on the territory of Maine, on May 19, 1605, and another at Chop's Point on the Androscoggin River, on June 13th of that year. Thus, close to four hundred years ago, from the beginning of its exploration and colonization, Maine was marked as the land of the Holy Cross.

Abandoning the venture on Holy Cross Island, which stands near the entrance of the river that divides Canada from the United States, the French settlers moved to Port Royal. From there in 1611 came the Jesuits Pierre Biard (1567-1622) and Ennemond Massé (1574-1646) who would plant the seeds of Christianity among the Passamaquoddies (at Pleasant Point) and the Penobscots (at Old Town). Having explored the rivers of Maine, they came in contact with the Native Americans and were cordially received by Betsabés (d. 1615), the chief of the Penobscots. While investigating a suitable place to establish a mission, Father Massé offered the First Mass, that is, the first recorded one in New England, on an island (presumably Swan Island) at the entrance of the Kennebec River, on November 1, 1611. That same year Father Biard also visited Matinicus Island where he set up the Holy Cross.

Backed by Antoinette du Pons (1570-1632), Marquise de Guercheville, the same two Jesuits returned to Maine, in late May of 1613, with two more Jesuits, Jacques Quentin (1572-1647), a priest, and Gilbert du Thet (1575-1613), a brother, and founded Holy Redeemer Mission (known as Saint Sauveur). Initially, the Jesuits hoped to plant the mission on the Penobscot at the juncture of the Kenduskeag River not far from Bangor. But they had been turned away from that objective by the crew for various reasons, including the weather. Thus, they decided to establish themselves with their horses, goats, sheep and supplies near what is Fernald Point, especially since the Native Americans, under Chief Asticou of the Penobscots, at what is now Manchester Point, were open to conversion.

Quite appropriately, the church that stands at Northeast Harbor today is named for St. Ignatius Loyola, the founder of the Jesuits, while the monument there commemorates the landing of the Jesuits in 1613. There, too, opposite Northeast Harbor, are Jesuit Field and Jesuit Spring, local attractions known to residents since the end of the nineteenth century.

Unfortunately, the English, under Samuel Argall (d. 1641), Admiral of Virginia, came upon the mission and destroyed it, killing Brother Du Thet. The latter had taken charge of the construction of the new mission and was defending it when he died at the foot of the mission cross, thereby becoming the first Jesuit to die in New England. Argall was determined to prevent the French from gaining a foothold in the area that he considered within the English grant to the Virginia Colony. As for the other Jesuits, Father Massé was left to fend for himself on the open sea but Fathers Biard and Quentin were taken captive to Virginia later that summer and, fortunately, after their release, they were able to make their way back to France. Significantly, that encounter between the French and the English proved to be the prelude to the long struggle between the two nations for control of North America.

Subsequently, the Franciscans also came to plant the seed of Christianity in what is now Maine. From 1619 to 1630, the Recollect Franciscans, who had a mission on the St. John River ministered to the Native Americans and the French. Then, from 1633 to 1648, another branch of the Franciscans, the Capuchins, from their base at Port Royal in Acadia, moved into the Penobscot River Valley where they cared for a chapel in 1635 at Pentagoet, a fort at what is now Castine. After Ste. Croix in 1604 and Saint Sauveur in 1613, this was the third chapel established in Maine. The efforts of the Capuchins were such that, on June 8, 1648, they dedicated the cornerstone of a second chapel there, Our Lady of Holy Hope, the name given the present Catholic Church which was established in Castine early in the twentieth century.

Unfortunately, by 1654, the Capuchin mission at Pentagoet had been terminated when an expedition sent by Oliver Cromwell took Bernadine de Crespy, the Capuchin superior, captive to England. However, the work of the mission was resumed in 1667 when Lawrence Molin, a Franciscan, took charge of the existing missions of Acadia. In 1670, when the site at Pentagoet fell into the hands of the French under Jean Vincent d'Abbadie, Baron de St.-Castin (1652-1707), a merchant and trader, after whom Castine was named, the mission underwent a rebirth. And, it is known that the old Capuchin mission at Pentagoet was still there on the Penobscot when Jean Pierron (1631-1700), a Jesuit, visited there in 1673.

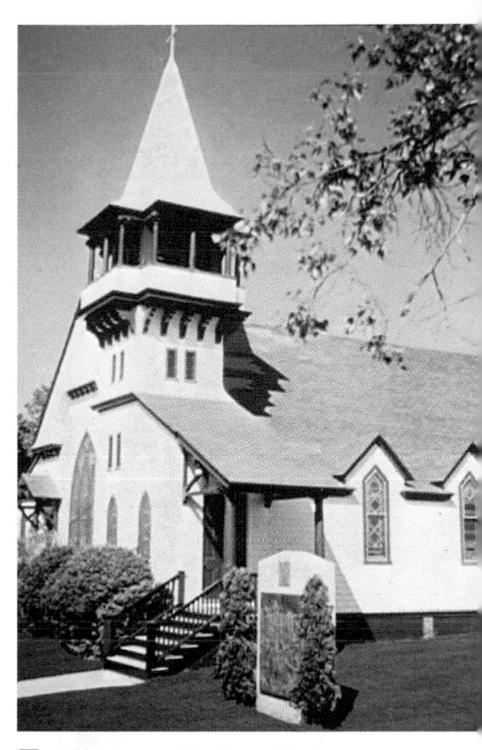

St. Ignatius, Northeast Harbor.

Mission Cross, Capuchin Mission, Castine.

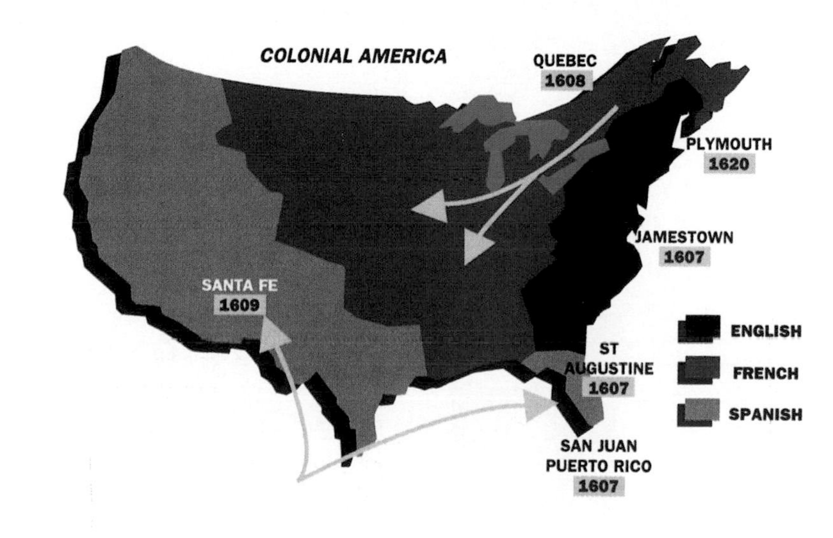

Meanwhile, before that, the Jesuits had returned to Maine at the request of the Abenakis with Father Gabriel Druillettes (1610-81), a charming, holy, and talented person who had recovered the loss of his sight in 1644. By this time, the English from Boston had established themselves within Maine as far as the Kennebec River. Since the Jesuits had assumed responsibility for the missions of New France, Druillettes set the foundation for the first parish of St. Mary of the Assumption with the chapel which he built on the Kennebec at Gilley's Point in what is now Augusta during mid-August of 1646. This chapel was the fourth established in Maine in the first half of the seventeenth century.

When Druillettes came upon "a small hospice of Capuchin Fathers," these missionaries, under their superior, Father Ignatius of Paris (d. 1662), asked the Jesuits in the following year not to interfere in the area of their apostolic work which stretched from Acadia to the Kennebec River. However, after the Abenakis complained, Father Côme of Nantes, Father Ignatius' successor, relented and, by 1650, the Capuchins were asking for the help of the Jesuits in the area where the former had established their chapel in 1648.

■ *Monument to former missionaries and pastors, St. Mary's Church, Augusta.*

Druillettes continued his work for a few more years. He established himself higher on the Kennebec River at Norridgewock which, like the surrounding area, he had already visited on his first arrival in Maine. It was a risky time for missionaries since St. Isaac Jogues (1607-1646), a brother Jesuit, was killed by the Iroquois in New York on October 18th, about two months after Druillettes had descended the Kennebec. Even though Massachusetts had passed a law against the Jesuits in 1647, Druillettes had returned to Maine to carry out two diplomatic missions for Quebec. These led him to travel south across what is now the York River to the New England colonies of Boston and Plymouth in 1650 and to Connecticut and New Haven in June of the following year.

Although Druillettes did not return to Maine after 1658, other Jesuits did so. The Assumption Mission, which he founded, was successful judging from the statistics given by Blessed François de Montmorency Laval (1623-1708), vicar apostolic for the area since 1658, who reported that some 200 baptisms took place there between 1660 and 1663. While Druillettes' diplomatic missions had failed to bring about an alliance between the French in Quebec and the New Englanders in Boston, his work among the Abenakis, who were protecting themselves, in the territory between the Ste. Croix and the Kennebec Rivers, from the Puritans in the South and the Iroquois in the West, flourished.

Moreover, in one of his three journeys among the Abenakis in Maine itself, Druillettes had offered the First Mass in Madawaska in 1651. Later the Catholic Penobscots, who centered themselves at what is now Old Town, became involved in that war between New France and New England, under Mugg (Mog), their leader, in the attack on the English colonists at Black Point in the area of Scarborough. In this way, the turmoil in the region found the Native Americans, to whom the blackrobes administered, involved in warfare. While the Abenakis were driven back into the Jesuit missions of Canada in August of 1676 during King Philip's War, the chapel which Druillettes had built at Gilley's Point was destroyed.

With the newly established Diocese of Quebec on October 1, 1674, Bishop Laval had left the Jesuits responsible for spreading the faith in Maine. As the struggle between France and England for the control of North America increased, the Jesuit missionaries of New France became involved in helping the Native Americans defend their lands against the incursions of the settlers from New England. By 1676, the Baron de St.-Castin, who had restored the French presence at Pentagoet, was the ally of both the Jesuits and the Native Americans and, during his time in the Penobscot River Valley, had defended his country's interest more than once.

In 1684, the Jesuit Jacques Bigot (1651-1711) had been authorized by the Bishop of Quebec to join Baron de St.-Castin in marriage with Matilda (1653?-1717?), princely daughter of Native American Chief Madockawando (1630?-1698) of the Penobscots, whose great rival was Chief Taxous (1690-1717), also known as (Moxus), of the Kennebecs. This marriage, which presumably took place in the 1680s, resulted in a strategic alliance with the French and the tribes between the Kennebec and St. John Rivers during the tumultuous last quarter of the seventeenth century. The baron, by remaining in the French trading post at Pentagoet during that period, left his name as a legacy to the area. The Recollect Father Claude Moreau cared for the Catholics of that region from his mission on the St. John River in 1680. And, later, Jacques Bigot was trying to revive the work of Father Druillettes when he built a chapel in the area of Norridgewock in 1686. In 1690, a Recollect priest named Simon took charge of the mission on the St. John.

As the wars continued between New France and New England, the Jesuits cared for a number of missions at the forts on the major rivers between the two sides. Meanwhile, in May of 1690, the Native Americans from the mission villages attacked Fort Loyall on what is now India Street in Portland and burned the city. Then, in the following year, under Chief Madockawando of the Penobscots and Worumbo, Chief of the Androscogggins, they attacked the Storer's Garrison in Wells. However, by 1693 the Penobscot chief was signing a peace (Phipp's Treaty) that was more favorable to the English than to the French. Around the time of the Treaty of Utrecht (1713), Joseph Aubery (1673-1756) had drafted a map which showed that these missions, existing since the end of the seventeenth century, really constituted a defensive perimeter for New France against New England.

The fort at Pentagoet, it should be noted, had been key in the French strategy to defend the region. However, with the passage of time, it became clear that a move of the mission up the Penobscot would provide both the French and the Native Americans better protection from the English. Consequently, Vincent Bigot (1649-1720), Jacques' brother, who had arrived in 1693, because of the baron's strategic concerns, established the mission at St. Ann's on Indian Island in 1694, where Father Louis P. Thury (1644?-1699) from the seminary in Quebec had paved the way after he had been installed by Jacques Bigot as the resident priest at Pentagoet in 1688.

Panawamské, the mission at Old Town on Indian Island, originated before the end of the seventeenth century and was a place where even white people worshipped, with a cemetery founded by Vincent Bigot in 1688. There is some evidence that others like Philippe Rageot, a priest from the Congregation of the Foreign Missions, were also involved in caring for the Penobscots between 1688 and 1732, even though the Jesuits had returned there in 1705. By 1694, a fort had been set up there for defense and for trade and a Catholic center with a house of worship. Thus, this became the sixth Catholic chapel constructed in Maine.

While the structure of the missions was the work of the Bigot brothers, the sons of a famous French family of viscounts, Sebastian Râle (1652-1724), another Jesuit, was also important. Associated with the mission on the Kennebec River since his arrival in 1694, this famous missionary was not far from Anmesokkanti (Amesconti), the mission which was Vincent Bigot's responsibility on the Sandy River, and where the priest's assistant was Prince Waxaway, one of the tribal leaders near Farmington Falls. There was another such mission at Pégouaki (Pigwacket) among the Pequawkets, a branch of the Abenaki, near Fryeburg on the Saco River in 1696. This was home for Catholic Indians like Atecouando,

Interior, St. Ann, Indian Island.

Tabernacle, St. Ann, Indian Island.

Pastor, deacon and parishioner at St. Ann's Parish, Indian Township.

Nescambiouit, who had been decorated by King Louis XIV of France, in 1705, and Paugus.

■ *Monument to Jesuit Mission, Northeast Harbor.*

Then, in the summer of 1698, a Jesuit mission, Naurakamig (Rockameka), was established by Vincent Bigot among the Native Americans on the Androscoggin River. This was in the area of Canton, Jay, and Livermore where there was a more fertile area than at the mission established on the Penobscot River. During the time of those missions, the worshippers among the Native Americans on the Androscoggin had so impressed a number of captives by their religious beliefs and practices that some of the New Englanders converted to Catholicism.

■ *Destruction of Norridgewock and death of Fr. Râle.*

Understandably, when the Bigot brothers left the scene, the number of chapels among the Native Americans of Maine by the end of the seventeenth century and even the schools associated with them, had increased because of those fortified missions. This was evident in the records of the destruction of the one at Norridgewock in 1705 since the report of that expedition by the English from Massachusetts described what was the first school in Maine. In recognition of this mission school, where Father Râle taught the Norridgewocks music, reading, and writing as well as religion, the Daughters of the American Revolution, which had set up one marker outside the cemetery to commemorate the ancient village in 1926, set up another inside the cemetery in mid-December of 2000 to credit Father Râle for the first school in Maine. Râle had himself told his relatives that a main church and two chapels, one dedicated to the Blessed Virgin Mary and the other to the Guardian Angel, marked his mission at one time.

Given what the Jesuits had done in establishing these missions, it is no wonder that Massachusetts, of which Maine became a part in 1669, passed another law against the Jesuits, on June 17, 1700. Vincent Bigot, who was aware of this hatred for the Jesuits, had been present at the capitulation of Pemaquid which members of his Abenaki flock had destroyed in 1696. Actually, Bigot mentioned that hostile attitude of the English in a letter to the English commander of the fort on the Saco River on September 24, 1700. Not surprisingly, in the following year, Lieutenant Governor William Staughton warned Father Vincent Bigot, in a letter of April 10th, to leave the area. Even though the Franciscans, who had maintained some contact with Pentagoet, eventually left Maine in 1703, other priests, including Vincent Bigot, not to mention Antoine Gaulen (1674-1740), a priest from the Congregation of the Foreign Missions, who ministered to the Native Americans on the Penobscot River and on Passamaquoddy Bay until 1732, were still in evidence.

Moreover, it must be noted that Vincent Bigot had participated as an advisor in the conference in Casco Bay (Kaskebé to the French) in June of 1701 and again in June of 1703. On such occasions, the chiefs of the various tribes, like Nescambiouit of the Pequawkets and Waxaway of the Abenakis on the Sandy River as well as Bombazine and Moxus for the Norridgewocks, arrived at the conferences with a fleet of canoes and in their tribal garb. Given the presence of Bigot and other Jesuits, it is not unlikely that Mass was offered in Portland at such times, if it had not been offered there earlier for the first time.

In August of 1703, when the inhabitants of the Jesuit mission on the Kennebec raided Wells, they took Esther Wheelwright (1696-1780), daughter of a prominent family in that town, as a captive. Brought by the Native Americans to their mission village, she was rescued by Father Vincent Bigot who sent her to Quebec where, having been instructed in the beliefs and practices of Catholicism, she became, in 1760, the superior of the Ursulines and was known as Mother Marie-Joseph de l'Enfant Jesus. Today there is a painting of this remarkable Maine woman in the Massachusetts Historical Society in Boston.

After the Bigot brothers left Maine, Jesuits like Sebastian Râle and others continued their work. One was Pierre de la Chasse (1670-1749) who took over the mission at Naurakamig from Vincent Bigot in 1701 and became a leading figure in keeping the Abenakis of the whole region loyal to the French. Another was 1701 Étienne Lauverjat (1679-1761) who, having replaced La Chasse in 1718, remained there for twenty years. Because of his balanced view of the struggle between France and England, Lauverjat, along with Râle and La Chasse, became a confidant of the Abenakis and, advised them in the Grand Council at Norridgewock in 1721. As in the Abenaki attack on Fort St. George in Thomaston in 1723, Lauverjat was present at the sites of the major events which involved his flock. So familiar had this Jesuit been with the family of St.-Castin that Lauverjat complained, in a letter of July 28, 1728, that the baron's sons were quite unlike their late father.

In the first quarter of the eighteenth century, the New Englanders intensified their efforts against the Native Americans and the Jesuits. As already indicated, that winter of 1704-05, they had destroyed the church and the school at Norridgewock. Then, in the winter of 1721-22, Thomas Westbrook and his men plundered Norridgewock, destroying the church, which had been rebuilt, and seized its mission bell and Father Râle's strong box, which are at the Maine Historical Society, and his Abenaki dictionary, which is at Harvard University. After Governor Samuel Shute had declared war against Father Râle on July 22nd of 1722, the New Englanders destroyed, on March 9th of the following year, Lauverjat's mission, his church and his residence, among the Abenakis on Indian Island.

Not surprisingly, that violence by the New Englanders triggered retaliatory actions by the Norridgewocks against towns like Scarborough when, on June 26th , the Native Americans took Mary Scammon, a resident of Saco, captive. Another raid followed in April of 1724 when two Mitchell boys, whose father was killed, were taken captive. Throughout his work among the Native Americans, Lauverjat had defended their religious freedom and their lands against the New Englanders. Scammon, who became known as Marie Seaman in Canada, married there in 1740 and refused to return to her native area in Maine even after she had inherited land there.

Against such a background, the allies of New France were on the defensive in the struggle between England and France for the control of North America. Since this was a religious as well as a political conflict, Father Râle incurred the wrath of the English who, centered in Boston, placed a price on his head. Having kept the Native Americans loyal to the French, centered at Quebec, like the other Jesuit missionaries who had cared for the missions at the forts on the rivers between New England and New France, Râle was determined to stand by his flock of Native Americans in the Kennebec River Valley and to defend their rights while caring for their pastoral needs and nourishing their religious beliefs and practices.

Though the Jesuit was willing to support the Abenakis in moving to the safety of the Jesuit missions in Canada, Râle stayed with them to protect their interests to his dying breath as long as they remained in Maine. Clearly, after the Treaty of Utrecht in 1713, the English commissioners had forced the Native Americans to accept very harsh conditions that were further tightened in the 1717 Treaty of Georgetown forcing them to agree to English settlements east of the Kennebec. It was at this conference on Arrowsic Island that the New Englanders found Râle to be a tough negotiator in defending his flock as he later did with his own life.

Tragically, Râle was eventually cut down in a surprise assault on his mission village at Norridgewock, Maine, on August 23, 1724. The vulnerability of the Native Americans was exposed when Father Râle, encircled by seven chiefs (among them were Bombazine, Carrabasset, Job, Mog, and Wissimemet), who tried to protect him, were killed with him. The news of the Jesuit's death caused the Protestants throughout the region to rejoice when they learned that this most famous Jesuit in the colonial history of New England had perished. While his enemies in New England in the eighteenth century saw the Jesuit as the major obstacle to their objectives until he was out of the way, Râle had truly demonstrated that he was the "Apostle of the Abenakis" for his flock. Many years later, the American

bishops regarded the Jesuit as a true martyr of the faith when, near the middle of the twentieth century, they submitted his name to Rome for beatification, with a number of other martyrs from North America.

In this connection, one contemporary report of the martyrdom of Father Sebastian Râle stated: "He dropped dead at the foot of a large cross that he had erected in the midst of the village, in order to announce the public profession that was made therein of adoring a crucified God." While this version from the viewpoint of the French, especially La Chasse, portrays the Jesuit as a martyr, it is one that is sustained by such experts on Râle as Antonio Dragon and Mary R. Calvert in contrast to the view of him as "a bloody incendiary" held by Samuel Penhallow (1665-1726), Râle's contemporary, and others who were sympathetic with the English cause. Certainly, the impartial view of John Francis Sprague, a later writer, defuses this harsh view of Jesuit.

■ *Monument to Fr. Râle, St. Sebastian Cemetery, Norridgewock.*

As Father Râle's War raged on for two years in the wake of his death, the Native Americans lost their lands with the eventual triumph of the English in the pivotal battle of Quebec in September of 1759. Among the forces of the Marquis de Montcalm, 245 Abenakis had enrolled, including thirty-six from Indian Island. Although Jesuits like Jacques de Sirême (1695-1747) took over as Râle's successor and rebuilt a chapel at Norridgewock, the martyrdom of the Jesuit with about thirty of his flock in August of 1724 forced many of the Abenakis to flee into Canada to the Jesuit mission on the St. Francis River or to take refuge among the Abenaki tribes with Lauverjat and his successors.

■ *Drawing by Louis Ewer of Indian Chapel at Norridgewock.*

Moreover, there were other Jesuit priests who cared for the Native Americans in Maine between the Kennebec River and the St. John River. There is evidence that Laurent-Thomas Corthier did so from 1742 to 1750, before he died back in France no earlier than 1762; that Pierre Audran, who later joined the diocesan clergy in France around 1792, was at his mission not too far from Augusta, on January 4, 1754; and that Pierre-Simon Gounon (d. 1764) was with the Penobscots from 1750 to 1755. Significantly, when the English commissioners at Fort Richmond complained about the trouble caused by this last Jesuit, the Native Americans responded: "We want no Jesuits to meddle with our treaties. All we require of them is to pray with us, and take care of our souls."

But the Abenakis had lost their lands and their religious freedom despite the agreements worked out with the Governor of Massachusetts. The latter could never really assure the Abenakis of a Jesuit because the anti-Jesuit laws were still in existence, making it illegal to grant such a request. Then, with the worldwide suppression of the Jesuits, on 16 August 1773, the Native Americans were without a priest. Consequently, there was not a blackrobe among them for at least a generation, especially after the former French lands came under English rule with the Treaty of Paris in 1763.

Thereafter, given the geopolitical change in the victory of England over France in North America, Catholics in the Thirteen Colonies came under the Vicar Apostolic of London, with whom there was no significant connection with New England. Here, where Massachusetts had incorporated Maine under its jurisdiction in 1776, there were entrenched anti-Catholics whose influence the circumstances of history would alter, particularly in the way its leaders approached the requests of the Native Americans for a priest. This came about in 1776 when Chief Joseph Orono of the Penobscots, whose ancestors were baptized by the Jesuits in the early part of the seventeenth century, demanded a priest as a condition for his people to support the American Patriots in their rebellion against the King of England.

Not wanting to lose any important help to the American cause and due to the efforts of Colonel John Allan, superintendent of the Eastern Indians, it became possible for an Augustinian priest, Hyacinthe de la Motte, a French naval chaplain during the American Revolutionary War, to visit the Native Americans for a few months in the summer of 1779. Then, with the tolerance of Catholics by Massachusetts in 1780, other French priests like

■ *Acadia National Park, Mount Desert Island.*

the Capuchin Frederic of Bourges went to the Penobscots while the Recollect Juniper Berthiaume went to the Passamaquoddies in the tradition of their Franciscan predecessors more than a hundred years previously. The French connection with the American cause made it possible for the Catholic Indians of Maine to support the cause of American Revolution when their request for a priest was reluctantly honored by Massachusetts as a condition for winning Indian support. At the same time, the French support of the American cause helped to tone down the anti-Catholicism of the Americans because a Catholic nation was helping the birth of the new American nation.

Meanwhile, the Acadians, about whom Henry Wardsworth Longfellow later wrote his epic, *Evangeline*, in 1847, were expelled by the English from Nova Scotia in 1755. Some of them had settled in the St. John River Valley until they were forced out of the area to make room for the British Loyalists who had fled for their lives from the former Thirteen Colonies once the Americans had issued their Declaration of Independence. By June of 1785, a number of these pioneering Acadians had moved up to the Madawaska territory in Aroostook County on foot settling above the Great Falls on the St. John River thereby planting the roots for what later became St. Basil's, the first Catholic Church in that area. That following year, they were visited by a priest who took care of their spiritual needs.

Certainly, by the time that the American Revolution had run its course, the Holy Cross had been planted firmly on Maine soil. From the time it was erected on the island bearing its name early in the seventeenth century and down to the first stirrings of the American patriots in the second half of the eighteenth century, it had been the shining symbol of the faith of the Native Americans in the river valleys of the St. John, the Penobscot, the Kennebec, the Androscoggin, and the Saco. Into these valleys came the missionaries like the Franciscans, Jesuits, and others, as well as diocesan priests from Quebec helping to plant the cherished symbol of Christianity.

Chapter 2

Maine Catholics in a New Nation

■ *Portrait of Bishop Jean de Cheverus by Gilbert Stuart*

After the victory of the Americans in the Revolution, the Catholic Church in the United States came into existence under John Carroll (1736-1815), a former Jesuit. Having served as Prefect Apostolic of the United States since June 9, 1784, he was named, on November 6, 1789, the first Catholic bishop of the United States. In this office, Carroll was responsible for Maine which came within his geographic jurisdiction as Bishop of the Diocese of Baltimore. This included the whole country throughout which parishes were developing so as to constitute the building blocks of his new diocese. In Maine, before the American Revolution, these nascent parishes had centered mainly around the Catholic inhabitants of Indian Island in Old Town and at Pleasant Point in Perry. In the next half century and more, they were moving beyond these early settlements to include English settlers and immigrants of Irish and French ancestry who migrated into this part of the Northeast.

■ *St. Patrick's Church and cemetery, Newcastle*

On May 17, 1791, not long after Carroll became bishop, the Native Americans made known to him their need for a priest. Responding to the problem in the early years of his episcopate, he sent to them three priests. After the Indians had lost their lands, Carroll realized that a resident priest would help to compensate the Catholic Indians, religiously and culturally, and to rehabilitate their poor status after many years of neglect.

■ *Kavanagh Mansion, Newcastle*

The Sulpician François Ciquard (1750-1824) was the first priest to help. He arrived among the Passamaquoddies at St. Ann's (Pleasant Point), on October 10th 1792, and remained there until August of 1794. Ciquard had come from France with Father François Antoine Matignon (1753-1818), another refugee priest from the French Revolution of 1789. During his two years in Maine, Ciquard strengthened the foundations of the Catholic communities on Indian Island and at Pleasant Point to which the Native Americans were being restricted. Though he moved to New Brunswick, Canada, in 1794, the Sulpician priest did visit the Native Americans in Maine on Indian Island in 1797.

After Ciquard, Jean-Louis Lefebvre de Cheverus (1768-1836), another French refugee, also helped to strengthen the foundations of the Catholic Church in Maine. Sent by Bishop Carroll in June of 1798, he was astonished to learn on his first visit that the Native Americans, who had been without a priest for years, were chanting one of the Masses by Henri Dumont (1610-1684), a baroque composer known to the Jesuits. While Cheverus was spending his summers with the Native Americans at Pleasant Point, he also cared for the Catholic community of Irish immigrants centered at Newcastle where he offered Mass at the home of the Kavanaghs.

Originally, there was a chapel in the area of Newcastle. Situated in Damariscotta Mills, it was known as St. Mary's of the Mills before Bishop Carroll formally established it as St. Patrick's in 1801, the name selected by Father Cheverus. During this time, Cheverus was embroiled in a civil dispute over his authority to perform the first Catholic marriage in Newcastle. The persons involved in this ceremony, on January 1, 1800, were James Smithwick (1777-1810), a ship builder, and Elizabeth Jackson (1782-1864). Rather than at St. Mary's Chapel in the cold of winter, the ceremony took place at the home of the Kavanaghs, the family of Edward Kavanagh (1795-1844), Elizabeth's nephew who became the first Catholic governor of the State of Maine in 1843.

Subsequently, in Wiscasset, Maine, on July 15, 1800, Attorney General James Sullivan sought to prosecute Cheverus for allegedly lacking the civil authority to officiate at the marriage. After a grand jury had indicted the priest, United States Congressman Silas Lee (1760-1814) defended Cheverus when the case went to trial the following October. However, in this criminal proceeding, of the three judges who sat in judgment, two of them (Theophilus Bradbury and Simeon Strong) were prejudiced against Cheverus while the third (Samuel Sewall) was a fair-minded jurist.

Even though Lee had successfully defended the priest, a civil action was scheduled against Cheverus for June of 1801. But, in a strange twist of events, Presiding Judge Bradbury, who wanted the priest to pay a fine of fifty pounds in the criminal case, was unable to prevail because, having fallen off his horse, he was in no condition to preside in the final proceeding. Thus, Cheverus, who had been vindicated in the civil suit, won vindication in the criminal suit and escaped an hour in the pillory.

In 1799, Bishop Carroll assigned Jacques R. Romagné 1762-1836), a third priest. Also a refugee from France, he succeeded Cheverus among the Catholic Indians of Maine working among both the Penobscots and the Passamaquoddies. Residing at Pleasant Point, Romagné, like Cheverus, ministered among the Irish and other Catholics in the Newcastle area and its neighboring towns. During these years, he saw a church built at Pleasant Point, by 1803, on land and money appropriated by the State of Massachusetts, of which Maine was still a part, and the new church of St. Patrick's at Newcastle by 1808.

Although St. Patrick's was not constructed when Bishop Carroll paid a visit to the church in Newcastle in October of 1803, he did offer Mass in the home of Matthew Cottrill for the expanding Catholic community which then numbered two hundred parishioners living within twenty miles of old St. Mary's Chapel. Due to an arrangement worked out by Father Matignon, Father Romagné resided with the Kavanaghs in Damariscotta and cared for the area's Catholics during the winter months from 1805 until 1818. With this advantage, Father Romagné was able to return to the reservation to care for his flock at Pleasant Point for the summer and fall.

While Bishop Carroll forged the link which preserved Christianity among the Catholic Indians of Maine during the first two decades when the United States came under its new Federal Constitution of 1789, Jean-Louis Lefebvre de Cheverus, his successor, built on that legacy. Appointed the First Bishop of Boston, on April 8, 1808, Cheverus, by this time, was very much acquainted with the problems of the Catholic Church in Maine. On July 17, 1808, authorized by Bishop Carroll, he dedicated, as bishop-elect, the new church of St. Patrick's in Newcastle, now the oldest Catholic Church in New England, and he visited Pleasant Point, on September 15, 1811, where he confirmed 122 Passamaquoddies instructed by Father Romagné. The latter, effective in keeping his flock neutral during the War of 1812, welcomed another bishop to Pleasant Point, Joseph-Octave Plessis of Quebec (1763-1825), a great grandson of a deacon of the Congregational Church in Deerfield, Massachusetts, in 1815.

Before he returned to France in 1818, Romagné brought about peace between two chieftains who had been disputing an election within the tribal community and even reached a financial settlement in which the Government of Massachusetts agreed to the care of the Native Americans in exchange for the latter surrendering their claims to lands that had been their legacy. Romagné's memory of his work in Maine was so strong that it led him to remember the Diocese of Boston in his will with a financial contribution.

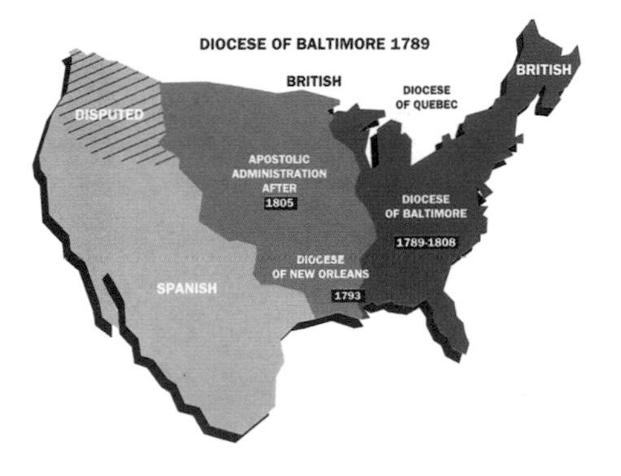

After the departure of Father Romagné to France for reasons of health, Bishop Cheverus, who had visited the Catholic centers of Maine and their surrounding communities in his circuit rides as a priest almost every summer during the previous two decades, appointed Father Dennis Ryan (1786-1852) as Pastor of St. Patrick's in Newcastle in 1818. Having left his native Ireland for Quebec, Ryan came into the Port of Boston on a captured ship during the War of 1812. When Bishop Cheverus ordained him, on Trinity Sunday, May 30, 1817, Ryan became the first priest ordained for the Diocese of Boston and the only Irish priest in Maine until 1826.

■ *Cottrill Mansion, Newcastle*

In the thirty years of his pastorate, Ryan became known as the "Apostle of Maine."

■ *St. Dennis, Whitefield*

■ *Interior of the first St. Dominic's Church, Portland*

Perhaps his greatest contribution under Bishop Cheverus was the establishment in North Whitefield of St. Dennis, a church named for his patron saint in 1818. It is one of the oldest of the Catholic centers in New England, along with St. Ann's in Old Town and St. Patrick's in Newcastle. In was in his last visit to the new state that the bishop, on June 30, 1822, dedicated the new church of St. Dennis, in North Whitefield before returning to Boston. Later, when Father Ryan went on to spend the rest of his life, from 1846 to 1852 in Illinois, St. Dennis was a flourishing parish of five hundred Catholics with ten missions (Augusta, Bangor, Bath, Belfast, Damariscotta, Gardiner, Portland, Thomaston, Waldoboro, and Wiscasset) which indicated the geographic scope of the pastor's activities.

Meanwhile, the Catholics centered around Newcastle, where James Kavanagh and Matthew Cottrill had established themselves in the shipping industry, were becoming influential as civic leaders. Though the Catholic community around North Whitefield was the larger of the two, some of those associated with St. Patrick's had played a prominent part by their defense of religious freedom in drafting the constitution for Maine when it entered the Union as a new state in 1820.

Two years before Cheverus was named Bishop of Montauban in France, on May 32, 1824, a Catholic parish was organized in Portland, the state's largest city. Named St. Dominic, it numbered about forty-five members who were located in a section of the city which was distinguished for its Irish settlement. If he did not offer Mass in his first visit, on July 24, 1798, Bishop Cheverus certainly offered Mass in Portland in his visits there for a number of days in the spring and summer of 1822. Between 1822 and 1827, Catholics used to gather in Beethoven Hall in the area of Monument Square (previously known as Market Square) for religious services.

On May 10, 1825, Benedict Joseph Fenwick (1782-1846), a Jesuit, was named second Bishop of Boston, a diocese which took in the whole of New England. A Maryland native, his tenure as bishop over Maine would be longer than that of either Bishop Carroll or Bishop Cheverus. While both Carroll and Cheverus had helped Maine Catholics adjust to the new religious environment of the United States, Fenwick would do still more by establishing a number of important parishes throughout the state.

At the outset of Fenwick's episcopate, there were eight churches in his diocese and half of these were in Maine. There were the shabby buildings on the reservations at both Pleasant Point (St. Ann's with about three thousand Passamaquoddies) and Indian Island (also named St. Ann's, with about four hundred Penobscots); the brick church of St. Patrick's at Newcastle with its tower bell cast by Paul Revere and the home parish for about a half dozen families of shipmasters; and St. Dennis, a wooden church in North Whitefield, with about four to five hundred Irish farmers in the Sheepscott Valley for whom Bishop Fenwick later, on August 10, 1838, dedicated a new church which still remains today with its historic cemetery. The Irish there were in sharp contrast to the few wealthy families centered in the area of Damariscotta and Newcastle where Bishop Fenwick found helpful advisors in the Cottrills and the Kavanaghs. That St. Patrick's did not receive a resident pastor until 1931 is an indication of the lack of growth of parishioners there.

Meanwhile, more immediate to the pastoral work of Bishop Fenwick were the needs of the Native Americans who wanted a resident priest. Within a year of his episcopal ordination, the new bishop assigned to them Virgil H. Barber (1782-1847), a former Episcopal minister, who had converted to Roman Catholicism in 1816 and had become a Jesuit priest. In July of 1826, Fenwick sent him to the Passamaquoddies and, in October of that year, to the Penobscots. Later, when Barber returned to Maine as a resident priest in 1828, he was more a "patriarch" in the eyes of the Penobscots for whom he opened up a new school that year and built a new church the next year. However, the bishop had paved the way for the these buildings when, on January 23, 1828, Fenwick had submitted proposals for the same to the state legislature.

Recalled to Maryland by his Jesuit superiors in 1830, Barber returned to Maine in 1832 to baptize the son of Thomas Cooney and his wife, the first white child baptized on the Penobscot River. At that time, the Jesuit was able to end the proselytizing efforts of Rev. Elijah Kellogg (1761-1842), a Protestant minister, who had been a thorn in Fenwick's side because of his attempts to draw the Native Americans on Indian Island and at Pleasant Point away from the Catholic faith of their ancestors.

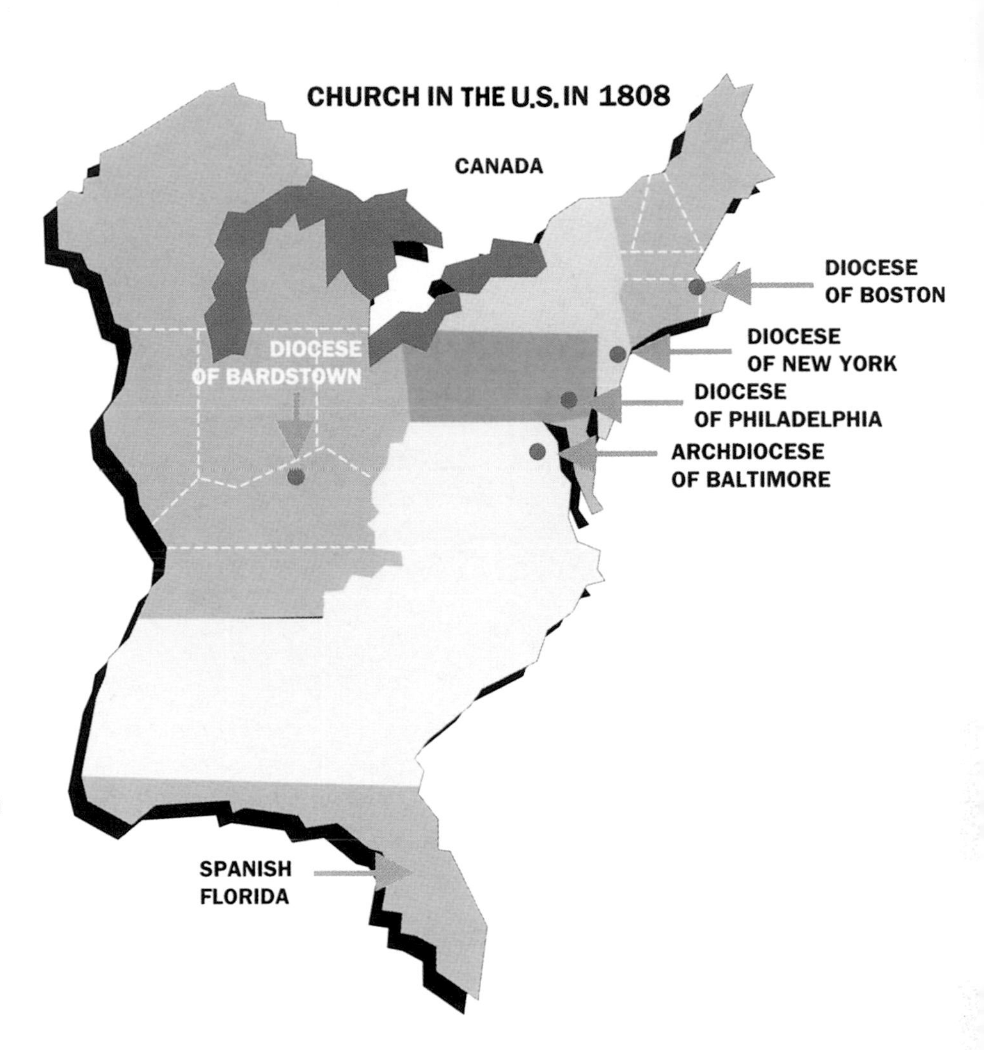

In the following years, Fenwick sought missionaries to carry on the pastoral work among the residents of the reservations. When, in 1835, he did so, Edmond Demillier and August Petithomme, priests of the Congregation of the Sacred Hearts of Jesus and Mary, commonly known as the Picpus Fathers, responded. In December of 1836, Patrick Ratigan took over among the Penobscots and remained there until the following June. Then, in 1838, Edward Murphy, recently ordained, brought new hope to the Penobscots until he was recalled in December of 1839. Still the Native Americans did not cease writing to the bishop for a resident priest in the remaining years of Fenwick's episcopate during which Father Thomas O'Sullivan tried to care for them along with his own parish in Bangor.

While the bishop was interested in Catholics like the Native Americans and the Irish, Fenwick, like Cheverus before him, was also interested in non-Catholics as his relationship with the Barber family indicated. However, the bishop's first official visit to Maine in the summer of 1827 found him saying Mass in a rented room of a building in Market Square in Portland, offering the first recorded Mass in Saco, on August 15th, in the home of Dr. Henry B. C. Greene (1800-48), a convert who later moved to Boston, becoming the first Catholic elected to the Massachusetts legislature; visiting Josue Mary Moody Young (1808-66), the convert son of a prominent New England family from Shapleigh; and, on July 19th, arriving in Eastport where he preached in the Congregational Church.

Actually, the instrument of Young's conversion to Catholicism was the Dominican Charles D. Ffrench, (1775-1851). He was an Irish priest, who began his ten years as pastor covering the seacoast from Eastport down through New Hampshire between 1828 and 1838. The son of an Anglican bishop, Father Ffrench was himself a convert to Catholicism, and he had baptized Young in October of the first year of his pastorate. When Ffrench became the first resident priest in Portland in 1827, Catholics numbered 150 out of a city population of 12,000.

While those developments reflected the growth of the Catholic community in Maine, it was evident that the priests who labored among the Native Americans had left a rich legacy to spur the bishop on to care for those who were most neglected in his diocese and to safeguard

■ *(published drawing)Bishop Benedict J. Fenwick*

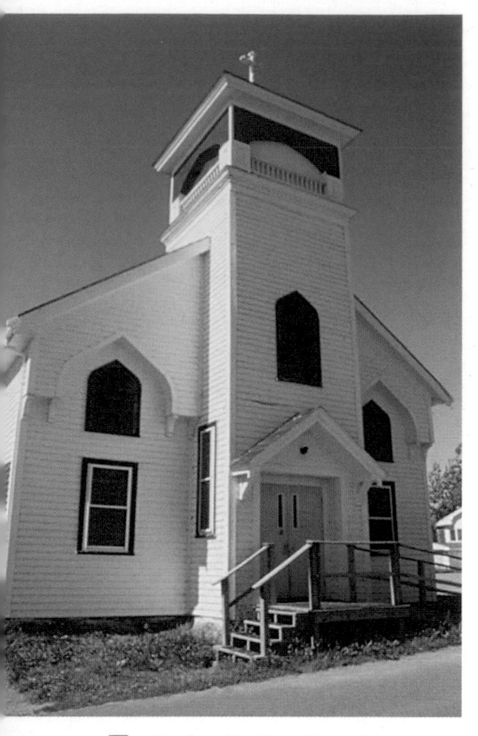

St. Ann, Indian Township

St. Bruno/St. Remi, Van Buren

their memory. This was evident when Bishop Fenwick dedicated the huge obelisk of granite at Norridgewock in memory of Sebastian Râle in 1833 and published The Indian Prayer Book by Father Romagné in 1834. Unfortunately, there were those who feared the growth of Catholicism in the Pine Tree State and did not hesitate to destroy the Râle Monument so that Fenwick, who endured the burning of the Ursuline Convent in Charlestown in 1834, had to rededicate the granite monument in his visit to Maine in 1838. Despite such bigotry, Catholicism was taking root throughout the state and this was particularly evident among the Irish, outside of areas like Newcastle and Portland, in places like Gardiner, Belfast, and Benedicta.

In Gardiner, the connection with the Catholics in Boston went back to the second decade of the nineteenth century when the First Mass was offered at the home of Martin Esmond (c. 1790-1832), the first Catholic of the town, whose wife, Jean (Jane) Stuart Esmond (1777-1867), claimed kinship to Mary Queen of Scots. It was in their home that both Boston Bishops Jean Lefebvre de Cheverus and Benedict Joseph Fenwick visited and offered Mass. Fenwick had honored the Esmonds by giving Mrs. Esmond, who had lost her husband and a son within a year, an English edition of the Catholic Bible in a visit there in 1833. Her son, John (1818-1833), a seminarian in Montreal, had been the bishop's hope for starting Maine's native clergy before his unexpected death. Despite her sorrow, Mrs. Esmond, operating her store on Water Street, nourished her husband's dream of a Catholic church which became a reality in the second half of the nineteenth century.

Further up the coast was Belfast which, like Gardiner, was a mission station of St. Dennis' in North Whitefield. The town was one of those on Cheverus' circuit and Fenwick was surprised to learn of the growing Catholic community there and how the Irish were attracted to its port from Canada just as they had come into Maine through Eastport. At Belfast, the origins of the church centered around the home William S. Brannigan (1810-1901) in the 1830s. In a letter of September 26, 1830, Fenwick wrote that there were 150 Catholics in Belfast at that time.

But, it was at Benedicta, a town in Aroostook County named for the bishop's patron saint, where Fenwick provided a social experiment for Irish immigrants. Located about ninety miles north of Bangor, the bishop sought to establish a Catholic colony there in 1833 and to found a Catholic college. The town was so isolated that people had to travel by boat from Bangor before taking a cart to the end of the dirt road after which they would have to walk the rest of the way. Here the settlers could obtain land as cheap as $2.25 an acre where the bishop hoped that his experiment in colonization would flourish. To provide for the pastoral needs of the colony, Fenwick established St. Benedict's Parish there in 1834.

In Fenwick' time, when the Irish were also arriving in Bangor, this city was the lumber center of New England and its immigrants had to go to St. Ann's on Indian Island to attend Mass. But, after Fenwick established St. Michael's Parish in 1832, the Irish built their own church so that they did not have to travel far for religious services. In fact, that link with the Penobscots proved beneficial to the new parish because the Native Americans came in full regalia to protect the construction of St. Michael's against bigots who opposed the presence of Catholics in Bangor and threatened to burn the church. Eventually, their efforts were crowned with success when Bishop Fenwick dedicated St. Michael's on November 10, 1839.

In addition to the Irish, the French had an even stronger presence in Maine. While their oldest roots in North America go back to the settlers of New France, the growing community of Acadians, which had settled around Madawaska, was of immediate concern for Fenwick. By the 1830s, there were about two thousand of them there, including Irish and Italians, in addition to those of French ancestry. St. Basil's Church, regarded as the mother church of the area since it goes back to July 7, 1793, is located on the northern shore of the St. John River in present-day New Brunswick. Before the end of the eighteenth century, the settlers on both sides of the river had their own priest when Sulpician Father Ciquard resided among them for a short time. That the flock was not abandoned is clear because other priests came to live among them, with one residing there in 1808, and another, Jean Elie Sirois, who was living there in 1831.

Not far away in Van Buren, where St. Bruno's was established in 1838, Father Antoine Gosselin had built a church before Governor Kavanagh sent James C. Madigan (1821-79) into the territory of Madawaska to establish schools there. In 1843, St. Luce's opened in Upper Frenchville and it was served by a French priest named Henri Dionne from New Brunswick who built a church in Wallagrass in 1851. Thus, before the Webster-Ashburton Treaty of 1842 clearly defined the boundary between the two countries and before these churches were formally brought into the territory of the United States, Catholics there were cared for by Canadian priests.

Away from the St. John River Valley, the French were moving into Maine from Canada after the road in the Kennebec River Valley linking the Americans and the Canadians was opened in 1830. This development paved the way for the settlement of Augusta, Skowhegan, and Waterville and the neighboring areas. In Augusta, where the Irish came to help construct the dam on the Kennebec and where St. Mary's was established in 1834, the Catholics converted the Bethlehem Unitarian Church on the corner of Cony and Stone Streets as a church of their own. In the case of Waterville, Father Moise Fortier paid a visit to the town in 1841 and administered the sacraments to Catholics because a number from his parish, in St. George's, Canada, had migrated there.

It was into the Skowhegan area that the ancestors of Margaret Chase Smith (1897-1995) and other French Canadians came. Elected to both the United States House of Representatives (1940-48) and the United States Senate (1948-72), she was the first Republican woman who became a serious contender for nomination to the presidency. Her ancestry descends from her Franco-American mother, Caroline Morin. Eventually, the area would be established as the Parish of Notre Dame de Lourdes in 1881.

Certainly, Bishop Fenwick's efforts to expand Catholicism in Maine were extraordinary if one considers some of the other churches and parishes which he helped to establish. One was Holy Name in Machias (1828) where a new church was built in 1845. Another was St. Joseph's in Eastport (1828), which had its church dedicated by Boston's bishop, on July 19, 1835. St. Mary's in Augusta (1834), a third, opened as a newly-built church in 1846 on State Street. A fourth, St. Mary's of the Visitation in Houlton (1839), had its own new church by the end of 1840. St. Mary's in Bath (1849), a fifth church, also traces its origins to Fenwick. And, St. Denis' in Fort Fairfield (1842), which was established as a mission covered from Benedicta, was a sixth church of the Fenwick era.

In Portland, towards the end of 1830, Bishop Fenwick actually spent about a month trying to inaugurate St. Dominic's Parish on a firm foundation. With the dedication of their church, the first Catholic church in Portland, on August 11, 1833, its parishioners, had grown to about 250 members in a decade. At the time, William Pitt Preble (1783-1857), the city's renowned jurist and owner of its newspaper, Eastern Argus, entertained the Catholics at the dedication of their first church. Since the bishop and the clergy were present, it is clear that Fenwick continued to reach out to others who were not of his own faith.

When Bishop Fenwick died on August 11, 1846, John Bernard Fitzpatrick (1812-66), a native of Boston, who had been named his coadjutor, on November 21, 1843, became Bishop of Boston. It was his responsibility to care for the Catholics in Maine for almost ten years before they had their own bishop. A year after succeeding Fenwick, Fitzpatrick spent two months, from July 23rd to September 10th, in Maine trying to come to grips with the problems of this vast area of his Boston Diocese.

Most significant during Fitzpatrick's years was the return of the Jesuits to Maine, a goal that the bishop accomplished in a meeting at the College of the Holy Cross in Worcester, Massachusetts, with the Jesuit Provincial, on

St. Joseph, Eastport

St. Mary of the Visitation, Houlton

June 9, 1848. Though Fenwick had already made use of isolated appointments of Jesuits like Virgil Barber on the reservations and James Powers as Pastor of St. Dominic's in Portland from 1844 to 1846, Bishop Fitzpatrick sought a more substantial commitment. In this agreement, the Jesuits, under the leadership of Father John Bapst (1815-1887), a refugee priest from Europe, were to revive the missions among the Passamaquoddies and the Penobscots and to care for Catholics in the surrounding towns. Meanwhile, in Portland, the state's leading city, the Catholic population had expanded from forty-three Catholics in 1822 to one thousand by 1846. By 1848, St. Dominic's, the city's only Catholic church, was too small and needed to be enlarged.

Certainly, the work of John Bapst, who arrived in Maine on August 11, 1848, and his Jesuit companions would constitute an important link between the Jesuits of the seventeenth and eighteenth centuries and those who came later to labor in the twentieth and twenty-first centuries. In the decade or so that they were in Maine, the Jesuits were in charge of eight churches and thirty-three chapels, branching out from their centers at Bangor and Eastport, to cover the area north from the Penobscot River Valley to Passamaquoddy Bay. Among the Native Americans, there were major problems because they did not have a resident missionary for years. Then, with Bapst present on the reservation in Old Town, the Jesuit tried to bring peace among the warring factions and to obtain facilities from the state for his flock, and a missionary's salary which was eventually approved and continued until its termination near the end of the twentieth century. It took a visit by Bishop Fitzpatrick himself, on September 3, 1849, and an assembly of Native Americans to try to straighten out those problems. That, as a consequence, a fifteen-foot cross was erected outside the church on the Penobscot Reservation is another indication of just how important was the legacy of the Holy Cross to the Catholics in what is the State of Maine.

Although the roots of St. Mary's Church in Bath go back to 1840, it was not established as a parish until 1849. In the subsequent years, the Know-Nothings made life quite uncomfortable for Catholics and their priests as they began to dominate state politics. In Bath, they burned St. Mary's, on July 6, 1854, underscoring the violence which erupted elsewhere in the state against Maine's Catholics during those days of flagrant anti-Catholicism.

In 1852, at Ellsworth, where Father James C. Moore , S. J. (1799-1868), had been pastor before Father Bapst, the latter had provoked Know-Nothings by complaining against Catholic students in public schools having to listen to the reading of the King James version of the Protestant Bible. By taking up residence on "Galway Green," as it was known, Bapst came in close proximity with his bigoted adversaries. However, the Jesuit was no stranger to controversy since, during his three years among the Native Americans, he had failed in his efforts to bring about peace among the divided Penobscots at Old Town.

But, in Bapst's new pastorate, bigots made known their objection to him by various acts of violence in 1854. On June 3rd, they broke the windows of the rectory. On June 6th, they smashed the windows of the church with stones. On June 13th, they badly damaged the old chapel, which served as a school, with a bomb. And, on July 15th, they failed to burn the new church where the priest was forced to hold classes. This escalating situation of violence led Bishop Fitzpatrick to order Father Bapst to Bangor until the controversy cooled. When Bapst returned to Ellsworth four months later, on the night of October 14th, a mob tarred and feathered him in an action that even a newspaper dominated by Protestants, the Eastern Argus condemned in its pages, on October 19th, of that same year.

Later, on December 8, 1854, when Bishop Fitzpatrick blessed St. John's Church in Bangor, the cornerstone contained a bottle with a relic of the tarring and feathering of Father Bapst. The church, which stands today as a national historical landmark in Bangor, was constructed during Bapst's pastorate with the Irish keeping watch over the building at night lest the Know-Nothings destroy it. Tragically, what happened in Ellsworth on that horrible night of October 1854, haunted the Jesuit during the decline of his health in the last six years of his life.

Mary Agnes Tincker (1833-1907), an author from Ellsworth, whose conversion under Bapst had helped to inflame the bigots in her native town, has left a record, The House of Yorke (1872), of what happened there. The daughter of prominent and respectable parents in Ellsworth, Tincker had qualified for teaching in the public schools when Father Bapst convinced her to teach in the old chapel school those students who had joined the protest against the reading of the Protestant Bible in the public schools. Actually, along with those on the reservations, that school in Ellsworth, before it was destroyed by bigots, was then one of the few Catholic schools in Maine.

In their pastoral work in Maine, Bapst and his Jesuit companions continued to ride the circuit through some thirty towns of the state while serving its nine thousand Catholics, Canadians as well as Irish and Native Americans, until 1859. The eight chapels which were under construction when the Jesuits arrived in Maine in 1848 were completed by the spring of 1852. That year Bapst became the superior of the mission and acquired a good reputation as a builder of churches as he remained at Ellsworth. Though the first church at Winterport was not completed until 1853, St. Gabriel's (1850) was established there. And, under Bapst's leadership, the Jesuits opened a mission, St. Mary's, at Trescott in 1853, and converted a store at Pembroke into a church, St. John's, thereby providing another mission in 1854.

In Waterville, in 1851, Bapst himself opened St. John's Chapel (1851-74), the first Catholic church in that town. While it served at least three hundred French Canadians, there were many more of them in the surrounding towns, who cultivated crops on the farms and cut down trees in the forests. Significantly, to avoid provoking the dominant nativist population in those days of the Know-Nothings, the new church was constructed without a tower and a bell.

While there were many signs of hope for the future, one disappointment resulted from the time of Fitzpatrick's predecessor. That was the colonization project launched by Fenwick in Benedicta. There the building which was to be a college was crumbling, and the sawmill, which had been constructed to help the local economy, remained unused. However, as a colonization project, according to articles in the Boston Sunday Herald (June 30, 1907) and Boston Sunday Globe (November 10, 1929), Benedicta was perhaps the most successful utopian experiment in Maine.

■ *(published drawing)*
Bishop John B. Fitzpatrick

The development of the Catholic Church continued under Bishop Fitzpatrick just as it had under his predecessor. By the middle of the nineteenth century, not only had Bishop Fenwick passed from the scene but his predecessors who held episcopal jurisdiction over Maine had also gone to God. John Carroll, who had been promoted to First Archbishop of Baltimore, on April 8, 1808, died in Baltimore, on December 3, 1815, and John Cheverus, who had been elevated to Cardinal-Archbishop of Bordeaux, on February 1, 1836, died at Bordeaux on the following July 19th. With the Catholics of Maine increasing in numbers, a new era was dawning as they looked towards the second half of the nineteenth century. Compared to some hundreds of Protestant churches in Maine by 1850, the number of Roman Catholic churches constituted a mere fraction of Christian churches.

Chapter 3

Portland's First Bishop

■ *Bishop David Bacon*

■ *Episcopal ring, Bishop Bacon*

■ *Coat of arms of Bishop David Bacon*

On December 8, 1854, Rome appointed David William Bacon (1815-74), First Bishop of Portland, Maine. Born in Brooklyn, New York, on September 15, 1815, the son of William and Elizabeth (Redmond) Bacon, he prepared for the priesthood under the Sulpicians in Montreal and later at Mount St. Mary's in Emmitsburg, Maryland. Ordained a priest by Archbishop Samuel Eccleston, S. S., (1801-51) of Baltimore, on December 13, 1838, Bacon was selected to fill the new see created by Rome on July 29, 1853, after Henry B. Coskery (1808-72), Vicar General of Baltimore, had refused to accept the appointment as the first bishop-elect. Among the other candidates for bishop was Anthony F. Ciampi (1816-93), the Jesuit President of the College of the Holy Cross who, when he had learned in February of 1854 that he was being considered, begged his provincial superior to help sidetrack his possible appointment. Incidentally, on that very day, on which the Diocese of Portland was established, Josue Mary Moody Young, a convert to Catholicism, was named Bishop of Pittsburgh thereby becoming the first Maine native to be chosen a Catholic bishop.

Bacon, former pastor of Brooklyn's Our Lady of the Assumption Church, was consecrated, on April 22, 1855, by New York's Archbishop John J. Hughes (1797-1864) at Immaculate Conception Church in that city. Hughes was assisted by Bishop John B. Fitzpatrick of Boston, who was then the Apostolic Administrator of the Diocese of Portland, and Bishop John Loughlin of Brooklyn. While the new bishop was formally installed by Bishop Fitzpatrick as bishop in Portland's St. Dominic's Church, on May 31st, this was not Bacon's first visit to the state since he had been present when Bishop Fitzpatrick had blessed the cornerstone for St. John's Church in Bangor the previous December. Among the few priests present at Bacon's installation were Father Basil Pacciarini (1816-84), the Jesuit superior, and Father Bapst, under whose direction at least five new churches were listed in the Catholic directory of 1855. These were mainly in the larger cities of the state, not in most of its smaller towns where the Catholic faith was practically unknown when Bacon became bishop.

■ *Episcopal staff, Bishop Bacon*

The Diocese of Portland, which had six priests and eight churches at its founding, included the State of New Hampshire as well as the State of Maine. It did not include what became the American part of the Madawaska territory which had been incorporated into the Pine Tree State in 1842. Since New Hampshire eventually became an independent diocese under Denis M. Bradley (1846-1903) as First Bishop of Manchester, on June 11, 1884, this history will not be concerned with the Granite State. Although the Madawaska territory did not formally come under the Diocese of Portland until 1870, this history must include developments there.

When Bishop Bacon took over the new diocese, French Canadians were coming into Maine to work in the cotton mills and the Irish were arriving from Boston to build the railroads. It was at a time when Protestants, who were fearful of Catholicism gaining the upper hand, began organizing into nativist political groups. One of these, known as the Order of the Star Spangled Banner ("The Sons of Uncle Sam"), had members who were both anti-Catholic and anti-Irish and they had captured city hall in both Augusta and Portland. In the state capital, for example, where they had the support of *The Kennebec Journal* and the state legislators, the mayor and the city councilors were known to be members of the Know-Nothing Party. Even the election of Republican Governor Anson B. Morrill in Maine that year was viewed as a victory for the Know-Nothings. At the time, Rev. Charles Augustine Egan (1821-95), Pastor of St. Mary's, had to cope with that government as Catholics in Augusta's public schools were forced to listen to the King James version of the Bible and have the Lord's Prayer recited in the Protestant manner. Incredible as it may sound today, such discriminatory practices were upheld by Maine's Supreme Judicial Court.

Back in 1846, Maine outlawed the manufacture and sale, but not the consumption, of alcohol. This was the nation's first prohibition law and gave the impression that it was aimed at the growing Irish population in Maine. If there had been any doubt about that interpretation, it was erased in 1851 when another law was passed against the consumption of liquor. During this period, the Irish were not permitted to become firemen, legislators, or policemen. Exactly how distorted was this bigoted view is evident from the 1860 census which lists somewhat more than three hundred Irish in Augusta out of a population of seven thousand residents.

Even though the Know-Nothings were eventually thrown out of office, their impact on the 1850s throughout New England, if not the nation, was considerable. This was particularly true in 1854 in Maine where, as already mentioned, a Catholic church was burned in Bath in July and a chapel destroyed in Ellsworth in October. In November of the following year, when the cornerstone for a new Catholic church in Bath was about to be dedicated, bigoted protesters prevented this from taking place. On April 27, 1856, other bigots destroyed the Catholic church which the Jesuits had constructed in Ellsworth. Fortunately, the Know-Nothings were unable to prevent the dedication by Bishop Bacon of St. John's Church in Bangor on October 12th of that year. Nevertheless, all these anti-Catholic incidents were not isolated events in Maine, as can be seen from what happened to the Catholic community in the area of Auburn and Lewiston.

After the Irish arrived in Auburn during the 1840s to help in the construction of the mills and the railroads, the First Mass was offered there by Father James O'Reilly in 1848 and in Lewiston by Father Charles McCullion in 1850. Having obtained an old Baptist church in Auburn during the early 1850s, the Catholics moved it to Lincoln Street in Lewiston where they remodeled it for their own use. Although this was the first Catholic church in the area, the Know-Nothings wrecked it in 1855. When the Catholics responded by immediately rebuilding their church, the anti-Catholics destroyed it once more by setting it on fire. Such was the little-known background of what became St. Joseph's Church in Lewiston which was established in 1857, with Father John Cullen as the first resident priest. Bishop Bacon blessed the church's cornerstone, on June 13, 1864, and dedicated the new structure of St. Joseph's, on June 13, 1869.

St. John, Bangor

Furthermore, the efforts of Catherine Mangan O'Donnell (1826-1913), a native of Ireland and a devoted daughter of the Catholic Church were very significant in that development in Lewiston. This city had attracted the Irish ever since Patrick, her husband, a contractor, had constructed the canal and the mill for Continental Mills. Although Patrick died in 1863, the O'Donnell home, which had been the center for Catholic worship in Lewiston since 1850, was one that was honored by Bishop Bacon on his visits to the city. Eventually, the dream of the O'Donnells was realized long before Mrs. O'Donnell died in 1913 when St. Joseph's Parish came into being in 1857 and St. Patrick's Parish in 1887.

Moreover, in Portland, where the city government was dominated by Know-Nothings, Monsignor John O'Donnell (d. 1882), the bishop's vicar general, felt constrained to ask for police protection in mid-October of 1855 because it was not safe for Catholics to go out

Fr. John Bapst, SJ

■ *Interior, original Cathedral Residence Chapel, Portland*

■ *Bishop Bacon, dedication of Cathedral cross, Portland*

at night. His church, St. Dominic's, which was suspected of being a depot for arms against the Protestants, had its windows smashed. The pastor himself was stoned, and his rectory was damaged. What happened in Portland recalled the situation of Catholics in Philadelphia in 1844 when, during the riots there, two Catholic churches were burned, and in New York City where the government would not provide protection for Catholics.

Before the Diocese of Portland opened Calvary Cemetery in South Portland in 1858, Western Cemetery, which is located not too far away from St. Dominic's, served as the first cemetery where Irish Catholics were buried in the city. Near the end of the twentieth century, the Ancient Order of Hibernians, on August 15, 1999, erected a monument there bringing attention to a forgotten section of it as "The Catholic Ground" where Irish Catholics had been interred during the nineteenth century.

Though the municipal situation in Portland was not easy for Roman Catholics, Bishop Bacon did not let it deter him from his plans to build up the diocese. Having purchased land on Cumberland Avenue for a second church in the city, he was bent on the construction of his own Cathedral in Portland, in a part of the city where he was establishing a second city parish in 1856. Bacon had John Doyle, a Brooklyn architect, draw up plans for his Cathedral Chapel. Soon, in May of 1856, its cornerstone was dedicated and the chapel was completed by the end of 1863.

As for the Cathedral itself, the bishop would have to wait. He liked the work of the architect Patrick C. Keeley (1816-96), whose neo-Gothic style became popular, as evident in such churches as the Cathedrals in Boston and Providence, not to mention St. John's in Bangor and St. Francis Xavier in New York. However, the Civil War intervened to halt any immediate progress in construction. Even after the cornerstone was dedicated, on May 31st, 1866, there was a further delay after a devastating fire swept through the city, on July 4, 1866, destroying the episcopal residence, the elementary school, the convent of nuns, and the girls' academy. Faced with this tragedy in his see city, Bishop Bacon was forced to raise funds by touring the northeast, visiting cities and towns in Canada as well as in the United States. Fortunately, his efforts were crowned with success when he dedicated the Cathedral of the Immaculate Conception, on September 8, 1869, almost two months before he left, on November 9th, for the historic First Vatican Council. By that time, Portland's Roman Catholic population had climbed to three thousand.

Two of the new parishes in Bishop Bacon's diocese were established where the Jesuits were in charge. One was St. Bernard's in Rockland which goes back to 1857 (originally St. David's) and where Father Anthony F. Ciampi was ably assisted by Cornelius Hanrahan, the leading Catholic of the town, in building Rockland's first Catholic church. Both persons got along so well together that they were still exchanging letters many years after Father Ciampi and the other Jesuits had ceased their missionary work in Maine.

The other church was St. Mary of the Assumption which Bishop Bacon established in Biddeford in 1858. The street on which the original church stood was name Vetromile Street in memory of Eugene Vetromile (1819-81), a native of Italy, who served the new diocese as a Jesuit from 1854 to 1858. With the departure of the Jesuits in 1859, Vetromile put himself at the service of the Diocese of Portland and became the Pastor of St. Mary's (1860-67) in Biddeford.

■ *Immaculate Conception, Calais*

A scholar who served the Penobscots at Old Town and the Passamaquoddies at Pleasant Point, Vetromile wrote a book, The Abenakis and Their History (1866), which was based on his personal experiences among them.

He continued to serve those Native Americans later while caring for Calais (1865-70), Eastport (1872-76), and Machias (1879-81). Of these churches, Calais, like Machias had been under construction when the Jesuits had arrived under Father Bapst. In 1864, when Bishop Bacon established the area as the Parish of the Immaculate Conception at Calais, this new parish replaced St. Joseph's in Eastport in embracing the geographical area of St. Croix Island where the first chapel had been established by the French in 1604.

By 1870, the French-speaking population of Maine numbered about a quarter of the state's Catholic population. In Biddeford, St. Joseph's was established that year for the Franco-American population which had moved to that area from Quebec. These Catholics were able to go to their own church rather than "the Irish church" of St. Mary's, and the parish was able to open its own cemetery which was blessed in 1871. Unfortunately, as will become evident, Bacon had, unwittingly, laid the foundation there for a future battle between the pastor, Jean-François Ponsardin, and the bishop's immediate successor in the see of Portland.

The Franco-American population of Waterville continued to grow during Bishop Bacon's time. Their first resident priest was Jean-Jacques Nicolyn (also Nycolin), born in Lyons in 1802, whom the bishop had Father John Bapst install as pastor in May of 1855. Though Nicolyn was transferred to Old Town (St. Joseph's, now Holy Family) in 1862, his parish included a mixture of Franco-Americans and Irish-Americans by mid-century. Father David J. Halde, Nicolyn's successor from 1870 to 1880, led a drive for a new church to seat six hundred people, Bishop Bacon dedicated it as St. Francis de Sales, on June 14, 1874. To this was attached the church in North Vassalboro which was built in that same year and out of which would evolve the Parish of St. Bridget in 1911. And, to provide for the deceased of the growing Catholic community, Halde purchased land in 1873 for a cemetery.

With more French-speaking immigrants descending into Maine from Canada, Bishop Bacon continued to provide for them during the period after the American Civil War, when the French increasingly wanted their own national parishes. In 1870, the bishop established Saint Peter's in Lewiston, where Father Pierre Hévey (1831-1910) became the resident pastor. There, about one thousand French Canadians had been cared for by Clement Louis Mutsaers (d. 1882), a curate assigned to them from St. Joseph's in 1869. Given that the French-Canadians were arriving in Lewiston at the rate of one hundred or more a day after the Civil War, the Franco-Americans could no longer be cared for adequately at St. Joseph's. Consequently, a new parish was organized for them called St. Pierre with a new church which opened in 1873. Eventually, this parish became known as Saints Peter and Paul.

Original St. Mary's Church, Biddeford

Not too far away, the Franco-American population had also settled along the Sabattus River and its people found jobs when the first mill in Lisbon Falls opened in 1874. As these immigrants increased, they could be found in the cotton mills in Lisbon and the wool, saw, and paper mills in Lisbon Falls, not to mention their presence in Lisbon Center. To care for them, Holy Family Parish was established at Lisbon Falls in 1914.

On August 16, 1870, the Congregation of the Propagation of the Faith in Rome finally transferred the jurisdiction of the American section of Madawaska, which was on the southern bank of the St. John River, from the Canadian Diocese of St. John, New Brunswick, to the Diocese of Portland, as the Americans living there had desired in petitions to both Bishop Bacon and Rome. This was the only realistic solution given the confusion that arose over the lack of the proper registration of births, deaths, and marriages of Americans residing under Canadian ecclesiastical jurisdiction.

With towns and villages like Fort Kent and Van Buren coming under his jurisdiction in Aroostook County, Bacon visited Madawaska in the fall of 1870. From Fort Kent, where St. Louis was established as a new parish in that same year, the migration of Catholics had gone from the juncture of the St. John and the Fish Rivers and followed the flow of these waters down to

Fr. Pierre Hévey (right)

■ *St. David, Madawaska*

other French-speaking settlements like Wallagrass and Eagle Lake. In 1860, Father Charles Sweron (d. 1908), known as the "Apostle of Madawaska," began his work in the area by fixing his residence at St. Luce's.

In that part of Madawaska, Van Buren had also joined Fort Kent in welcoming Bacon in the fall of 1870. With the territory's change in jurisdiction, the bishop had to cope with the Congregation of the Holy Cross, the only group of male religious in his diocese, the Jesuits having departed more than a decade earlier. The bishop told the religious in Van Buren that he wanted to have diocesan priests operating St. Bruno's Parish. He had not realized that the religious priests had come into the area with the understanding that they would found a college. With that goal thwarted by the bishop's plans, the Holy Cross Fathers let Bacon know that they were leaving his diocese. Fortunately, this did not dampen Bacon's interest in education because the 1875 edition of the Catholic directory for his diocese indicates that a number of parochial schools was established for the inhabitants of his expanded jurisdiction.

■ *Mausoleum, St. Peter's Cemetery, Lewiston*

Perhaps the most interesting of the parishes in region of Madawaska was St. David's which the bishop established to honor his patron saint in 1871. Even though Bacon had been somewhat indifferent to acquiring the new territory, the change of jurisdiction marked the triumph of the people's attempt to bring the American side of that area into the Diocese of Portland. Certainly, Bishop Bacon had to be pleased when he blessed the bells for St. David's in August of 1872.

Yet, it can be said that Bishop Bacon had accepted the solution and did his best to implement Rome's decision for a people whose ancestors planted the faith in the area. A cross and a plaque in the present St. David's Church marks the site from which the early Acadians crossed over the St. John River from Canada to form the origins of the Catholic community. There fishing, farming, and lumbering became important for those looking to earn a living in the late eighteenth century and through at least the first half of the nineteenth century. The church there today, which is listed by some as worthy of preservation as an architectural gem, was designed by Timothy G. O'Connell (1868-1955), the architect of many Catholic structures in New England.

St. Joseph had been honored in the Diocese of Portland with a number of churches named for him and Bishop Bacon had added to them with those churches in Biddeford and Lewiston. In 1862, the bishop continued this practice with one in Ellsworth and another in Old Town where the churches had been constructed under the Jesuits and where the parishes were ones which John Bapst himself had helped to establish. A third parish was in Gardiner where the Esmond Family had been pioneers and Jane Esmond had been a guiding force until the new church finally opened there in October 1858. When she died, on June 29th of 1867, Mrs. Esmond could rejoice that the dream of the first Catholic family of Gardiner had been realized when Bishop Bacon dedicated that church to St. Joseph, on June 14, 1863.

With the departure of the Jesuits during the early years of his tenure as bishop and of the Holy Cross Fathers during his later years, Bacon did not have in the Diocese of Portland any permanent religious until the Sisters of Mercy arrived in Bangor, North Whitefield, and Portland. These religious women would eventually staff the schools, orphanages, and hospitals within the diocese thereby providing a substructure for the many charitable and educational works of the Catholic Church.

After Bishop Bacon had asked Mother Frances Xavier Warde (1810-84), in his letter of March 22nd, 1865, whether the Sisters of Mercy could take care of Bangor starting the following May, her response was to send Mother Gonzaga O'Brien (1834-1920). By opening the first mission of her congregation in Maine at Bangor on August 5th of that year, this superior of the Sisters of Mercy became their foundress in Maine. Traveling incognito to avoid inciting the non-Catholic population of the state, the Sisters of Mercy arrived in Bangor to find that the convent, which the pastor was building, not yet ready. Nevertheless, once they were settled in the city with their own convent, these pioneer Sisters of Mercy in Bangor proved to be a blessing in providing Bishop Bacon with a day academy, a boarding school, and an evening school for working girls.

In North Whitefield, where Father Edward Putnam (d. 1863), a convert and a painter, was the pastor, the Sisters of Mercy were able to establish a convent school and an orphanage. After Putnam's death, Father James Peterson, his successor, and Father Daniel W. Murphy, whom the bishop had put in charge of building schools, saw a school for girls open in 1871. Zealous as he was to build, Murphy was determined to set up schools elsewhere in the diocese. With the gift of a house, money, and an orchard from Winifred Kavanagh (1805-83), the project had been successfully launched. The benefactress sent two of her nieces to be educated by the Sisters of Mercy and encouraged her non-Catholic friends to send their daughters there. Because of her generosity, Bishop Bacon was able to plan a school for girls in Portland which was completed under his successor.

The third foundation of the Sisters of Mercy in Maine was in Portland where the bishop had obtained land for a convent in 1869 not too far from his own Cathedral where the school situation was somewhat different. Prior to inviting the Sisters of Mercy, Bishop Bacon had the Sisters of the Congregation of Notre Dame from Montreal run the schools in Portland. In October of 1864, the bishop opened St. Aloysius, the first parochial school in the city, and the sisters staffed this and what was Notre Dame Academy. Before the school was destroyed in the fire of 1866, it had 270 students and, after the fire destroyed it and it reopened in 1867, it had as many as 400 students, thereby demonstrating its popularity. Evidence of the school can be found in Mary Raymond Higgins' study of the Sisters of Mercy as well as in the street records of the City of Portland's Department of Public Works.

At St. Dominic's School, which began in 1865 and where the first classes were held in the church before the school building opened in 1867, the enrollment had gone from 380 students before the fire to 300 students in 1868 after the bishop had hired lay teachers to fill the gap following the departure of the sisters to Canada. Though the Sisters of Notre Dame had returned to Portland for a short time by 1868, the situation had so changed that they did not see a future for their work in the city.

It was in reply to Bishop Bacon's initial request for help to staff an orphanage, that three Sisters of Mercy came to Portland on May 31, 1873. But, since the bishop's real needs were in education, his letter to Mother Warde, on July 23, 1873, resulted in twenty sisters arriving in the fall of that year to take care of his schools in the Cathedral Parish as well as the one in St. Dominic's Parish. As a result of the bishop having his pastors follow a policy of setting up parochial schools in their parishes, Bacon's achievements in education were quite ambitious when one recalls that it was not until the Third Council of Baltimore in 1884 that the American bishops approved a fixed policy of having "a Catholic school in every parish."

Bishop Bacon had acquired a reputation as a orator and a scholar. Although he appeared physically strong, he suffered from a bladder condition which sapped his strength towards the

St. David, Rockland

Diocesan Sisters of Mercy, South Portland

St. Francis' Cemetery, Waterville

last years of his life. However, he did not use his condition as an excuse to avoid responsibilities which he bore with courage. At the First Vatican Council, like eighteen other American bishops, including Archbishop John McCloskey (1810-85) of New York, Bacon had petitioned the Holy See to avoid a formal declaration of papal infallibility as church doctrine because it was inopportune. Not unlike other American prelates who had faced the wrath of the bigoted Know-Nothings, the Bishop of Portland did not want to stir up non-Catholics needlessly against Catholics.

That they were practical considerations involved in Bishop Bacon's stand became evident four years later when, in 1874, James G. Blaine (1830-93), proposed an amendment to the United States Constitution prohibiting any public funds to be used to educate students in schools under religious auspices. Even though this proposal was defeated, it spurred action in the state legislatures so that at least thirty-four states, including Maine, passed such a law aimed directly at the Catholic school system which had grown larger than ever in Maine. Because of his way of proceeding, Bishop Bacon had contributed to the development of the Catholic school system in the State of Maine and helped to safeguard the religious as well as political freedom for his flock.

There is no doubt that Bishop Bacon was held in high esteem by his contemporaries within the American hierarchy. He was not only very close to Archbishop McCloskey, later the first American cardinal, but, on January 29, 1860, he was the only American bishop to accompany Pope Pius IX on his first papal visit to the North American College in Rome. After Bishop Fitzpatrick died, Bacon had assisted McCloskey in consecrating, on February 13, 1866, John J. Williams (1822-1907) as Bishop of Boston; and, in 1872, he had assisted the Archbishop of New York in consecrating, on April 21st, Bishop Francis McNeirny of Albany and, on April 28th, Bishop Thomas Francis Hendricken of Providence.

Having made his first *ad limina* visit to Rome in 1859, Bishop Bacon hoped to anticipate his fourth visit that was due for 1874. Unfortunately, his health underwent a reversal during the winter before his departure. As a consequence, his subsequent sea voyage to Europe indicated that Bacon should be taken to a hospital. After landing at the Port of Brest in France, he spent much of his time recuperating in a hospital. He recovered enough to celebrate the Feast of the Assumption, but suffered a relapse shortly thereafter. Archbishop McCloskey joined him in France in late October and both returned to New York where, in St. Vincent's Hospital, Bishop Bacon died, on November 5, 1874, a few hours after his arrival.

Bishop Bacon was fifty-nine years of age at his death. Given his reputation as a scholar and his association with McCloskey, not to mention his links with New York, it is not unlikely that Bacon might have succeeded his friend as Archbishop of New York had death not intervened. At least, it was the opinion of William H. O'Connell, who became one of his successors, that Bacon was in line to be McCloskey's coadjutor and that he had already been appointed to that office prior to his unexpected death.

When Bishop Bacon's body was brought back to Portland for the funeral, his flock was very much grieved. After the solemn obsequies under Bishop John Williams of Boston as chief celebrant at the Funeral Mass and Archbishop McCloskey as the eulogist, Bacon was buried in the Cathedral crypt which he had prepared for himself and for members of his family. That Archbishop McCloskey later dedicated a bronze altar to the Sacred Heart in St. Patrick's Cathedral in memory of Bishop Bacon is further testimony of the high regard in which the late Bishop of Portland was held and of the possibility that he might have been in line as his coadjutor to become the next Archbishop of New York.

Nevertheless, Portland's first Catholic bishop had accomplished much in the twenty years when he led the diocese as its first shepherd. Certainly, he reflected both "Courage and Hope" ("*Robur ac Spes*") which he had used as his motto. He left behind a diocese which then consisted of Maine and New Hampshire with 80,000 Catholics, fifty-two priests fifty-eight parishes, twenty parochial schools and six academies for girls at the time of his death.

Chapter 4

The Nation's First Black Catholic Bishop

With death of Bishop Bacon, Rome appointed, on February 12, 1875, James Augustine Healy (1830-1900) as the second Bishop of Portland. Born in Macon, Georgia, on April 6, 1830, he was the eldest son of an Irish immigrant and cotton planter, Michael Morris Healy (1796-1850), and of his wife, a mulatto slave girl and a native of Georgia named Mary Eliza Clark (1813-50) who bore her husband nine other children (five sons, one of whom died in infancy, and four daughters). Though their 1829 union in wedlock may have been valid in the eyes of the Catholic Church, it was not recognized by the State of Georgia, nor were their children, as products of a mixed racial union, permitted to receive an education in the South. Consequently, the father moved the boys to the North where they were being educated by the Quakers until he had a chance meeting with Bishop Fitzpatrick of Boston while traveling along the Atlantic coast. This led Healy to transfer his sons to the newly-founded College of the Holy Cross in Worcester, Massachusetts, where they were baptized, on November 14, 1844, and continued their education. In 1849, James was a member of the first class to graduate from Holy Cross and its valedictorian.

Subsequently, James began his studies for the priesthood at the Grand Seminary in Montreal and continued them at St. Sulpice in Paris where, on June 10, 1854, he was ordained in the Cathedral of Notre Dame, by Archbishop Marie Dominique Auguste Sibour (1792-1857). Healy, then, became Chancellor of the Diocese of Boston in 1857 and Pastor of St. James Church in the South End of Boston where he served Irish immigrants from 1866 until his appointment as Bishop of Portland, a diocese with which he was familiar because of his summer visits there to the Catholic enclave of Irish immigrants in Damariscotta. On June 2, 1875, Healy was consecrated bishop in Portland's Cathedral of the Immaculate Conception by Archbishop John J. Williams, his close friend, who was assisted by Bishop Francis McNeirny of Albany, New York, and Bishop Patrick Thomas O'Reilly of Springfield, Massachusetts. The consecration was the first of a Roman Catholic bishop in Maine and the first of a black American as a Roman Catholic bishop in the United States.

While the choice of Healy was incredible for those years when the rigid patterns of segregation were emerging in the country, it was not surprising to anyone who knew him. The new shepherd had all those qualities which have been recognized as essential for true leadership: intellectual gifts, common sense, devotion to the welfare of others, and strength of character. During one of his visits to Maine some time before his appointment, James Peterson, pastor in North Whitefield, had publicly denounced the visiting priest because of his race. Although Healy had grown accustomed to meeting such opposition with tact, tolerance, and wit, the priests and people of the Diocese of Portland sought to compensate for such a disgraceful attitude by making the new bishop feel welcome. In his first pastoral letter, Bishop Healy aimed to prevent a case like his own from arising by prohibiting his priests from using the pulpit for such public denunciations. After serving as pastor in Rockland for thirteen years, Peterson returned to his native Ireland in 1889.

In his see city, Healy's efforts on behalf of the Irish on Munjoy Hill, a section of the city not too far from his own Cathedral, were particularly noteworthy. At the outset of his tenure as bishop, there was a chapel for the poor, on the corner of Congress and Sheridan Streets, dedicated to St. Aloysius Gonzaga, a Jesuit saint. Further, up the hill, on the Eastern Promenade, the bishop could be seen, during the new snow of winter, with his sleigh drawn by his horse hauling children who were hitching a ride. Even walking around the Cathedral block and in the yard of the Kavanagh School, boys

Bishop James Augustine Healy

Bishop Healy's travel diary

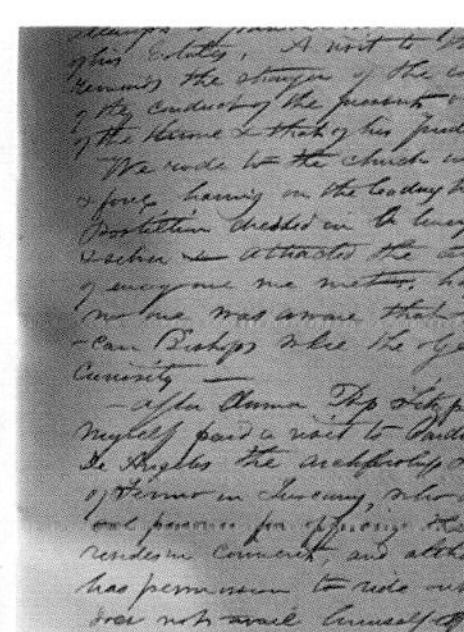

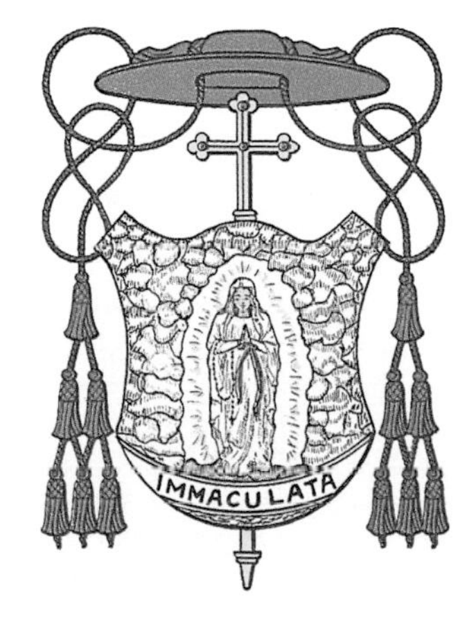

Coat of arms of Bishop James Augustine Healy

le 20 avril 82

Cher M. Hevey,

Et moi aussi, je veux de tout mon cœur éviter un procès par lequel M. Halde sera tellement flétri qu'il aura de la peine à trouver une position ailleurs. Je ne puis accorder un Exeat tant que ses affaires restent dans cet état. J'espère qu'il évitera des censures plus graves et plus notoires en réglant ces affaires de suite.

Il faut savoir que ces comptes ont été réglés, il y a six ans, avec des peines inconcevables de la part de l'Evêque; ensuite reconnus et promulgués d'année en année.

C'est au Métropolitain qu'il faut appeller de ces décisions de votre ami en J.C.

+James Aug. Healy
Ev. de Portland.

P. Hevey

■ *Copy of correspondence, Bishop Healy*

■ *Cruets used by Bishop Healy, Cathedral, Portland*

■ *The former Our Lady of Mount Carmel, Lille*

and girls would flock to Healy, especially when he had goodies from the kitchen at the Cathedral. And, on learning of the condition of the poorer families, the bishop, known for his love of the poor, would bring food to their homes to make sure that they were properly nourished.

One Jesuit visitor to his see city wrote in the Woodstock Letters in 1884 that: "There is far more drinking going on in Portland than any city of its size in the Union." While that might have been a social problem for the Irish, it did not dampen the bishop's attitude towards them. His experience in dealing with the Irish in Boston during the Civil War and after had taught him how to love these immigrants who were the day laborers, dock workers, and longshoremen in Portland and whose heritage he shared through his own father. Unlike his predecessor and successor, he took his turn in administering to them and to others the sacraments in his own parish and in the mission stations of Falmouth, Gorham, and Westbrook.

As the leader of Maine's Catholics, Bishop Healy depended on the assistance of informed and qualified Catholics in the state in facing the problems of his geographically vast diocese. While the debt incurred by Bishop Bacon was less than $125,000, it was an amount with which Bishop Healy had to contend as he sought to build necessary churches and schools. Unfortunately, within a week of his consecration as bishop, fire destroyed the church and the rectory in Machias thereby adding to his burdens though, in this case, the insurance helped to compensate for the damaged property.

In addition to appointing Father John E. Barry (1836-1906), the first native of Maine (Eastport) ordained for the Diocese of Portland (June 29, 1864) as his vicar general, Bishop Healy sought the advice of prominent lay Catholics. Among these were the Madigans, James C. of Houlton and his sons, Albert W. and John B., later a justice of the State Supreme Court. In Portland, the Cunninghams, James and Frank W., contractors, and Charles McCarthy, a clothier, were very influential. Elsewhere, there were persons like Thomas J. Lynch, a banker in Augusta; James Donahoe and Cornelius Hanrahan, pillars of the church in Rockland, whose generosity lightened the financial burdens of the diocese; and James Reynolds of Gardiner who helped the bishop in building a home for the elderly and a convent in Portland.

Then, of course, there was Winifred Kavanagh, the generous benefactress from the Damariscotta area and close friend of the bishop and his sisters, who had provided a gift of $25,000 for a school for girls in Portland. Healy was able to carry to fruition the plans for the Kavanagh School, which his predecessor had launched, by opening it in 1877 with 450 girls at a cost of $23,000 for its construction.

As Bishop of Portland for a quarter of a century, Healy expanded the frontiers of Catholicism into the cities and towns of his diocese among the Irish and the French. The steady stream of the Irish into Bangor and Portland and the French into Biddeford, Lewiston, and Waterville stressed the need for more priests and more parishes in his diocese. Although the statistics at the start of Healy's tenure are impressive, a more realistic view of the picture in Maine requires that they be reduced by half since they also included New Hampshire which remained a part of the Diocese of Portland until the expansion of the French Canadians into that region made it necessary to set up another diocese centered at Manchester in 1884.

In the case of the establishment of new parishes, the growth was remarkable because Healy more than doubled those already in existence, especially by extending the Catholic Church beyond the larger cities where he established three French-speaking churches at St. John the Baptist (1877) in Brunswick, at St. Augustine's (1887) in Augusta, and at St. André's (1899) in Biddeford, while he also established two English-speaking ones at St. Patrick's (1887) in Lewiston and at Sacred Heart (1896) in Portland. In Brunswick, not unlike other cities and towns, the cotton mills which were constructed by their Yankee owners at the falls of the Androscoggin River, drew the French Canadians there in the last part of the nineteenth century.

Moreover, in the smaller towns of the state, where many of the immigrants from Canada were drawn to work in the leather, paper, and textile mills, Bishop Healy built most of his churches for those of French-speaking background, as in the case of St. Hyacinth's (1879) in Westbrook, and Our Lady of the Sacred Heart (now Sacred Heart) in Caribou (1881). Elsewhere he established St. Gabriel's in Winterport (1877), Sacred Heart in Winn (1881), St. Sylvia's in Bar Harbor (1883), and Sacred Heart in Yarmouth (1900) as separate parishes for the general Catholic population. The parish in Winn, which centered northeast of Bangor on the Penobscot River, was larger than the State of Rhode Island.

St. Gabriel, Winterport, 1850's

Once the diocese in Maine had been separated from New Hampshire, Bishop Healy was freer to develop his large territory where the French-speaking faithful made up the majority. Understandably, he provided other churches for them as St. Anne's (1885) in Lisbon, Notre Dame (1887) in Springvale, St. Agatha's (1889) in St. Agatha, St. Joseph's (1890) in Wallagrass, Immaculate Heart of Mary in Fairfield (1891), St. Ignatius of Antioch (1892) in Sanford, St. Mary's (1892) in Eagle Lake, St. Anthony's (1892) in Jackman, St. Ann's (1893) in Dexter, St. Charles' (1894) in St. Francis, St. Rose of Lima (1894) in Jay, and Holy Rosary (1896) in Caribou. Others like St. Mary of the Nativity (1893) in Presque Isle, St. Teresa's (1896) in Brewer, St. Thomas Aquinas (1898) in Dover-Foxcroft, and St. Martin of Tours (1899) in Millinocket had a significant French-speaking minority among the parishioners.

Churches were also established in a number of the cities and towns for the English-speaking Catholics after the split in the diocese of New Hampshire from Maine. This was clear at St. Joseph's (1885) in Farmington, St. Michael's (1886) in South Berwick, St. Mary of the Assumption (1888) in Orono, St. Ambrose's (1889) in Richmond, Sacred Heart (1889) in Hallowell, St. Vincent de Paul (1890) in Bucksport, St. Francis of Assisi (1891) in Belfast, and St. Denis' (1894) in Fort Fairfield which had been established as a mission in 1842.

Foremost among the religious in the diocese were the Sisters of Mercy. They helped Bishop Healy with institutions within Portland itself, starting with the Kavanagh School. For Native Americans, they opened the state school near Old Town at Indian Island in 1878 and, in 1879, the schools at Dana Point and at Pleasant Point where the state built the schools and provided the salaries for the nuns. In 1881, they began St. Joseph's Academy for girls in Portland's Deering section, where the bishop had purchased an extensive estate and established a mission chapel on Walton Street in honor of St. Joseph. Then, in 1885, they were at Immaculate Conception in Calais and at St. Joseph's in Old Town followed by schools at St. Mary's in Biddeford in 1892 and at St. Mary's in Bangor in 1896.

St. Anthony, Jackman

Of the French Canadians, who constituted the largest Catholic bloc next to the Irish, with enclaves throughout his vast diocese and whose language he spoke quite fluently, Healy was particularly mindful. Hoping to provide for these new arrivals, who eventually numbered about 43,000 during his tenure, the bishop invited the Jesuits to open a college in Van Buren, a town incorporated in 1881 taking for its motto, "In Hoc Signo Vinces," the same as Holy Cross, his alma mater. One of them, Edouard Hamon (1841-1904), a Canadian, was prominent in visiting the French-speaking areas of his diocese, in giving missions and retreats, and in founding at St. Joseph's in Biddeford the League of the Sacred Heart with 400 parishioners in 1886.

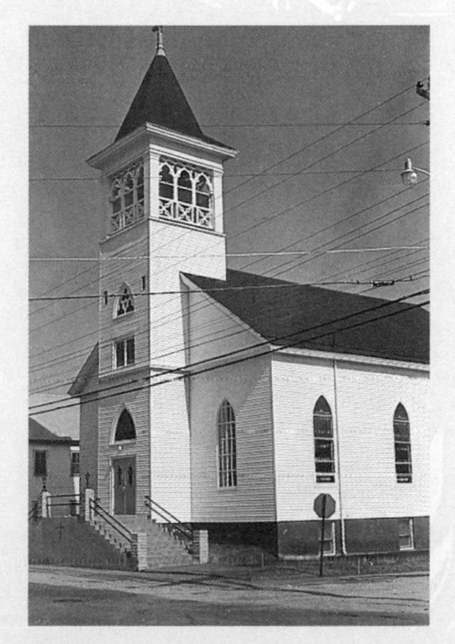

St. Anne, Lisbon
First Mass was celebrated on Easter Sunday 1886

St. Agnes, Pittsfield, c. 1915

Notre Dame de Lourdes, Springvale

To care for the French-speaking Catholics of his diocese, Bishop Healy welcomed a number of women religious into his diocese. In Lewiston, for example, there were at least three groups of nuns who were involved in education. The Sisters of Charity (Grey Nuns) opened Notre Dame de Lourdes in 1878, the Dominican Block in 1883, and the Healy Asylum in 1893. The Congregation of Notre Dame began a school at St. Joseph's in 1881 and one at St. Patrick's in 1884. And, the Daughters of Our Lady of Sion, who replaced the Sisters of Charity at the Dominican Block in 1892, started one at St. Louis in nearby Auburn that same year and, in 1894, a school in Brunswick's St. John the Baptist Parish which had, in 1886, lost seventy-four parishioners, mostly children, from an epidemic of diphtheria.

Also, other women religious of French Canadian background were helpful throughout the diocese. The Sisters of the Good Shepherd began St. Joseph's, an elementary and high school in Biddeford in 1882, and operated Sacred Heart, an elementary and high school in Van Buren in 1891. The Ursulines opened up parish schools at St. Francis de Sales in Waterville in 1888, and at St. Augustine's in Augusta in 1892. Then, there were the Sisters of the Presentation of Mary who began a school at St. Hyacinth's in Westbrook in 1894, the Little Franciscan Sisters of Mary who did so at St. Joseph's in Wallagrass in 1898, and the Congregation of Our Lady of the Rosary which started the Bailey School at St. Luce's in Frenchville in 1899.

Although the Sisters of Charity helped the bishop with the staffing of Our Lady of Lourdes, the Catholic hospital in Lewiston, and the Sisters of Mercy took care of St. Joseph's Hospital and Home for Aged Women in Portland, the major charitable work which occupied Healy's attention was the care of the orphaned children. In 1887, he had St. Elizabeth's Orphanage transferred from North Whitefield to High Street in Portland and took a personal interest in the welfare of the children there, going so far as to purchase a rather extensive piece of property on Little Diamond Island in Casco Bay where they could enjoy the summer. While the bishop had in Lewiston the Healy Asylum as an orphanage for boys, an orphanage for girls was attached to the hospital operated there by the Sisters of Charity.

In addition to the women religious, Bishop Healy successfully invited the first religious men into the diocese since the priests of the Congregation of the Holy Cross departed under his predecessor. The Dominican Friars came to St. Peter's in Lewiston in 1881 to take over that parish where Father Pierre Hévey, during the previous decade, had built it into a vigorous center of 5,000 Franco-American Catholics. With the help of the Marist Brothers, teachers for the boys, and the Daughters of Our Lady of Sion, teachers for the girls, these religious developed St. Peter's into a dynamic center for French-speaking Catholics. In fact, towards the end of the nineteenth century, there were nine priests and five brothers among the Dominicans stationed there, not to mention at least two dozen Daughters of Our Lady of Sion. Among the other male religious, the Brothers of the Christian Schools were teaching at St. Mary's in Bangor where, due to the efforts of Father John W. Murphy (d. 1892), the school became a significant educational center.

Since the Jesuits lacked the manpower to undertake the foundation of a college, the Marist Fathers, who were placed in charge of St. Bruno's in Van Buren in 1884, opened St. Mary's College (1886-1926) there as an institution that actually helped in the Americanization of the French-speaking citizens. Even though some of Healy's critics place him with the conservatives in the classic controversy between the Americanizers and the Europeanizers, Healy respected the French language and did not believe, as did Peter Paul Cahensly (1838-1923), a leading Catholic layman of the time, that learning English in adjusting to American society would lead to a loss of one's Catholicism.

Bishop Healey's tenure in Maine was very fruitful in the growth of the Diocese of Portland. There was an increase of parishes from about twenty-five in Maine at Bacon's death to about sixty when Healy died, a jump of about thirty-three more parishes with a resident priest. At the same time, there were missions and stations which increased to almost seventy, as twenty-two schools, eighteen convents, and a small number of hospitals and orphanages were added to those already existing. In many of these developments, as in the case of the schools, the bishop was assisted by the Sisters of Mercy who staffed these institutions, especially the English-speaking ones, even though their American foundress, Mother Mary Xavier Warde, clashed with Healy on a number of administrative issues, as her biographer Kathleen Healy has observed. While the bishop and Warde were able to work together, it does appear that Healy could have interfered less with the work of the nuns. In any case, the relationship improved under Sister Mary Teresa Pickersgill (1843-1922) who became the first Reverend Mother of the Sisters of Mercy in Maine in 1884. That the women religious who worked in his diocese found in their bishop a gentle shepherd whom they loved and respected indicates that Healy was not an unreasonable person.

One of Healy's major problems as bishop was with the French Canadian community in Biddeford where Jean-François Ponsardin, Pastor of St. Joseph's (1870-77), gave him trouble. Twice within a short span of five

St. Joseph, Biddeford

St Joseph's Convent, Motherhouse of the Sisters of Mercy, Portland

years this pastor had serious administrative differences with the bishop who wished to remove Ponsardin due to the latter's handling of the finances of the parish. Unfortunately, the Biddeford pastor sought to turn the disagreement into a clash of personalities which Healy defused by twice offering Rome a way out of the controversy with his resignation. In the end, Ponsardin was upheld in both a canonical and a civil proceeding and was reinstated by the bishop as pastor. However, Healy so acted in 1881 with the understanding that Ponsardin, being so vindicated, would immediately resign. On May 9, 1883, Bishop Healy had the consolation of dedicating the new church of St. Joseph's after Pierre E. Dupont, its new pastor (1877-1915), had straightened out the church's finances.

Nevertheless, though Ponsardin eventually left the diocese, the clash between him and the bishop, had dragged on for five years and brought out a sharp side of Healy's personality which was generally charming, pleasant, and warm. The bishop held the First Diocesan Synod in 1885 and the State granted his diocese the Corporation-Sole Charter on February 25, 1887. Both measures would help future bishops avoid any problems like those which arose in the case with Father Ponsardin because the Bishop of Portland alone would henceforth be the owner of the parish property. Eventually, Ponsardin returned to France after he ran into similar difficulties in the Diocese of Denver in 1888. Yet, Ponsardin's connection with Maine was not completely severed even after Healy's death since the Diocese of Portland was paying him a retirement pension as late as January of 1908.

During his twenty-five years in Maine, the number of Catholics in the state increased from about 40,000, when Healy arrived, to short of 100,000 by the time of his death on August 5, 1900. Understandably, given at least 50,000 people of French-speaking background in Maine by the 1890s, close to half of those Catholics came from this group. Healy's first year in office saw the bishop travel the vast expanse of Maine and confirm 4,000 youth and preach about 100 sermons. The subsequent years were not much different when schools were provided not only for those of Irish and French backgrounds, but also for the Native Americans. Children flocked to him, the orphans loved him, and the poor found in him a helping hand in time of need. Although he was on friendly terms with Catholics and non-Catholics, especially with Henry Adams Neely, the Protestant Episcopal Bishop of Maine (1867-99), Healy had to endure the contempt of religious bigots in the state legislature. This was clear, for example, when he went before it to defend the rights of those Catholics confined to public institutions to have the services of Catholic chaplains.

The Knights of Columbus, which was established in New Haven, Connecticut, in 1882, founded its first council in Maine, No. 101, in Portland on August 12, 1894. About five hundred knights came to Healy's see city, having chartered out of Boston the steamer *City of Portland*, especially for the induction ceremony. This group of Catholic laymen was devoted to helping the widow and the orphan as well as to defending Catholicism against the attacks of bigots. Given his conservative instincts and his suspicion of secret societies, not to mention his condemnation of the Knights of Labor, Bishop Healy was understandably apprehensive about fraternal societies. However, within two years, Maine had at least ten councils of the Knights of Columbus and 600 members under Portland's Joseph A. McGowan, who became Maine's First State Deputy on May 30, 1896, with Father Thomas H. Wallace (1846-1907), approved by Healy, as their First State Chaplain. Today Bishop Healy is honored by that order since the Fourth Degree section of the Knights of Columbus has its province in the region of New England named for him.

As a bishop in New England, Bishop Healy was, because of his friendship with Archbishop Williams of Boston, very influential. "We are just like two brothers," said Williams. "No one was more dear to me than he." While this was clear in decisions like Healy's founding of the Conference of the St. Vincent de Paul Society in Maine just as Williams had established in Boston in 1861 the first such conference in New England, it was more evident in the appointment of bishops. That most of the other bishops in New England towards the end of his life, including Denis M. Bradley (1846-1903), his successor in New Hampshire, were alumni of the College of the Holy Cross was more than a coincidence since Bishop Healy's counsel, which Archbishop Williams cherished, was often followed.

Therefore, if the Bishop of Portland was a beloved *outsider* because of his race, he was a beloved *insider* because of his character. While his advice as a counselor was cherished, his talents as an orator were also much in demand as evident when he preached at the dedication of the cornerstone of Our Lady of Perpetual Help Church in Boston, on May 28, 1876, and when he preached at the Archbishop Williams' Silver Jubilee Mass as a bishop, on March 12, 1891.

There are those who believe that Bishop Healy failed to become a national voice on the racial issue because he did not speak out at the Third Plenary Council of Baltimore in 1884 and at any one of the five Afro-American Catholic Conferences between 1889 and 1894. Although he was one of the better speakers among the bishops in the United States, administrative priorities and personal concerns cannot be overlooked in dealing with such an evaluation of his career. With respect to that Council of Baltimore, Albert S. Foley, his biographer, shows that Bishop Healy did help to move the other bishops to provide assistance to black Catholics and to eliminate any discrimination in the churches just as he refused to tolerate any segregation of the 300 black Catholics within his own Diocese of Portland. As for the Afro-American Conferences, Bishop Healy had gladly supported these gatherings as a way to improve the lot of black Catholics. What is sometimes overlooked is that Healy's primary responsibility was for the welfare of his Catholic flock in his own diocese at a time when the majority in the nation and in the state was against his race and his religion. In this connection, a recent study by James M. O'Toole's has evoked a debate about the latter's view that the Healy brothers, who were really African Americans, conscientiously conducted themselves more like Irish Americans.

With respect to the Native Americans, who reflected the ancient roots of Catholicism in his own diocese, Bishop Healy certainly had a good relationship. This was evident in the late 1870s, in having the Sisters of Mercy helped him cut down on the rising intolerance in the nation by extending their educational ministries first to the Penobscots and then to the Passamaquoddies and the Micmacs. In his visit to Rome in 1879, he brought with him a pair of moccasins that the Native Americans had crafted for the Pope and which Leo XIII (1878-1903) wore at the audience attended by Portland's bishop. When James Fitton (1805-81), the renowned Boston missionary had passed from the scene in Healy's time, it was recalled that he had begun his priestly career by caring for the Passamaquoddies in 1828.

Moreover, on June 25, 1885, Bishop Healy himself had not forgotten that tribal nation when he addressed a letter to the Committee on Indian Affairs of the state legislature pleading for their rights in these

Fr. Alexandre L. Mothon, O.P., first prior, Dominican Friars, Lewiston

Former Dominican Priory, Lewiston

Calvary Cemetery, South Portland

words: "The Indians claim that they are not wards of the State; that they are a Nation, whose rights are guaranteed by Treaty with Massachusetts, and accepted by the State of Maine." Such lobbying for the weakest of his flock was characteristic of one who as Bishop of Portland had spoken against child labor and for the repeal of state laws discriminating against Roman Catholics. Later it was Healy who had encouraged Louis F. Sockalexis (1871-1913), a Penobscot, after whom the Cleveland Indians derived their team's name, to attend the College of the Holy Cross between 1894 and 1897, before the Maine native entered professional baseball and before the bishop became the first golden jubilarian of that same college.

Certainly, it is not altogether clear that Bishop Healy had anything to lose or anything to gain by speaking out or by remaining silent on national issues. If what he did now appears to be an error of judgment, it can be said that the bishop was willing to shoulder this burden, including many others like his own frail health. "I pray," Healy said of historians and others, "that they will be kind in judging my numerous faults, mistakes, and errors of judgment." Yet, that he was able to rise above whatever prejudices which he may have encountered either inside or outside of his church says much about the quality of Healy's character, the spirituality of which, was grounded on his devotion to Our Lady of Lourdes whose title, "*Immaculata*", he placed on his episcopal coat of arms.

The great outpouring of people at his funeral, on August 9, 1900, indicated that James Augustine Healy was a beloved shepherd of his flock. That the Vatican had honored him two months earlier, on the Silver Jubilee of his Episcopal Consecration, as Assistant to the Papal Throne, indicates how highly he was regarded outside the diocese. Today his memory is fixed in his diocese in South Portland's Calvary Cemetery which he had enlarged and where his remains lie in the earth under a huge Celtic Cross, made possible through the contributions raised by the children of the diocese. And, his legacy continues at the College of the Holy Cross where a residence hall was dedicated in his memory in August of 1967. That, in March of 1998, a panel of the State of Maine suggested that a portrait of the bishop be among those housed in a place of honor at the State House in Augusta says much more about the real stature of Bishop James Augustine Healy.

Chapter 5

A New Style of American Bishop

William Henry O'Connell (1859-1944) was appointed third Bishop of Portland, on February 8, 1901. Born in Lowell, Massachusetts, on December 8, 1859, the son of John and Bridget (Farley) O'Connell, he was ordained to the priesthood, on June 8, 1884, by Cardinal Raffaele Monaco La Valletta (1827-96) at St. John Lateran in Rome. Subsequently, Father O'Connell spent his first decade as a priest in the Archdiocese of Boston before he was appointed Rector of the North American College in Rome on November 21, 1895. Elevated to the rank of Monsignor, on June 9, 1897, he was consecrated bishop by Cardinal Francesco Satolli (1839-1910) with the assistance of Archbishops Rafael Merry del Val and Edmond Stoner, on May 19, 1901, in the Corsini Chapel of the Basilica of St. John Lateran.

When Rome had been confronted with strong opposition to the nomination to the Diocese of Portland of three English-speaking priests of the diocese (Edward F. Hurley, Thomas H. Wallace, and Michael F. Walsh), it was Cardinal Satolli who had suggested the name of O'Connell, one of his former students, and Pope Leo XIII approved. Obviously, what was behind the length of time it took to name the new bishop was the opposition of the French-speaking Catholics to the control of the leadership of the Catholic Church in Maine by the Irish. That Rome chose to ignore the recommendation of the American bishops for a priest from the Diocese of Portland was due to a certain uneasiness regarding the growing tension among the English-speaking (about 27,000), French-speaking (about 20,000), and bilingual (about 45,000) parishioners in the state.

After Bishop O'Connell was installed as Bishop of Portland, on July 4, 1901, amid the fanfare of exploding fireworks on the nation's birthday, it became clear that he was a different type of bishop. His charm, intellect, and patriotism attracted both Catholics and non-Catholics alike. On the death of President William McKinley the following September, he was called upon to deliver the brief oration at City Hall before four thousand people in Portland's civic ceremony held in memory of the President. When Theodore Roosevelt, McKinley' successor, visited the same city, the President was interested in seeing only O'Connell with whom the latter formed a warm friendship as the bishop did with the public officials of his see city and of the state itself. Such recognition of Portland's Catholic bishop was also evident when Maine's Governor John F. Hill had welcomed O'Connell on his arrival in Maine, with a public reception in Augusta, and when he and other dignitaries attended the Memorial Mass in the Cathedral of the Immaculate Conception for Pope Leo XIII, on July 28, 1903.

That year, when O'Connell declined the nomination as Archbishop of Manila in the Philippines, which the United States had gained in 1898 as a result of the Spanish-American War, it was obvious that Portland had a unique Catholic leader. O'Connell sought recognition among the economic, political, religious, and social elite within his episcopal city and the state. Two prominent citizens of Portland, William L. Putnam (1835-1918), a federal judge,

Bishop William H. O'Connell

Cardinal William Henry O'Connell's coat of arms

Msgr. Michael McDonough, Vicar General

and Thomas Brackett Reed (1839-1902), a former congressman, were among those who opened their doors to him. Such a reception helped the Catholic bishop to break down the barriers against Catholics in a heavily Protestant environment and to reach out to people of other faiths as well as to Catholics of diverse cultural backgrounds.

Having spent much of his time as a priest recently in Rome, O'Connell's knowledge of the clergy in New England was rather limited. In fact, as far as Maine was concerned, the only other priest that he knew when he came into the Diocese of Portland was Michael C. McDonough, as O'Connell later declared when that priest died in 1933. Understandably, then, O'Connell set out early in his tenure as bishop to explore by carriage, rail, and steamboat his vast diocese of almost a hundred thousand Catholics.

Former St. Ignatius Church and Convent, Sanford

To acquaint himself not only with the clergy but also with the laity and religious of the Diocese of Portland, O'Connell sought to familiarize himself with the needs of about fifty-five resident priests, at least thirty parishes with churches, almost eighty mission stations, and close to thirty chapels. In addition, the diocese had twenty-five schools and some 350 women religious who helped to operate them, along with three orphanages, two hospitals, and one home for the aged. That O'Connell was able to deal with almost every ethnic group in its own language, including newer immigrants like the Italians, was an important asset for the new bishop in learning about Maine's Catholic population.

In his less than five years as Bishop of Portland, O'Connell established a number of parishes so that some fifteen new churches were added to the diocese. Among these were St. Mark's (1902) in Ashland (Sheridan), St. Louis in Auburn (1902), St. Mary of Lourdes (1902) in Lincoln, St. Athanasius (1902) and St. John the Baptist (1905) in Rumford, and St. James the Greater (1905) in Baileyville (Woodland). While these may appear to be few, they were evidence of the church expanding outside of his see city, especially with more mission stations rather than parishes.

Yet, O'Connell did not get along too well with the French-speaking Catholics outside of Portland because, unlike Bishop Healy who respected their culture, the new bishop emphasized the need for them to become assimilated into American society. Although O'Connell stood solidly with the conservatives in Pope Leo XIII's condemnation of the Americanism (*Testem Benevolentiae*, January 22, 1899) on its theological points, the Bishop of Portland realized that it was very important for the immigrants to become culturally assimilated into American society, a process that is better described as Americanization than as Americanism. That he drew such a distinction between religion and culture was evident in his decisions directing the Franco-Americans to speak English, rather than French, in their churches and in their schools.

In the case of the parishes, O'Connell announced in early October of 1905 that he would establish Sacred Heart, a parish in Waterville for the Irish. In doing so, the bishop included some of the French-speaking families of St. Francis de Sales in the new parish. This was not unlike his establishment of St. Athanasius for the French-speaking families in Rumford in 1902 when the bishop turned it into a church for the Irish by forcing the French-speaking families to build a new church, St. John the Baptist, just around the corner from their original church. At the same time, O'Connell sought to bring about assimilation by replacing the French-speaking nuns with English-speaking Sisters of Mercy who took over the parish school in Brunswick in 1905.

Moreover, in dealing with the parishes within his diocese, O'Connell instructed his priests be careful to avoid debts. To this end, he demanded that an annual report of the parish include information on its finances, attendance at Mass, and special collections. Since, as bishop, he was completely responsible for the financial situation of the diocese, he wanted to have the final say with respect to any parish constructions. If a pastor failed to adhere to these guidelines, O'Connell would not hesitate to correct him. To a prominent laymen like Thomas E. Vose, a clothier in Lubec, who had continually pressed the bishop since late November of 1903 to establish Sacred Heart, the mission chapel of Machias, as a new parish, O'Connell responded: "While I am happy to organize distinct parishes, I must in duty see to it that such parishes will be self-supporting."

In the pursuit of his supervision of the parishes, the bishop was known to have clashed with some pastors. One, John M. Harrington (1856-1926), Pastor of St. Mary's in Orono, acted on his own with his plans for a new church. Another, Adolphe O. Lacroix (1858-1938), Pastor of Notre Dame de Lourdes in Skowhegan, approved of a loan for construction in his parish without consulting the bishop. And, a third, Narcisse R. Charland, Pastor of St. Francis de Sales in Waterville for many years (1880-1923), who had been, after Healy's death, the French-speaking clergy's candidate for bishop, disagreed with O'Connell on the erection of Sacred Heart Parish because it would break up his own parish. While O'Connell prevailed in demanding accountability, he had planted the seeds of a bitter controversy for his successor in the plans for a parish for the Irish in Waterville.

Although the priests of the diocese increased by twenty during O'Connell's tenure, he lost some exceptional ones. Of these, Michael J. O'Brien (1842-1901) and Richard John Duddy (1844-1905) are particularly noteworthy. Monsignor O'Brien, vicar general of the diocese and favored by the French-speaking Catholics as an English-speaking candidate to succeed Bishop Healy, was Pastor of St. Mary's in Bangor and had welcomed the new bishop and pledged the loyalty of the clergy to him just four months before his death on November 12, 1901. Father Duddy, the first native of Portland to be ordained a priest (1869), served in the Diocese of Portland at Lewiston, Old Town and Winterport, before his death, on February 17, 1905, as a member of the clergy of the Diocese of Manchester.

Choir, St. John the Baptist, Brunswick, c. 1908

During O'Connell's tenure, a number of schools were opened throughout the state. The Sisters of Mercy opened one at St. Ignatius' in Sanford in 1903. The Sisters of the Good Shepherd opened St. André School in Biddeford in 1901. The Dominican Sisters arrived from France in 1904 to teach at Saints Peter and Paul in Lewiston. The Daughters of Wisdom opened Notre Dame de la Sagesse, an elementary and high school, at St. Agatha in 1904, and Our Lady of Mount Carmel School at Lille in 1905. The Congregation of Notre Dame opened a new facility, the Wallace School, named for the parents of Monsignor Thomas H. Wallace, at St. Patrick's in Lewiston in 1905. The Little Franciscan Sisters of Mary opened St. Louis

Parish Band, St. John the Baptist Parish, Brunswick, c. 1900

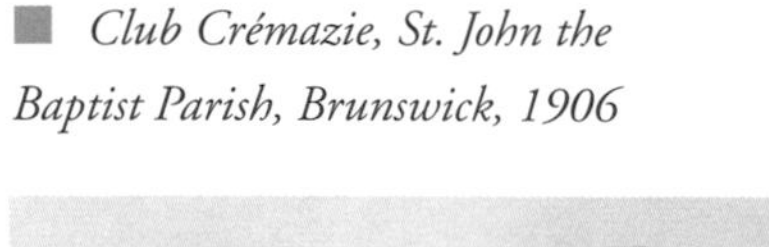

Club Crémazie, St. John the Baptist Parish, Brunswick, 1906

St. Mary's Church Choir, Biddeford, 1900 (photographer unknown)

School at Fort Kent, in 1906. And, this same year, the Sisters of St. Joseph opened the Sacred Heart Convent School in Jackman. It is noteworthy that most of those were in areas of French-speaking Catholics whose migration into Maine had declined during the first decade of the twentieth century due to the prosperity in Canada.

Given his background in Rome, O'Connell was a man of culture and sought to display this in his own Cathedral. After a generation of service, the building was in need of renovations and the new bishop undertook the task with a personal interest. "If in all America there is a better equipped Cathedral in all that pertains to the dignity of worship, and the glory of the House of God, I do not know it," he declared with obvious satisfaction at the completion of the project in 1903. To mark his contribution, O'Connell donated the new window above the main altar and dedicated an altar in memory of each of his predecessors. Likewise, his love of liturgical music was evident in two of the new Cathedral windows which symbolized this.

A wave of newer immigrants from Southern Europe like the Italians and from Eastern Europe like the Poles forced the bishop to look to the future. They were outnumbering the flow of French Canadians and Irish into the Diocese of Portland since the end of the nineteenth century and Bishop O'Connell urged his priests to welcome these people and provide for their spiritual welfare. Recalling the immigrant origins of the Catholic Church in the United States, the bishop reflected in first pastoral letter (*Ad Clerum*), of May 31, 1903, on the incredible development of Catholicism because of the contributions of the Irish, the Germans, and the French. One of those newer immigrant who had settled in Rumford in 1903 was a tailor from Poland whose son, Edmund S. Muskie (1914-96), became in 1954 the first Catholic to be elected by the voters as Governor of Maine. In 1904, Bishop O'Connell instructed his flock through another pastoral letter dealing with the authority of the Church of which he was its chief leader in the state.

Apart from Catholic organizations like the Knights of Columbus, which had been founded in 1882 as a benevolent society, Bishop O'Connell, like other members of the hierarchy, was apprehensive about Catholics joining organizations which threatened their beliefs and practices. To counteract those societies that offered cultural, financial, and social benefits in an era of joiners, the bishop sought to attract Catholics to such activities as Catholic Reading Circles and the Catholic Union for Men. Though women had a number of societies to occupy their attention, O'Connell was particularly effective in sponsoring, with the help of Catholics and Protestants in 1902, the Working Men's Club on Commercial Street which, in attracting dock workers, railroad workers, and ordinary laborers in Portland, became a very prestigious social club in Maine. Likewise, to care for the younger men, the bishop provided Catholic clubs with benefits similar to what Protestant youth derived from the Y. M. C. A.

O'Connell's last years in Portland were marked by his Roman approach to his office. On July 1, 1904, he held the Second Diocesan Synod, a meeting of representatives of the diocese summoned with a view to shaping decrees to help advance the life and mission of the Roman Catholic Church under his jurisdiction. On Sunday July 24th that same year, when Cardinal Satolli visited the city, he became the first cardinal to do so, as he presided at Mass in the Cathedral. Later, on November 24th, O'Connell sailed for Rome and did not return to Portland until February of 1905.

In mid-September of 1905, after Russia and Japan had signed a treaty of peace on September 5th, Bishop O'Connell went to Japan as papal envoy to Emperor Mutsuhito who had been reigning since 1867. Obviously, O'Connell had been selected for the mission because of his friend, Rafael Cardinal Merry del Val, who was the Papal Secretary of State. By this time, the bishop, ever concerned about the impression he was making in Rome, had been appointed Assistant at the Papal Throne by the Pope, St. Pius X (1903-14). That the treaty between Japan and Russia had been concluded within the boundaries of the Diocese of Portland at the Portsmouth Naval Shipyard in Kittery, Maine, may have been relevant to Rome's choice of O'Connell rather than another American bishop for the mission.

Although O'Connell's major objective was to inaugurate diplomatic relations between the Vatican and Japan, he was also to sound out the government about the possibility of opening a Jesuit school in Japan. In pursuing this objective, the bishop emphasized the special bond between the Jesuit St. Francis Xavier and the Japanese people. O'Connell secured the cooperation of the Japanese Foreign Ministry through its representative, Prince Taro Katsura (1848-1913), who was very enthusiastic about the proposal for a Catholic university in Tokyo.

At the time, when the French, as allies of Russia, the country recently at war with Japan, sought to thwart the papal mission, they did not succeed because O'Connell's competence and the help of Lloyd C. Griscom, the American Ambassador to Japan (1902-06), acting under instructions from President Theodore Roosevelt to help the Bishop of Portland, prevailed. The Meiji Emperor Mutsuhito received the papal envoy very cordially as the latter presented him, on November 10, 1905, a letter of July 21st of that year from His Holiness. Very appreciative of the O'Connell mission, the Emperor conferred on him, through his representatives, on November 20th, the Order of the Sacred Treasure, the nation's highest honor and, after he had delivered a Latin address to the society, on November 22nd, the Imperial Education Society of Japan elected O'Connell as a fellow member.

Much of O'Connell's attention during his years in Portland was given to matters outside of the diocese from which he was absent almost twenty-five percent of the time. For his successful mission to Japan, from which he returned to Rome, on January 10, 1906, the Holy Father, named O'Connell Archbishop Coadjutor to Archbishop Williams of Boston, on February 8, 1906. In the eyes of Rome, the mission had exceeded anything the Vatican had expected and the Bishop of Portland had proven himself to be an ideal diplomat. Some years after O'Connell said farewell to the Diocese of Portland, on September 9, 1906, the Jesuits opened, in 1913, Sophia University for which he had so effectively prepared the way.

Considering his short career in Maine, O'Connell saw his diocese expand to 110,000 Catholics, his priests grow by twenty to 121, his churches increase by at least fifteen to 104 within five years, and his schools rise from some thirty to thirty-seven. Despite his absences from Maine, O'Connell found time to revamp the administrative structure of his diocese by reorganizing the curia and placing the

Quoddy Head Light

institutions and the parishes of his diocese on a firmer foundation. He shaped his own Cathedral into a model parish with the renovation of its structure, the reduction of its debt, and its emphasis on liturgical life with the splendor of its music and ritual.

At the same time, O'Connell projected a new style for an American bishop in extending his interest to the public at large in the state, the nation, and even around the world. But, in doing so, O'Connell, whose lifestyle was rather pompous compared to the simple one of his predecessor, conducted himself as a prince in sending money to Rome, especially the $2,500.00 or so derived from the annual collection for Peter's Pence. Since Portland was not a wealthy diocese, its bishop needed to add to the collection from his own or other sources if he wished to impress Rome.

Unfortunately, O'Connell's departure in 1906 left a cloud over his years in Portland. To what extent he wished to impress Rome with money when the United States was still a mission territory is not altogether clear. What is clear is that, despite his insistence on accountability from his pastors and from his own household, O'Connell left the diocese in debt until this was called to his attention by his successor. The latter, as James M. O'Toole, O'Connell's biographer has shown, conducted his own investigation and found that his renowned predecessor owed the Diocese of Portland funds that could take it out of debt. To O'Connell's credit, he recognized his error and came through with a check for $25,576.09 that cleared the debt in the eyes of his successor. While he sought to live up to his motto of demonstrating "Strength in Difficulties" ("*Vigor in Arduis*") as a bishop, William H. O'Connell could have avoided such an error on his departure to Boston had he been more careful to regard himself as one who was a servant of the church rather than the church itself.

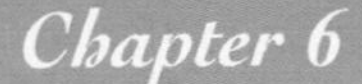

Chapter 6

Maine's Americanizing Bishop

Louis Sebastian Walsh (1858-1924) was appointed the fourth Bishop of Portland on August 3, 1906. Born in Salem, Massachusetts, on January 22, 1858, the son of Patrick and Honora (Foley) Walsh, he was ordained a priest in St. John Lateran in Rome, on December 23, 1882, by Cardinal Monaco La Valletta, the same prelate who, two years later, ordained O'Connell. Walsh had served as the Superintendent of Schools (1887-1906) for the Archdiocese of Boston and was consecrated a bishop, on October 18, 1906, by Archbishop Williams who was assisted by Bishop Thomas Daniel Beaven of Springfield and Bishop Matthew Harkins of Providence, in Portland's Cathedral of the Immaculate Conception. That day, Walsh's predecessor, Archbishop O'Connell, his junior in the priesthood but senior in the episcopacy, was seated in the sanctuary to witness the transition.

As in the succession to Healy, the Franco-American community, which then claimed a majority of the parishes and of the Catholic population in the Diocese of Portland, had once more attempted, as Kenneth B. Woodbury, Jr., has demonstrated, to have one of their own (Narcisse R. Charland of Waterville, Pierre E. Dupont of Biddeford, or François X. Trudel of Old Town) appointed as the new bishop. Although more than half the parishes of the diocese were French-speaking and the Irish were easily outnumbered by a margin of two to one, the attempt, launched by *Le Messager*, Lewiston's leading French newspaper from 1880-1966, failed in good part because some leading French-speaking priests refused to go along with what was viewed as opposition to assimilation into American culture. Nevertheless, the new bishop was an exceptional choice since he had already been regarded as a possible successor to Healy and as a coadjutor for Williams before he was chosen for Portland.

As Bishop Walsh attended to the needs of his diocese, significant changes were taking place. Not long after his predecessor had succeeded Williams, on August 30, 1907, as Archbishop of Boston, Rome removed the United States from the jurisdiction of the Congregation for the Propagation of the Faith in 1908. Subsequently, Americanization on the cultural level, became more of a policy for the bishops as the nation was no longer mission territory, a development that was also affirmed in the elevation of Archbishop O'Connell to the College of Cardinals, on November 27, 1911. In engaging in the acculturalization of the immigrants to American society, Walsh, like his fellow bishops, upheld the doctrine of the Catholic Church, including its condemnation of the theological points of Americanism, while turning Catholic immigrants into Americans.

Having attended the College of the Holy Cross from 1876 to 1877, Bishop Walsh was mindful of the contributions of the Jesuits to the history of his diocese. If anything marked his tenure as a bishop, it was his sense of the history of the Catholic Church in Maine which came through in his work in establishing parishes throughout the state. In Portland, in particular, new milestones were achieved in providing for the spiritual welfare of the recent Catholic immigrants who were of Italian and of Polish background.

In the case of the Italians, most of whom came from the southern part of Italy, they were cared for by Father Antonio J. Petillo (d. 1938), native of Salerno, who came to Portland as an assistant at the Cathedral between 1907 and 1909. Then, when Father Agnello Santagnello arrived in Portland, on July 1, 1910, Mass was offered for the Italians in the Kavanagh School until the diocese purchased an old stable on Federal Street which F. W. Cunninghan & Sons converted into a chapel for $2,642.00. This was blessed just in time for

Bishop Louis S. Walsh

Interior, present Cathedral Residence Chapel built by Bishop Walsh

Coat of arms of Bishop Louis Sebastian Walsh

St. Mark, Sheridan

Christmas of 1911 as a mission of the Cathedral for which Santagnello cared until he left the diocese in December of 1913. With Father Petillo's return to the diocese on August 1, 1914, his work at St. Peter's was formally resumed, on April 11, 1915. Again Petillo ministered to the Italians for a second time until his final return to Italy in early November of 1925.

In the case of the Polish Catholics, the bishop opened a mission for them at St. Dominic's, on April 6, 1915. Father John Sciskalski, a Vincentian, cared for them in the basement of St. Dominic's Church until Father Peter M. Pojnar (1890-1959) was appointed to minister to them in 1917. In 1924, a church and hall were constructed for $60,000.00 by F. W. Cunningham & Sons on the land that had been purchased in 1915 at the corner of Danforth and Emery Streets for $7,700.00. By that time, the Catholic Polish community at what is St. Louis Parish (1923) numbered 200 families in Portland.

Fr. Peter Pojnar, pastor of St. Louis Parish, Portland

Elsewhere, Bishop Walsh provided for other ethnic groups when the local pastor could not take care of these new immigrants. In Lewiston, where some Lithuanian immigrants had settled and were working in the shoe industry, Father Norbert Pakalins, as a priest at St. Patrick's, was caring for them in 1916. And, in the central region of the state in 1922, Father Joseph Award cared for the growing Syrian population in Waterville.

Further, due to the leadership of Father Honorius Frastacky, a Franciscan, Saints Cyril and Methodius was founded, on September 8, 1923, for the Slovaks in Lisbon Falls. This new church had 300 families and about 1500 souls in that area which included Lisbon and Lisbon Center as well as Danville and South Chisholm, with its cotton, paper, saw, and wool mills. These families were separated from Holy Family Church, where they had given the original altar for that church back in 1899, before Holy Family itself was finally established as an official parish in 1914.

One of the pastors who provided for other nationalities in his parish was Father Joseph M. LeGuennec (1876-1941), Pastor of St. Rose of Lima in Jay, whose missions covered almost a handful of counties. At Gilbertville, for example, in the summer of 1916, when Bishop Walsh visited there to administer Confirmations on July 2nd, there was a mixed congregation with parishioners whose native language was either Italian, French, or English. That day the bishop preached in all three languages to the congregation. If any pastor could not provide for these national groups in their own language, the bishop's policy was to have the pastor invite a priest of their own ethnic background to visit them at least twice a year to carry on their heritage.

Moreover, very much impressed with Sebastian Râle, Bishop Walsh honored the memory of this Jesuit martyr by dedicating a church in 1907 in memory of his patron saint, St. Sebastian's, in Madison, and by rededicating the monument which was set up at Norridgewock by Bishop Fenwick in the nineteenth century. Having acquired the land at the site of the old mission, Walsh invited Father Thomas J. Campbell, S. J., of Fordham University to give the main address at the dedication ceremonies held there, on August 22, 1907. Perhaps the strongest evidence of Bishop Walsh's interest in Maine's Catholic history was what he did to celebrate the tercentenary of the planting of the mission on Mount Desert Island.

Having already built a chapel at Northeast Harbor in honor of St. Ignatius Loyola, the Founder of the Society of Jesus, Walsh dedicated, on August 6, 1913, a church of granite honoring the original Jesuit mission and naming it Holy Redeemer, thereby changing the name of the parish which had been established as St. Sylvia's in 1883. With most of the bishops of New England and the Apostolic Delegate present, Walsh joyfully asked: "Am I not right, therefore, in feeling and saying that the vision of 1613 in France and on this Island has been more than fulfilled in 1913, on this day?"

Very much interested in the Catholic history of New England, as his publication of the study, *Origin of the Catholic Church in Salem* (1890) demonstrated, Bishop Walsh commemorated the golden jubilee of St. John's Church in Bangor in 1906, the centenary of St. Patrick's Church in Newcastle in 1908, the centenary of St. Dennis' Parish in North Whitefield in 1922, and the golden jubilee of the Sisters of Mercy in Bangor in 1915 and in Portland in 1923. Two of the more remarkable of these religious women, Sister Mary Gertrude (1848-1923), a cousin of Winifred Kavanagh, and Sister Stanislaus Finn (1856-1918), superior of the orphanages in both North Whitefield and Portland, passed on to God during Walsh's years as bishop. Their devotion to the church was not unlike that of Catherine Mangan O'Donnell, a pioneer of Catholicism in Lewiston.

St. Sebastian, Madison

But, Walsh's love for history was manifest above all in 1908 when he founded, with the help of priests like John E. Kealy (1863-1934) and Philippe E. Desjardins (1876-1969), the Maine Catholic Historical Society which published, *The Maine Catholic Historical Magazine*, a monthly between 1913 and 1916 and, irregularly, as a quarterly between 1916 and 1928. Devoted throughout his life to the Jesuits and their history, the bishop established a parish in honor of St. Francis Xavier in Winthrop in 1913 and blessed a chapel under that same saint's patronage at Brownville Junction in 1916. To conduct the retreats of his priests, at the famed Poland Spring House, where he was an honored guest of members of the Ricker Family, who operated the resort, the bishop chose the Jesuits. Later, before death overtook him, Walsh's sense of history had led him to plan a celebration for the bicentennial of Father Râle's martyrdom during 1924.

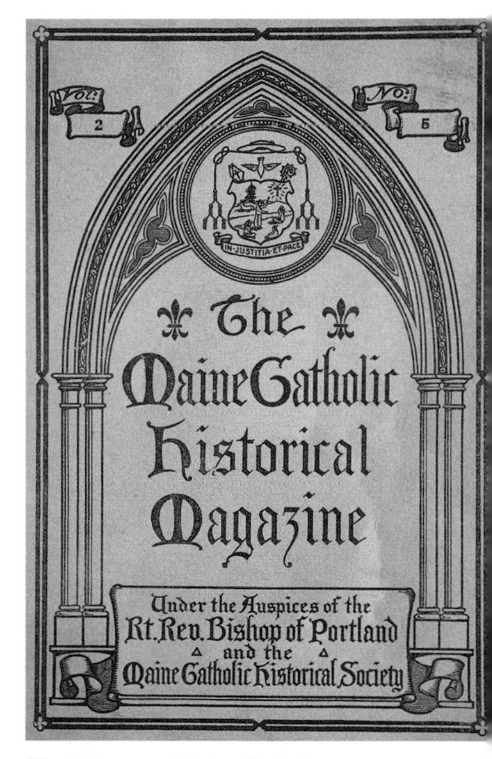

Vol: 2

No: 5

IN-JUSTITIA-ET-PACE

The Maine Catholic Historical Magazine

Under the Auspices of the Rt. Rev. Bishop of Portland and the Maine Catholic Historical Society

Title page, Maine Catholic Historical Magazine

There were other parishes which Bishop Walsh established as well throughout his time as bishop. Holy Family in Daigle and Sacred Heart in Waterville in 1906 were among the first. At Daigle, the first church build in 1906 was destroyed by fire within year and rebuilt in 1907. These woes of Bishop Walsh were minor compared with his problems with the Franco-American community in Waterville where O'Connell had decided to give the Irish families

Original St. Catherine of Siena Church, and Oxford Country Fairgrounds, c. 1915

in the Parish of St. Francis de Sales their own Parish of the Sacred Heart. As Michael J. Guignard has shown, when Walsh followed through on this by placing 1150 of the Franco-American population in the new parish with 250 Irish Catholics, he incurred the wrath of the majority for creating this bilingual parish. One of those opposed was Dr. Jean-Louis Fortier of Waterville, a close friend of the city's older pastor and the leader of its Franco-American community which was bent on the preservation of its religious and cultural practices as well as its customs and language.

Mount Merici Convent, Waterville

Unfortunately, that clash came about at a time when the Franco-Americans were becoming increasingly frustrated with Bishop Walsh who made himself even more notorious than O'Connell with his assimilationist policies. These were evident in replacing French-speaking with English-speaking pastors of Irish background, delaying the construction of a new church for Saints Peter and Paul in Lewiston, and requiring a special collection for the Irish orphans in Portland after he had closed a home for French orphans in Biddeford, not to mention his expectation that all Catholics, regardless of ethnic background, support the churches, the schools, the rectories, and the cemeteries of the diocese. After enduring what it regarded as intolerable practices of assimilation for a few years, the Franco-American community decided to act in its own defense when it judged that what Walsh was doing was neither reasonable nor just with respect to the church properties in the French-speaking centers of Biddeford, Lewiston, and Waterville.

Consequently, Franco-American Catholics decided to bring about a change in the 1887 law making the diocese a corporation sole in the person of the bishop by seeking to incorporate parishes individually as was the practice in Quebec. In this way, they would assure the survival, *la survivance*, of their religious and cultural heritage against the forces of cultural Americanization at a time when the total Catholic population of the state numbered 125,000.

After both sides appeared in Augusta to state their case on March 7, 1911, matters began to get out of control. On May 9, 1911, the bishop placed six members of the Franco-American leadership committee under an interdict, thereby forcing them to appeal to Rome. While Rome agreed on the interdiction, it did not agree on the ownership by the bishop. However, in the details of the decision by the Roman Congregation, it was clear that its decision of August 10, 1911, favored a corporation council for each parish while still preserving the absolute power of the bishop. Though the Franco-American lobby still tried to change the law to favor its view of ownership, it failed to do so in its last attempt, on February 20, 1913, especially after the bishop's letter of the previous January 30th had exposed how dangerous to the administration of his diocese was their position.

In the end, the state legislature, as it had throughout the controversy, backed Walsh who proposed a slight amendment to the law to allow for parish corporations not unlike those in other Catholic dioceses while not jeopardizing his authority. After the bill was signed by the governor on March 22, 1913, Franco-Americans who had held out saw that their cause was hopeless, especially since their funds had run out and they were no longer united. Thus, the matter came to an end leaving only a legacy of bitterness among some of those involved in the controversy.

Perhaps the saddest moment in the whole controversy came when Dr. Fortier died in Waterville, on June 4, 1911, as the protesters were gathering in Biddeford to coordinate their efforts to change the state law. Fortier had

St. Bridget, North Vassalboro

spent almost two months in Rome prior to Walsh's appointment lobbying for a Franco-American to succeed O'Connell as bishop. The news that Walsh would not allow Fortier, who had publicly opposed the bishop's views, to be buried from the church with a funeral Mass stunned the Franco-American community, especially since the deceased leader was not one of those under the bishop's interdict. Thereafter, no matter what Walsh did, as is evident from Robert Rumilly's history of the Franco-Americans, the bishop would never be viewed as a friend of the Franco-Americans in Maine even though he had set up at least four parishes for them (one in Sanford and three in the Auburn and Lewiston area).

Parish growth during Walsh's times continued at a steady pace. There were other new parishes like St. James in Kingman, St. Mary's in Lewiston, and St. Ann's at Pleasant Point in Perry established in 1907. These were followed by St. Martha's in Kennebunkport and St. Joseph's in Portland in 1909; Notre Dame in Waterville in 1910; Holy Cross in South Portland and St. Bridget's in North Vassalboro in 1911; St. Peter's in East Millinocket and Holy Family in Greenville in 1912; Sacred Heart in Lubec 1913; St. Catherine of Siena in Norway in 1914; St. Raphael's in Kittery, Most Holy Trinity in Saco and St. Mary's in Westbrook in 1916; St. Louis in Limestone in 1919; St. Agnes in Island Falls, St. Peter's in Bingham, and St. Joseph's in Hamlin in 1920; St. Matthew's in Limerick in 1921; St. Patrick's in Portland in 1922; and Sacred Heart in Auburn, St. Remy in Keegan, Holy Cross and Holy Family in Lewiston, St. Christopher's on Peaks Island, and Holy Family in Sanford in 1923. While the church grew quickly in Androscoggin, Aroostook, Cumberland, and York counties, its growth was slower in Washington, Somerset, Piscataquis, Penobscot, Oxford, Kennebec, and Hancock counties.

Former St. Catherine of Siena's Church, Norway

A number of prominent priests died during Walsh's tenure as bishop. One was the popular Father Narcisse Charland in Waterville who had been mentioned as a possible bishop and was certainly the favorite of the Franco-American community to succeed Bishop Healy on whose council he had served. Born on August 10, 1848, in Richmond, Quebec, he became known as the renowned pastor of St. Francis de Sales in Waterville. Charland had been responsible for bringing the Ursulines from Trois Rivières in Quebec to that Maine city in 1888 at a time when Roman Catholics numbered about 3,000 out of a city population of 7,500. At his death, on January 19, 1923, Father Charland was honored by the mayor of the city who ordered the city's flags flown at half-staff until the conclusion of the pastor's funeral when he was buried in St. Francis Cemetery.

St. Raphael, Kittery

Other priests of Walsh's time were Charles W. Doherty (1846-1910), François X. Trudel (1843-1917), Thomas F. Butler (1846-1917), and Charles W. Collins (1870-1920). Doherty, a native of Portland and Pastor of St. Mary's in Augusta from 1886 to his death, was eulogized by Timothy P. Linehan (1847-1922),

Bishop Walsh laying the cornerstone of St. Patrick's Church/School, July 17, 1922

Fr. Arthur Décary

Fr. Joseph Marcoux, the "Apostle of the Fish River"

Pastor of St. Mary's in Biddeford, at his funeral as the first in the diocese to die as a pastor in office. Trudel, a native of Canada, was ordained by Bishop Bacon in 1871 and elevated to the rank of monsignor in 1904, serving as the pastor at Old Town for almost forty years. Butler, a native of Galbally, Ireland, and Walsh's classmate at Holy Cross, was ordained in Paris, on May 22, 1880, and served as Pastor of St. Joseph's in Ellsworth (1881-94) and of St. Joseph's in Lewiston (1894-1917). And, Collins, a native of Ellsworth and a graduate of Holy Cross in 1891, had served as vicar general for both Bishop Healy and Bishop O'Connell and became a pastor with the rank of monsignor before he transferred to the Archdiocese of Boston in 1915.

Among other outstanding priests of the diocese, three others can be mentioned. There was Joseph P. Ahern (1859-1922) who was the pastor at Eastport for at least a quarter of a century. A second was Jeremiah McCarthy (1843-1923), the Pastor of St. Mary's in Bangor, who served as a priest for almost a half century after he was ordained by Bishop Healy. And, a third was Charles E. Woodman (1852-1924), a native of Saco (his former home was the rectory of the first Catholic Church there) and of Puritan ancestry who converted to Catholicism and become a Paulist Father in a career which he pursued outside of Maine.

Also, there were some prominent lay persons who died during Walsh's years as bishop. One was Frank W. Cunningham (1846-1915), one of the leading contractors in New England, whose firm had been responsible for building a number of churches and other buildings for the diocese. Another was Emily Poole Baxter (1875-1915), the sister of Governor Percival P. Baxter (1876-1969), whose travels in Europe had led her to convert to Catholicism which she devotedly practiced as a generous member of Sacred Heart Parish in Portland. And, a third was Charles J. McCarthy, Jr. (d. 1921), whose counsel on problems relating to the operation of the Diocese of Portland the bishop had come to value.

Walsh's work as a priest, it will be recalled, had been in Catholic education. A founder of the Catholic Educational Association in 1904, he continued this work by raising the enrollment of students in the Catholic educational institutions of his diocese from less than nine thousand to over twenty thousand and saw these institutions increase so that one college, nine academies, and sixteen parish schools opened in Maine during his tenure in office. Many of these schools were under the Sisters of Mercy who became more firmly established in Maine during Bishop Walsh's years in Portland.

The exceptional achievement in education when Walsh was bishop was the founding of St. Joseph's College for Women in 1912. This began as St. Joseph's Academy which opened its doors to girls in 1881 and provided for their formal primary and secondary education. The culmination of this experience was the new college which received its civil charter from the State of Maine in 1915. Very effective as a leader in all this was Mother Mary Xaveria Toohey (1869-1938), its foundress, who made it possible for women to obtain a bachelor of arts degree.

Among the nine academies, there were the schools that Bishop Walsh opened in Portland in 1909. One was Cathedral High School for girls which was rated very highly by the State Department of Education under Sister Mary Norberta Fitzgerald (1922-25) as principal. The other was the Catholic Institute which, having used the old motherhouse of the Sisters of Mercy for a grammar school for the boys and girls from the city parishes until 1917, then evolved into a high school for boys taught by the priests of the diocese. Other schools in the city included Holy Innocents' Home, opened in 1907; and parochial schools, which were inaugurated at St. Joseph's in 1915 and at St. Patrick's in 1923; in addition to King's Academy for Girls in 1919 (merged with St. Joseph's Academy in 1927).

Elsewhere in the diocese, with the help of the Sisters of Mercy, the bishop started Our Lady of Mercy in Bath (1909), St. Mary's Academy in Houlton (1911), St. Michael's Home in Bangor (1911), St. Edward's School in Bar Harbor (1913), St. Mary's School in Augusta (1914), St. Mary's Catholic High School in Orono (1916), St. Benedict's High School in Benedicta (1922), Holy Cross School in South Portland (1922), and St. Theresa's School in South Brewer (1922).

Relative to St. Edward's, Louise Drexel Morrell (1863-1943) of Pennsylvania, a summer resident in Bar Harbor, hosted with her husband, a congressman, at their summer cottage, *Thuristane*, her saintly sister, Katharine Drexel, the nun canonized by Pope John Paul II, on October 1, 2000. The Morrells supported the parish in Bar Harbor in 1918 with a convent as well as a school which is now the home of the Bar Harbor Historical Society.

As teachers in the schools of the diocese under Bishop Walsh, the Ursulines opened Immaculate Heart of Mary at Fairfield and Mount Merici, an elementary and high school in Waterville, in 1911. Then they began elementary schools at Notre Dame de Lourdes in Skowhegan in 1913, at St. Mary's in Lewiston in 1916, at Notre Dame in Springvale in 1919, at Notre Dame in Waterville in 1920, at St. Rose of Lima in Jay and at Holy Family in Sanford in 1923.

In addition to the Ursulines and the Sisters of Mercy, there were five other groups of religious women in teaching during Bishop Walsh's time. The Sisters of St. Joseph began St. Michael's in South Berwick in 1909 and St. Anthony's in Jackman in 1912. The Sisters of Ste. Chretienne inaugurated St. John the Baptist in Rumford in 1914. The Little Franciscan Sisters of Mary pioneered St. Mary's at Eagle Lake in 1916. The Sisters of the Good Shepherd started Champlain School in Van Buren in 1920. And, the Dominican Sisters moved into the new facility of the Saints Peter and Paul which replaced the school in the Dominican Block in 1924.

So dedicated had Bishop Walsh been to Catholic education throughout his life that he sought to have the state change its attitude towards Catholic schools. Since the public school system was regarded as a sort of "Protestant Public School System," it is not surprising that, with the bishop seeking such change, he encountered criticism for trying to enlist state aid in the expansion of Catholic education. After the state had given financial aid to Protestant schools, Walsh argued that it could not deny similar assistance to Catholic schools. As he pointed out in an article, "Catholic Public School System," published in *The Lewiston Journal* for January 2, 1923, those schools were free schools which saved the state and local government much money.

St. Joseph's School, Portland

Baseball Team, St. Mary's Church, Augusta, 1921 (courtesy Dan Hickey)

Dedication of Holy Family Church/School, Sanford, c. 1923

Understandably, the bishop, who was quite familiar with public issues before the legislature, did not hesitate to lobby for laws which helped Catholics and against those which hindered them. Coming into office when reform legislation was being advocated by the Progressives before the United States entered World War I, Walsh favored some legislation like liability for employers, fair hours for workers, government inspection of food, compensation for workers, and arbitration in labor disputes. But, on the question of the schools, he did not hesitate to lobby with city officials in Portland and with representatives and senators before the state legislature in 1915 to obtain for Catholics a fair share of the State Public Fund when he estimated that Catholic schools saved the government, in Portland alone, some $60,000.00.

St. Brendan's Summer Chapel, Biddeford Pool

For Bishop Walsh, as William L. Lucey, one historian of the diocese has pointed out, it was unfair that parish schools did not get a share of the money from the fund which was based on all the students in both public and parochial schools. Although, the bishop favored an amendment in 1915 to the fund that would allow this to take place, it never came about. Subsequently, Walsh was able to prevent the passage of an amendment to the state constitution that would prohibit funds to sectarian education. That Maine rejected it showed the good sense of the people, Protestants and Catholics alike, with whom Walsh continued to have good relations despite the legislative battles over education.

Foremost among Walsh's critics were the members of the Ku Klux Klan, a national organization which opposed not only Catholics, including the immigration of Franco-Americans, but also blacks and Jews. It had expanded to include, according to one estimate, about twenty-five thousand in Maine by 1924. Because R. Owen Brewster (1888-1961), a Republican, was opposed to state aid to parochial schools and running for governor, Bishop Walsh spoke out bluntly against him in late October of 1923, especially since his candidacy had the backing of the Klan.

Unfortunately, the bishop died in spring of the next year and Brewster, with the help of the Klan, won the primary and the election. As John Syrett has shown, after exercising its influence in the 1923 elections in having the council-manager type of government implemented in Portland, the Klan was such a political force in the 1924 elections that it helped to elect Brewster as the Governor of Maine and members of the state legislature, not to mention the impact that it had previously had on the school committees and the governing bodies of the various cities and towns. Two years before his death, Walsh revealed what he was experiencing in the fight for the schools when he wrote in his journal that 1922 was "the most trying in my life." And, after his death, when the clergy gathered for its annual retreat at the resort near Mt. Kineo in Rockwood, from July 7 to 11, 1924, the Klan burned a cross after setting off three loud explosions.

Nevertheless, while Bishop Walsh, like his predecessors Healy and O'Connell, could rely on the Cunninghams and the Madigans, he also had a special ally in Peter Charles Keegan (1850-1931), a lawyer and banker from Van Buren who was very influential within state politics and kept the bishop posted on attempts by the legislators to pass laws prohibiting state aid to private institutions. With information coming to him from different sources upon whom he could rely for advice, the bishop was acutely sensitive to the major social, political, and economic issues and problems.

Beyond his work as a bishop and an educator, Walsh was very much involved in the development of the National Catholic Welfare Conference, the agency through which the American bishops sought to bring about a solution to America's social problems by advocating a just wage and fair working hours and by opposing child labor. Though the National Catholic Welfare Conference was not very enthusiastic about women's suffrage, the bishops had sought to organize their activities during World War I to meet the needs of society through the National Catholic War Council. During World War I, in a policy that Walsh understood, the American bishops had encouraged their pastors to have their parishioners volunteer for the war effort and to buy bonds to demonstrate their patriotism as Americans.

After the war, in 1919, the National War Council became the Catholic Welfare Conference. The Bishop of Portland was very instrumental in bringing about this new agency through which the American bishops could cooperate in contributing to the welfare of the Catholic Church and its people in the United States. Thus, Bishop Walsh, a friend of James Cardinal Gibbons (1834-1921) of Baltimore, leader of the American hierarchy, and of Patrick Cardinal Hayes (1867-1938) of New York, staunch backer of the conference, reached beyond the frontiers of his diocese to advance the cause of American Catholicism.

Moreover, in his role on the National Catholic Welfare Conference, Bishop Walsh clashed with Cardinal O'Connell of Boston who sought to have the postwar organization eliminated even though the latter had previously backed the National Catholic War Council. Whether or not this was an ideological conflict or a clash of personalities is not altogether clear since the Boston prelate did not really have much affection for his Portland successor who had spent much of his efforts as the spokesman of a number of his brother bishops in seeking the removal of O'Connell from Boston during the last five years of Walsh's life. This came about because of the cardinal's reluctance to discipline a priest, James P. E. O'Connell (1884-1948), his nephew and his chancellor (1912-20), who had caused a public scandal for the church in Boston by secretly marrying a woman in a civil ceremony.

Not unlike the start of Walsh's tenure in Portland, the end of his tenure was marked by a confrontation with O'Connell who, it appears, would have been removed to Rome by Pope Benedict XV (1914-22) had more American bishops supported the action. That Walsh was older in age and in the priesthood may have had something to do with the rivalry between the two. In the end, O'Connell had the last word, as a priest of the diocese who was an altar boy at Walsh's funeral recalled years later. Standing over the casket of his deceased successor in the See of Portland, the cardinal shook his head faintly praising Walsh with these departing words: "He tried hard!"

Certainly, Walsh's tenure as Bishop of the Diocese of Portland was quite remarkable. From 1906 to 1924, the number of priests increased from 121 to 167, parishes grew from fifty to ninety-five, mission churches from thirty-seven to seventy-three, schools from twenty-five to fifty-six, and sisters from 482 to 670. Relative to the latter, two new motherhouses were established, one for the Sisters of Mercy in Portland, and another for the Ursulines in Waterville. And, for the administration of the diocese, the chancery was housed in the Guild Hall, built on the corner of Congress Street and Franklin Avenue in Portland in 1923.

Having established the charities of his diocese on a firm foundation, the bishop had the religious women involved in the operation of hospitals. In addition to St. Joseph Hospital and Home for the Aged in Portland, his tenure as bishop saw the opening of Queen's Hospital in his see city during the spring and fall of the 1918 influenza epidemic which afflicted one out of every four Americans and was responsible for at least 600,000 deaths in the United States. In response to a public appeal for help by Walsh, Marion Weeks, daughter of Stephen A. Weeks, a prominent surgeon, provided her mansion so that the Sisters of Mercy were able to set up a hospital on State Street between Congress and Deering Streets with twenty-five beds during the epidemic. So severe had the influenza become that children who had been orphaned by the

St. Michael's Center, Catholic Charities Maine, Bangor

Mural of St. Patrick, St. Patrick's Church, Portland

Funeral procession of Fr. John McGinnis, escorted by Knights of Columbus, St. Ignatius Church, Sandford, October 1924

epidemic could occasionally be found at the altar rail in Portland's St. Dominic's Church awaiting Catholic families to take and raise them as their own.

Elsewhere, the Sisters of Charity of St. Hyacinth continued to operate St. Mary's in Lewiston, the Little Franciscan Sisters of Mary were caring for Northern Maine General Hospital at Eagle Lake, the Sisters of Mercy were at Madigan Memorial Hospital in Houlton, the Daughters of Wisdom were operating a hospital at St. Agatha, and the Daughters of Charity of St. Vincent de Paul were about to operate a hospital in Waterville. Likewise, the other charitable works of the Catholic Church under Bishop Walsh were evident in St. Anthony's Guild, a home for working girls in Portland, St. Louis Home for Boys in West Scarborough, St. Michael's, a home for orphans in Bangor, and an asylum for the sick in St. Agatha, not to mention the other charitable institutions which already existed in his diocese.

The Knights of Columbus, the largest Catholic lay organization in the state, had grown to twenty-four councils by the end of World War I. During the war, at least 650 of its members in Maine had served in the armed services, including Father Edward B. Henry (d. 1919) of Governor Kavanagh Council, No. 1423, from North Whitefield, and Father Constantin A. Chauve of Madawaska Council, No. 1635, a Marist from St. Bruno's in Van Buren, to whom France awarded the Croix de Guerre for heroism during the war. At the end of the war, John F. Daily, father of the Most Rev. Thomas V. Daily (b. 1922), Bishop of Brooklyn and Supreme Chaplain of the Order, was the State Deputy of the Knights of Columbus in Maine. Understandably, in the controversy over the schools the Klan had not hesitated to attack the Knights who had always supported Bishop Walsh. And, this was at a time when Catholics were viewed as culturally as well as religiously separate from their fellow citizens with their own network of churches, schools, hospitals, and social organizations.

"Portland has been singularly favored in its prelates ---- they have all been men of piety, great scholarship, good judgment and great executive ability," declared the editor of the city's newspaper, *Eastern Argus*, when Louis S. Walsh was announced as the fourth Bishop of Portland in 1906. After his death, on May 12, 1924, the editor of *The Portland Press Herald*, in stating that the late prelate was "one of the outstanding citizens of the State," proved that Walsh turned out to be all that was expected of him at the start of his tenure as Bishop of Portland.

Certainly, since the bishop had made it a special point to stop off at Pontalier, France, the birthplace of Sebastian Râle, on the way back from his last trip to Europe within a month of his death, the French-speaking community should have found him a far more acceptable prelate at the end of his life than at the beginning of his episcopacy when he clashed with them over his Americanizing policies. That the University of Maine had conferred on him an honorary degree as early as June of 1908 was indicative of how quickly the Catholic bishop made friends in a state where Protestants outnumbered Catholics. In expanding the charitable, educational, and religious institutions of his vast diocese, Walsh had lived up to his motto, "In Justice and Peace" ("*In Justitia et Pace*") leaving the Diocese of Portland better than he found it. Like Portland's first bishop, Walsh was buried in the crypt of the Cathedral, the renovation of which he had undertaken in 1921. Cardinal Hayes honored him by his presence at the funeral and Bishop Philip R. McDevitt (1858-1935) of Harrisburg, another friend, who had preached at Walsh's consecration as a bishop, was the eulogist.

An Experienced Bishop

Following the death of Bishop Walsh, Rome acted in its usual deliberate manner and appointed John Gregory Murray (1877-1956) as the fifth Bishop of Portland, on May 29, 1925. Born in Waterbury, Connecticut, on February 27, 1877, the son of William and Mary (Connor) Murray, he graduated from the College of the Holy Cross (1897) and pursued his studies for the priesthood at the American College in Louvain, where he was known as "The Pearl of Louvain" because, down to his time, he was its brightest student. Ordained a priest at Louvain, on April 14, 1900, by Bishop Joseph F. Van der Stappen (1846-1908), a learned liturgist, Murray was consecrated, on April 28, 1920, Titular Bishop of Flavias by Giovanni Vincenzo Bonzano (1867-1927), Apostolic Delegate to the United States, in St. Joseph's Cathedral, Hartford, Connecticut, with the assistance of Bishop John Joseph Nilan of Hartford and Bishop Thomas Joseph Shahan, Rector of the Catholic University of America. Having served as Auxiliary Bishop of Hartford from November 19, 1919, the new bishop was unlike any of his predecessors, already an experienced bishop.

Murray's appointment was very interesting in that it was a benchmark in the declining influence of William Cardinal O'Connell who failed to secure the appointment of Monsignor Michael J. Splaine (1875-1951), his loyal aide, as the successor to Bishop Walsh. Rome chose, instead, an auxiliary of Bishop Nilan, a diocesan bishop who had staunchly supported Walsh in his attempt to have O'Connell unseated in Boston. In this appointment, one cannot overlook the hand of Genevieve Garvan Brady (d. 1937), a devout Catholic from Hartford who, with Nicholas (d. 1929), her husband, had a villa, Casa del Sole, in Rome and were good friends of Archbishop Bonzano, one then thoroughly familiar with the scandal in Boston. That Brady left Murray $250,000.00 in her will, as John Cooney points out in his biography of Francis Cardinal Spellman (1889-1967) of New York, is a strong indication that the influence of this woman, who became a papal duchess in 1927, cannot be discounted.

Murray was not altogether unfamiliar with Portland. He had actually substituted for Walsh during the ceremonies of Holy Week when the Bishop of Portland was in Rome in 1924. Murray came back the following year to take care of those same ceremonies while the diocese was waiting appointment of its new bishop. Thus, Murray was known to the priests of the diocese when he was installed as their bishop, on October 12, 1925.

At the outset of his tenure as bishop, Murray faced the problem of growth. To provide for the expansion in the number of Catholics, the bishop needed to establish new parishes. That the times were prosperous at the outset of his tenure enabled the Bishop of Portland to obtain the credits necessary for such construction. The banks, which had considerable confidence in the ability of the Catholic Church to pay its debts, were quite willing to invest in loans to accommodate the various pastors who were responsible for the new buildings in their parishes.

One of the newly constructed churches was St. Joseph's located in section of Portland known as Deering. Established as a parish in 1909, it was the first one set up in the episcopal city since Sacred Heart in 1896. Originally a small wooden church on Walton Street, St. Joseph's was replaced by Murray with the formal dedication, on September 6, 1931, of an impressive English Gothic structure which became the heart of the parish physical plant on Stevens Avenue in what was one of the more upscale sections of the city. Its architectural style was not unlike the new church building which Bishop Murray had dedicated in Augusta for St. Mary's of the Assumption in 1927. Such expansion was an indication that Catholicism was flourishing.

Bishop John Gregory Murray

Cathedral of the Immaculate Conception, Portland

Coat of arms of Bishop John Gregory Murray

Bishop Murray laying the cornerstone to the new St. Mary's Church, Augusta on October 3, 1926. (Courtesy Dan Hickey)

In his six short years, Bishop Murray was able to establish about two dozen new parishes in rural and urban parts of the state: St. Ann's on Indian Island in Old Town, St. Joseph's in Brewer, St. Margaret's in Old Orchard Beach, St. Theresa of the Infant Jesus in Mexico, and St. John the Baptist in Winslow, all in 1926; Our Lady of Peace in Berwick, St. Joseph's in Mars Hill, Our Lady of the Lakes in Oquossoc, and St. Agnes in Pittsfield, all in 1927; St. Mary's in Old Town, Our Lady Queen of Peace in Boothbay Harbor, St. Mary's in Wilton, and St. Theresa's in Stockholm, all in 1928; St. Francis Xavier in Brownville Junction, Christ the King in Hebron, St. Leo the Great in Howland, St. Thomas Aquinas in Madawaska, St. Ignatius in Northeast Harbor, Notre Dame de Lourdes in Saco, and St. Ann's in Peter Dana Point, all in 1929; and St. Charles Borromeo in Brunswick, St. Gerard's in Grand Isle, and St. John's in St. John, all in 1930.

Writing in his first pastoral letter at Christmas of his first year in office, Bishop Murray indicated that he was pleased with his visits to parishes after his first two months in office. In that time, he had been to about half of the parishes in the diocese and was very impressed with the number of children and adults he had confirmed. Since he was inclined to travel, he resumed his visitation the following spring and summer so that his first year turned out to be a very busy one in acquainting himself with the priests and people of his extensive diocese. So concerned was he about the sick in his parishes that he urged pastors to visit them at least once a day. The bishop himself would often visit the sick late in the evening at old Queen's Hospital in Portland.

Moreover, there were other parish developments of interest during these years. In Waterville, the diocese welcomed the establishment in 1927 of St. Joseph Maronite Church for the Syrian community with Joseph E. Awad (d. 1955) as pastor. And, starting on November 1, 1930, Mass was offered for the new Parish of St. Charles Borromeo by Father Thomas W. Dunnagan (1895-1939) in the chapel of Bowdoin College. This arrangement, unusual for that time, was possible due to the kindness of Bowdoin President Kenneth C. M. Sills (1879-1954), and it continued until part of the parish church under construction was available for use at the end of January 1931.

Our Lady Queen of Peace, Boothbay Harbor

Notre Dame de Lourdes School, Saco

At the same time, Bishop Murray expanded the Catholic school system throughout Maine. Within six years, he opened at least fifteen parochial schools: Holy Family in Lewiston, with the Sisters of St. Joseph de Lyons and St. Theresa of the Infant Jesus in Mexico, with the Sister of Ste.-Chretienne in 1926; and Holy Cross in Lewiston, with the Sisters of the Presentation of Mary in 1927. Then in 1928, came the opening of St. Joseph's Orphanage (for the girls moved from St. Mary's Hospital to the Marcotte Home which the Grey Nuns had opened in 1926) in Lewiston, with the Sisters of Charity; Saints Peter and Paul (for the boys in upper grades) in Lewiston, with the Brothers of Sacred Heart; Ave Maria Academy in Sabattus, with the Dominican Sisters; St. Francis de Sales (for boys in the upper grades) in Waterville, with the Brothers of Christian Instruction; St. Mary's in Westbrook, with the Franciscan Sisters; and St. John the Baptist in Winslow with the Ursulines. And the trend continued with St. Louis High School in Biddeford, with Brothers of Christian Instruction; Holy Rosary in Caribou, with the Ursuline Sisters; St. Athanasius in Rumford with the Sisters of Mercy; and Notre Dame de Lourdes in Saco, with the Sisters of the Presentation of Mary in 1929. In 1930, there was Ste. André's (for boys in the upper grades) in Biddeford, with the Brothers of the Sacred Heart; and St. Remy in Keegan, with the Sisters of the Good Shepherd. And, in 1931, came Notre Dame Institute (an elementary, high, and normal school) in Alfred, with the Brothers of Christian Instruction; Stella Maris in Biddeford, and St. Bernadette in Lisbon, with the Sisters of the Presentation of Mary in 1931. Also, noteworthy in education was the merger in 1927 of King's Academy in Portland with St. Joseph's Academy under the Sisters of Mercy.

Of particular interest in education were developments on the high school level. The Catholic Institute, which was founded as a high school in 1917, was renamed Cheverus in 1926 to honor the memory of one of the state's early missionaries, and Father Clarence H. Coughlin (1891-1959), who was later Chancellor of the Diocese of Portland (1924-52), served as its first principal. Since prospects for the expansion of their college in Van Buren had looked bleak from the time of Bishop Walsh, the Marists decided to close it in 1926, the year when Bishop Murray named Father Daniel J. Feeney, the first Diocesan Superintendent of Schools (1926-32). However, the Marists did accommodate the bishop by converting their physical plant into a high school which lasted until 1932.

Former SS Cyril and Methodius, Lisbon Falls (photograph, diocesan archives)

Boys' Graduation Class, St. Dominic's School, Portland, 1926

More enduring among the high schools of the diocese was the one named for John Bapst which was opened in Bangor in the fall of 1928 with the diocesan priests and the Sisters of Mercy as teachers. The school was the result of plans set in motion by Bangor's two pastors, Thomas J. Nelligan (1871-1959) of St. John's, who had served as principal at Cheverus in Portland during its early days, and Martin A. Clary (d. 1927) of St. Mary's, a former chancellor of the diocese (1912-14). After Father Clary died, Father Timothy H. Houlihan (1878-1941) who succeeded him continued the cooperative effort that led to the opening of an educational center for young men and women of the parishes in the Bangor area. Certainly, in considering the expansion of education on both the primary and secondary levels, the growth was significant with 19,137 students in parish schools when Bishop Murray came to Portland compared to 23,290 when he left. The

St. Thomas Aquinas, Madawaska

Original St. Charles Borromeo Church, Brunswick

total number of school children under Catholic auspices, including orphanages and the reservations, came to 24,549.

In dealing with parishes and schools, Bishop Murray was confronted with a fire, on January 19th, 1927, which erupted from a spark that ignited a sanctuary wreath and destroyed both the St. Ann's Church and Convent on the reservation for the Passamaquoddies at Pleasant Point in Perry. To rebuild, the Indians wanted the state, which had the obligation of providing a church for them, to provide $20,000.00 only to find that there would be no more than $6,000.00 available. With the $6,000.00 insurance money, the allocation by the state would cover only ten percent of the projected construction cost of $60,000.00 for a fire-proof church and convent. Consequently, Bishop Murray was forced to raise the money by two appeals to the faithful of the diocese in the following summer. This brought in $8,679.26 so that the total money available was about $20,000.00 for the estimated cost. Since the reservation was then under St. Joseph's in Eastport, Father Joseph S. Sullivan (d. 1957) succeeded in starting the construction of a brick church with a convent in 1928.

As the Great Depression dawned with Black Friday, on October 18, 1929, it was becoming more and more difficult for the diocese to rely on special collections for its works and the bishop, as corporation sole, was forced to borrow more from the banks. This was particularly true if he were to keep open the charitable institutions of the diocese which cared for orphaned children and aged adults, in addition to the sick. Yet, despite the needs of his own diocese, Murray was always open to the needs of others as was evident when he encouraged Catholics to help the Red Cross in its drives to raise money for relief to the people stricken by the disaster in Florida in 1928 and by the drought in the Midwest in 1931.

Yet, it is not surprising that a true sense of social consciousness characterized Bishop Murray. Like his predecessor Bishop Walsh, he was involved in the work of the National Catholic Welfare Conference. As a member of its administrative arm, Murray's concern and responsibility for the welfare of others extended beyond the borders of his own diocese and of his own faith. While he supported the fundraising for the Catholic University of America near the end of his time in Portland, the bishop was also recognized for his efforts in helping to solve society's problems within the State of Maine. This was affirmed when Benjamin Brewster, the Episcopal Bishop of Maine (1916-40), in the farewell dinner given in honor of Murray at the Portland Elks Club at the end of his tenure, praised the latter for advancing social welfare and reform.

That was clear in the strong contribution to health care which the diocese continued under Murray. While Sisters' Hospital (later known as Elizabeth Ann Seton Hospital) in Waterville, under the Sisters of Charity of St. Vincent de Paul, had been launched with the approval of his predecessor some thirteen years before Walsh's death, it was never opened until the day of the latter's death. In this way, with the other hospitals in Eagle Lake, Houlton, Lewiston, Portland, and St. Agatha, the Catholic Church had a very strong role in health care in the State of Maine. Murray even added to all this by providing for the poor Catholic children in Portland a dental clinic on Free Street before he finished his work in the city.

As the chairman of the legal department of the National Catholic Welfare Conference, Bishop Murray was in an office with a national perspective since his department was responsible for examining state and federal legislation to make sure that it did not conflict with Catholic social principles. That, of course, left the bishop vulnerable to critics on the national level who chose to accuse him of playing politics, as did *The New Republic*, on July 4, 1928, for allegedly supporting United States Senator Frederick Hale (1874-1963) when the latter was challenged by Governor Owen Brewster in his re-election campaign. In fact, Brewster was governor when the Indians found it difficult to obtain money from the state and he had actually gone on record in favor of amending the state constitution to prohibit funds for parochial and private schools. However, since Murray had not made any comment regarding the election in a letter that summer to the pastors requesting more funds for the rebuilding of the physical plant at St. Ann's in Pleasant Point, the national journal was in error.

One of the enduring legacies of Bishop Murray's years in Portland is *The Church World*, the diocesan newspaper, which was established on May 18, 1930. Its first issue, which appeared in tabloid form, on July 18, 1930, was edited by Father John F. Conoley (d. 1960), pastor of the parish in Hebron. *The Church World*, which also contained articles written by the bishop himself, was recognized, after a year in circulation, by *The Catholic Transcript*, the newspaper of Murray's home diocese of Hartford, as having "taken its place among the strong Catholic newspapers in the United States."

St. Joseph Cemetery, Biddeford

As the economic, political, and social consequences of the Great Depression made themselves felt during the early 1930s, Bishop Murray sought to lighten the burden for his people whose families were falling apart and to instill confidence in the ability of the diocese to pay its debts in a poor state like Maine. But, as the diocese fell deeper into debt, the mantle of office became heavier. It has been said that the influential Mrs. Brady had told him: "My dear bishop, I can't get you out of debt, but I can get you out of Portland." Whether or not that story is true, Murray was transferred to the archiepiscopal see of St. Paul in Minnesota, on October 29, 1931.

By that time, John Gregory Murray had achieved six fruitful years in Maine. He left a diocese of 175,191 Catholics which had an increase of resident pastors from ninety-five to 126, of churches from 168 to 183, of priests from 176 to 216, and of religious women from 670 to 964. However, the bishop did not have the skill required to control the diocese's spiraling indebtedness of millions of dollars which it was enduring during the economic crisis of the times as a consequence of the construction costs undertaken during the boom years of the 1920s. Among these was the complete renovation of the Cathedral with the installation of an Italian marble main altar for the celebration of the Diamond Jubilee of the Diocese of Portland at which Cardinal O'Connell and a number of other bishops had been present, on May 21, 1929.

Throughout his tenure as Bishop of Portland, inspiration, love, and wisdom had characterized Murray's devoted service to the Catholics of the Pine Tree State. This was a true reflection of his motto, "*Mea Omnia Tua*," words of Our Lord taken from St. John, 17: 10: "Yes, all who are Mine are Yours, and Yours are Mine, and in them I am glorified." Customarily, the bishop would like to walk in the late evening and talk with the people he met on these sojourns, including non-Catholics who found him to be very courteous and cordial. That same humane touch was not forgotten by those who knew him back in his native city of Waterbury which, within two years of his death, on October 11, 1956, named a park in his memory, on January 27, 1958. When St. Paul was mourning Murray, President Dwight D. Eisenhower happened to be campaigning in the city and praised its archbishop as "a great citizen, a civic and spiritual leader," words with which few could disagree.

Our Lady of the Lakes, Oquossoc

Chapter 8

The Shepherd Who Bore the Heavy Burden

Bishop Joseph McCarthy and Archbishop Richard J. Cushing accompanied by two Franciscan friars

Pectoral cross, Bishop McCarthy

Coat of arms of Bishop Joseph McCarthy

On May 13, 1932, Rome appointed Joseph Edward McCarthy (1876-1955) sixth Bishop of the Diocese of Portland, Maine. The son of Eugene and Johanna (Collaty) McCarthy, he was born on November 14, 1876. Like his immediate predecessor, the new bishop was a native of Waterbury, Connecticut, and an alumnus of Crosby High School and the College of the Holy Cross (1899). Having attended the Seminary of St. Sulpice, he was ordained a priest at the Church of St. Sulpice in Paris, on July 4, 1903, by Bishop Félix-Jules-François-Xavier Jourdan de la Passardiére (1841-1913) who was Auxiliary Bishop of Paris and Titular Bishop of Roséa. Though McCarthy later served as the vice rector of St. Thomas Seminary in the Diocese of Hartford, he was very reluctant to accept his appointment as bishop. However, in deference to the wishes of Pope Pius XI (1922-39), McCarthy did so and faced the future trusting in God.

On August 24, 1932, in the Cathedral of the Immaculate Conception, McCarthy was ordained a bishop by Auxiliary Bishop Maurice Francis McAuliffe of Hartford who was assisted by Bishop John Joseph Nilan of Hartford and John Bertram Peterson of Manchester with Archbishop Murray delivering the sermon. It was the first time that an episcopal ordination was broadcast by radio in Maine.

Early in his years as bishop, McCarthy learned about the generosity of the people of his diocese. In the late spring of 1933, when fires in Ellsworth and in Auburn left hundreds of people homeless, he called upon the faithful in special collections to provide clothing, food, and shelter for the victims. Then, in 1934, when he realized that the charitable institutions within the greater area of Portland were in distress, McCarthy launched a drive for funds. This was so successful, especially in the southern part of the state where his see city was located, that it became an annual program, thereby providing a cushion for the social, pastoral, and educational programs and services during the difficult years of the Great Depression. This fundraiser, which eventually became a state-wide appeal, customarily launched in the spring, was the basis for the annual charity drives by the diocese.

Pastoral staff, Bishop McCarthy

Certainly, the chief challenge confronting Bishop McCarthy was the need to shore up the finances of his diocese in order for it to survive. Given the economic situation of the nation, the Catholic Church in Maine had to protect its own properties, valued at nineteen million dollars, from foreclosure. At that time the diocese was at least four and a half million dollars in debt, mostly to banks which could sue to recover the money owed to them. Since all church property came under the bishop as the sole corporation responsible for the same, it was up to McCarthy to remove the debt of the parishes facing financial problems, especially because of the construction boom of the prosperous 1920s. To do this effectively, the bishop consulted businessmen like John J. Cunningham, lawyers like Francis W. Sullivan, and priests like George P. Johnson, to draft a solution which Rome eventually approved in the spring of 1935. At about the same time, the bishop appointed Father James E. Burke (d. 1951) Auditor of the Diocese of Portland to make sure that its resources were preserved.

Consequently, on July 1, 1936, a bond issue was set in place offering the property of the Diocese of Portland as its basis. With the pastors of the diocese pledging their cooperation, a special plan, which was drawn up under the guidance of the Reconstruction Finance Corporation, called for parishes to come through with the payment of an annual assessment thereby enabling the bonds to come due on July 1, 1956. Much to the satisfaction of the First National Bank in Portland, which handled their sale, the bonds purchased (among the original major parties which had purchased the bonds was Harvard University) had so exceeded expectations by the end of the first year that Bishop McCarthy announced that the diocese had not only paid the annual interest but had decreased the principal by $100,000.00. With a refinancing in 1938, the burdensome debt was decreasing annually through the diligence of the bishop and the support of the pastors. The Diocese of Portland looked forward to the projected liquidation of its debt by November 1, 1963. Meanwhile, all those parties which had lent money to the diocese were assured of recovering their investments because Bishop McCarthy was successful in restoring confidence in the ability of the Catholic Church to pay its debts, especially since his diocese could not exceed an indebtedness of half a million dollars.

Although McCarthy was not as free as his predecessors to expand the physical plants of his parishes, several churches were built by July 27, 1948, when his powers as a residential bishop were restricted because of his declining health. Among the parishes which he established were St. Ann's in Danforth (1933), St. Ann's in Bradley (1934), Star of the Sea in Stonington (1934), St. Joseph's in Sinclair (1936), and St. Christopher's in York Harbor (1946). "I have tried to borrow loans as to come to the rescue of other priests," the bishop wrote to the pastor in St. Agatha's in April of 1935, "and every bank sends back word that we are already in the diocese borrowed beyond our limit."

St. Ann, Danforth

SS Peter and Paul, Lewiston

Despite the limitations placed on construction by the diocesan debt, McCarthy participated in at least one magnificent achievement. That was his consecration, on October 23, 1938, of Saints Peter and Paul in Lewiston, a church which had been envisioned near the end of the nineteenth after the arrival there of the French Dominicans and which is the pride of the Franco-American community. This Gothic structure, financed by the sacrifices of the French Catholics of that city during the Great Depression, stands as the largest Catholic church in Maine, with a seating capacity of 2,200 and, next to the Mission Church in Roxbury, Massachusetts, which at the time sat 2,500, as the second largest Catholic church in New England.

Former Our Lady of Wisdom Newman Center, University of Maine, Orono

■ *25th Anniversary Celebration, Fr. Wilfred Ouellette, St. Joseph (now Holy Family), Old Town*

■ *Bay View Convent, Good Shepherd Sisters, Saco*

■ *Marie Joseph Spiritual Center, Presentation of Mary Sisters, Biddeford Pool*

■ *First graduating class, St. Dominic's High School, Lewiston, June 1945*

Notwithstanding the restraints imposed by the diocesan debt on the construction of churches and schools, education expanded on all levels. On the highest level, there was the expansion of colleges, due in most part to the religious of the diocese. The Franciscans opened Collège Séraphique (1939-53) which became St. Francis College (1953-78), along with a high school, in the resort area of Biddeford Pool near the mouth of the Saco River. In this period, Bishop McCarthy set up Our Lady of Wisdom (1946) as a center for Catholic students at the University of Maine in Orono, thereby inaugurating a campus ministry in the diocese.

The Oblates of Mary Immaculate opened a seminary in Bucksport (1941) on the former site of the seminary of the Eastern Maine Methodist Conference before they converted the Byrne Estate at Frenchmen's Bay in Bar Harbor into a junior college (1944). When this property was spared in the catastrophic fire on Mount Desert Island in 1947, the Oblates, in thanksgiving, built a shrine to Our Lady of Fatima, with columns donated from the nearby estate of United States Secretary of the Treasury Henry Morgenthau (1856-46). Later their educational complex was incorporated as Oblate College and Seminary (1949-67). Earlier, on November 25, 1948, they had established themselves in Augusta at the site of the former Governor Hill Mansion by converting it into the St. Paul's Retreat House and Cursillo Center.

Other Catholic groups had educational centers within the diocese even though they were not under the control of the diocese. The Brothers of the Sacred Heart opened Sacred Heart Juniorate (1945) in Winthrop. In the case of the Brothers of Christian Instruction, who had been established on Shaker Hill Road in Alfred for twenty years, they set up La Mennais College (1950-60) as their house of studies before they moved it to Canton, Ohio, where it became Walsh College (1958). Today a monument of J. M. Robert de La Mennais (1780-1860), their founder, marks the site.

On the secondary and primary levels of education, there were about 25,000 students in the parochial and private schools when Msgr. John J. Barrett (d. 1968) was Superintendent of Schools for Bishop McCarthy. As for secondary education, a number of the high schools were opened or underwent changes. John Bapst in Bangor came under the Xaverian Brothers (1933); St. André High School in Biddeford opened under the Sisters of the Presentation of Mary (1937); Sacred Heart Academy in Jackman was placed under the Sisters of St. Joseph (1940); St. Dominic's in Lewiston opened as a high school for boys on Bartlett Street under the Brothers of the Sacred Heart (1941) before it opened a section for girls under the Dominican Sisters (1946); Cheverus in Portland was given over to the Jesuits (1942); and, Marie Joseph Academy in Biddeford Pool was inaugurated as a boarding high school for girls under the Sisters of the Presentation of Mary (1948). Of these schools, only Sacred Heart Academy in Jackman and Marie Joseph Academy in Biddeford Pool were independent of the local parishes.

In the case of the Jesuits, apart from their preaching of missions and retreats, they had been absent as a group from the state for close to a century and the bishop's invitation to them brought back the successors of the early missionaries of Catholicism in Maine. Initially, the Jesuits, under the leadership of W. Edmund FitzGerald (1901-78), took charge of the operation of the Cheverus High School plant on 100 Free Street, next to the old Jefferson Theater, until it was purchased by Sears Roebuck & Company in 1945. At the same time, the Jesuits were very helpful in providing priests to minister for the diocese, especially on the weekends during World War II on the islands in Casco Bay and at other military installations in Maine.

Cheverus was then relocated to the old St. Aloysius School on Cumberland Avenue with an annex for the freshmen at the old Vaughan Street Public school before a new physical plant was dedicated, under Robert A. Hewitt (1897-1978), on April 1, 1952, at the site of the old Winslow Estate on Ocean Avenue. Much of this was made possible due to the generous benefactions of Mr. Byron Miller of F. W. Woolworth and his wife at the intervention of Father Edmund F. Walsh (d. 1962), Pastor of Sacred Heart in Yarmouth. Though Bishop McCarthy even envisioned a college operated by the Jesuits, history has proved that this was not a realistic objective.

At the same time, a number of parishes had both primary and secondary levels of instruction. St. Martin of Tours in Millinocket came under the Congregation of Our Lady of the Rosary (1939), and St. Ignatius in Sanford under the Brothers of the Christian School (1940). Still other schools provided upper grades for boys like Notre Dame in Waterville (1938) under the Brothers of Christian Instruction, St. Mary's in Lewiston (1939) under the Brothers of the Sacred Heart, and St. Joseph's in Old Town (1946) also under the Brothers of the Sacred Heart.

A number of religious sisters staffed many of the schools operated under auspices of the various parishes. The Sisters of Mercy staffed Immaculate Heart of Mary School in Fairfield (1934), St. Mary's in Westbrook (1947), St. Joseph's in Farmington (1947), and St. Mary's in Old Town (1947). The Sisters of the Good Shepherd, in addition to operating the Lincoln Public School in Grand Isle (1938), opened St. Mary's in Caswell (1944), Hill School in Connor (1944), St. Joseph's in Hamlin (1944), and Sacred Heart in North Caribou (1946). The Ursulines opened St. Joseph's in Waterville (1945). The Sisters of St. Joseph opened St. Joseph's Academy in South Berwick (1936). The Holy Rosary Sisters opened the Dewey School in Frenchville (1945) while the Sisters of the Presentation of Mary opened the Harding and Roosevelt Public Schools in St. John's (1947). The Daughters of Wisdom opened the Montfort School in St. Agatha (1948) and staffed three schools (Acadia School, Evangeline School, and St. Thomas Aquinas School) in Madawaska (1949). And, the Little Franciscan Sisters of Mary took care of the Market Street School in Fort Kent (1950).

Former St. Hyacinth's Church, Westbrook, November 20, 1941 (courtesy of St. Hyacinth's Historical Society)

Just as there had been changes in religious groups which operated some of the high schools during Bishop McCarthy's years, so there were similar changes in the primary schools. The Ursulines were replaced by the Sisters of Mercy at Immaculate Heart of Mary in Fairfield in 1934. The Sisters of Mercy, who were at St. Louis Home and School for Boys in Scarborough since it opened in 1920, were replaced by the Sisters of Charity (Grey Nuns) who had purchased the former Wayland Estate from the diocese in 1935 at the request of Bishop McCarthy. And, in 1938, the Sisters of Mercy were replaced by the Sisters of the Good Shepherd at St. Joseph's in Old Town.

In the field of education, moreover, the role of the religious teacher in the St. John River Valley had reached an interesting turning point

St. Gregory's Camp for Boys, 1948

under Bishop McCarthy. Francis Brassard, who studied this development, showed how the pastors of the area had taken the initiative in building and staffing the schools. While that was the case in Fort Kent, Madawaska, Van Buren and other towns in the river valley down to the 1930s, thereafter the school officials themselves, due to the lack of competent teacher during the 1940s and 1950s, turned to those religious teachers like Daughters of Wisdom, Good Shepherd Sisters, and others like, for example, the Brothers of the Sacred Heart, who were staffing Madawaska's public high school starting in 1952, to teach other subjects than religion. At the same time, in a number of these cases, without much argument over constitutional issues of church and state, property owned by the Diocese of Portland was leased to the various towns to make such education possible. In this way, Roman Catholics helped to solve the crisis in public education for the welfare of the children in the St. John River Valley.

Another dimension of education that received attention during Bishop McCarthy's years in office was the number of catechetical centers. These were operated by the Sisters of Mercy at Our Lady of Ransom in Mechanic Falls (1933), St. Joseph's in Gardiner (1938), Our Lady of the Rosary in Brownville Junction (1945), and Our Lady of the Sacred Heart in Presque Isle (1945). The Franciscan Sisters of the Atonement undertook the operation of catechetical classes at St. Bernard's in Rockland (1942) before undertaking a kindergarten at St. Matthew's in Limerick (1949).

St. Anthony's Friary, Francisan Friars, Kennebunkport

St. Francis Mission (formerly St. Francis Friary), Greene

In his role as teacher, Bishop McCarthy did not hesitate to speak out publicly on moral issues when Catholic morality was threatened. One occasion, which presented itself in the spring of 1941, was particularly noteworthy when there was a bill before the state legislature to extend sterilization to defective persons even when these same individuals had not been committed to a state institution. That was a time when such power had already been exercised in Nazi Germany where, on July 14, 1933, a law on compulsory sterilization had been promulgated opening the way to another, on 1 September 1939, ordering the elimination of the mentally ill and others who had been institutionalized. Such an exercise of the power by the state, as evident in Nazi Germany, was not only immoral but tyrannical. Understandably, McCarthy urged the faithful of his diocese to defeat the proposal which was a product of the eugenics campaign in the United States during the 1930s. Aimed at the non-white population like the Native Americans, it was racist and even anti-immigrant in trying to control the population and to rid the state of undesirable citizens. In the end, the bill was unanimously rejected by the State House of Representatives.

Of the religious groups which had come into the diocese under Bishop McCarthy, three are noted for their religious services. First were the Sisters Adorers of the Precious Blood who arrived on October 4, 1934, and established the Monastery of the Most Precious Blood at the old Fessenden Estate on State Street. The second is St. Anthony Monastery (and Shrines) operated by the Franciscan refugees from Lithuania who, in August of 1944, settled first in Greene, where they opened St. Francis Monastery (1943-76), before they purchased what is now their present site in Kennebunkport, on September 8, 1947, and set up St. Anthony High School there. And, the third, the Servants of the Blessed Sacrament, founded in Paris in 1858 by St. Peter Julian Eymard, Apostle of the Eucharist, attributes its official beginning in the United States to their arrival in Waterville during April of 1947. All three have become popular centers for the spiritual enrichment of the faithful since their establishment under Bishop McCarthy.

While the burden of the debt limited what the diocese could do in providing services for its faithful, still it did not frustrate works of the Catholic Church. Though this was most evident in a number of projects in Catholic education, it was also true with respect to Catholic hospitals in Portland, Bangor, and Biddeford. In his episcopal city, in 1943, McCarthy had the Sisters of Mercy open a new site on State Street renaming it Mercy Hospital to replace Queen's Hospital. In Bangor, he was successful in having the Felician Sisters of St. Francis take over the Paine Private Hospital in 1947 which they renamed as St. Joseph's Hospital. And, a third hospital, located in

Biddeford, was Notre Dame which came under the Religious Hospitallers of St. Joseph from Montreal when it opened in 1951. While none of these hospitals were under the control of the diocese at the time of Bishop McCarthy's death, they were like others independently owned and operated by religious communities.

The Bishop's journeys outside the urban centers of the state through the river valleys of scenic Maine were at times both consoling and surprising. This was particularly evident when, in his visitations to the parishes of the St. John River Valley, he witnessed the progress which the Acadians were making in fighting the Great Depression in the early years of the 1940s with the help of the Farm Security Administration of the New Deal. As Stewart Doty has shown, in dealing with their rural poverty, these hardy individuals, whose farm lives were bonded together by their cultural and religious origins, were able to obtain loans, improve farm practices, and introduce cooperatives. All this helped to bring about better times for at least 25,000 inhabitants of the region, most of whom were members of Bishop McCarthy's flock. Elsewhere, according to Dyke Hendrickson, as the workers were abandoning their enclaves, anglicizing their names, and voting for the Democratic Party, the social consequences of the Great Depression became evident in such efforts to obtain jobs and to improve themselves economically and socially.

Moreover, many people who met Bishop McCarthy in his diocese did so on his journeys throughout the state in conferring the Sacrament of Confirmation. At these times, his proverbial kindness and thoughtfulness were manifest in regard to the Catholics of Maine who had grown from 176,418 to 236,672 during his episcopate. Among those who witnessed his charity and generosity were the many young candidates for the sacrament. Of these, there were young men who also recalled how the bishop would have those from ethnic groups prone to drinking take the pledge of abstaining from liquor until they were twenty-one. Such a practice was not unknown in a church dominated by an Irish hierarchy acutely sensitive to such a shortcoming which tended to destroy the life of a family.

At the same time, Bishop McCarthy brought joy to minorities within his own diocese, as was evident in his visit to the Penobscots on Indian Island in 1947 when he was greeted by children and tribal leaders. Here the tribe had suffered the loss, through drowning, on May 6, 1934, of their beloved pastor, Matthew C. Descoteaux, following the destruction of his motorboat in the dangerous waters of the river. A friend of Democratic Governor Louis J. Brann (1933-37), the priest had been instrumental in obtaining road work for the men on the reservation during those uncertain days of the Great Depression.

Bishop McCarthy's vision was not restricted to Maine even though he seldom ventured outside the state. While Americans were coping with the Great Depression, he did not hesitate to urge them to support the efforts of Franklin D. Roosevelt, whose projects, especially the Works Progress Administration, were evident in Portland, in keeping people employed. Reportedly the first American bishop to have an audience with Pope Pius XII (1939-58), McCarthy was very loyal to the Holy Father during the troubled years of World War II and, like his brother bishops in the United States, was behind their statement, on November 14, 1942, denouncing the Nazi persecution of the Jews. In a message for Christmas 1947, McCarthy expressed, on December 20th that year, his deep appreciation for what Jews and Protestants, in addition to Catholics, had done to help their brothers and sisters in Europe and Asia to gain relief in the aftermath of World War II. And, in Portland itself his letters indicate that Bishop McCarthy was friendly with prominent non-

Mercy Hospital, Portland

St. Joseph's Hospital, Felician Sisters, Bangor

Bishop McCarthy (in straw hat) greets Penobscot children on Indian Island in 1947 (courtesy Catholic Charities Maine)

Ordination of Daniel J. Feeney as Auxiliary Bishop of Portland, September 12, 1946

Catholic citizens like Percival P. Baxter and Max L. Pinasky.

During his years, Bishop McCarthy was blessed with many devoted priests and the death of a number of them impoverished the diocese. One was Msgr. Michael C. McDonough (1860-1933), who served as vicar general for at least three bishops, including Bishop McCarthy. A second was Msgr. John W. Houlihan (1871-1945), who was one of three natives of Bangor (the other two were Charles Collins and Thomas J. Nelligan) ordained priests in Paris on May 19, 1894, and in whose memory the Knights of Columbus Council, No. 2983, in Portland was named. A third was Rev. Timothy J. Mahoney (d. 1938), the popular pastor in the Saco area. And, a fourth was Msgr. James A. Carey (1874-1953) who served as an army chaplain in World War I and as Pastor of Sacred Heart in Portland (1923-50). In that period, on April 22, 1944, William Cardinal O'Connell, one of McCarthy's predecessors, had also died.

Monastery of the Precious Blood, Portland

Of all the priests of the diocese, Daniel J. Feeney, Pastor of the Church of the Nativity of the Blessed Virgin Mary in Presque Isle, was selected, on June 22, 1946, to assist Bishop McCarthy in his declining years. In that appointment, Rome had for the first time chosen a native of Portland to serve as its bishop and for the first time chosen an auxiliary for the diocese. However, since Bishop McCarthy did not see any need for an auxiliary, he assigned Feeney as the Pastor of St. Joseph's in Lewiston from 1946 to 1948. With Rome thinking otherwise, on July 27, 1948, Pope Pius XII gave Bishop Feeney the powers of a residential bishop, and this enabled Bishop McCarthy to enter into retirement with ease and with dignity. In doing so, he was able to reside on the Western Promenade where, in 1938, he had purchased the former residence of Morris McDonald. By this time it had became the residence of the Bishop of Portland while the Cathedral Rectory became the residence for the auxiliary bishop and the priests of the parish.

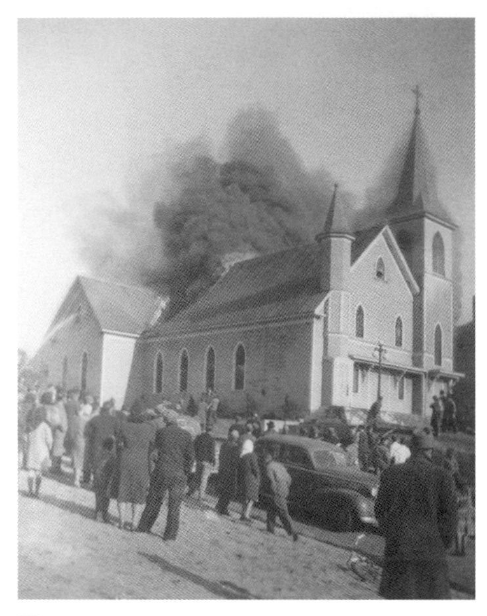

St. Rose of Lima, Jay, destroyed by flames on April 4, 1948

Having spent the last seventeen months of his life helpless in Mercy Hospital, Bishop Joseph E. McCarthy died on September 8, 1955. His life was a true reflection of his motto, "For me to live is Christ" ("*Mihi vivere Christus est*," Phil. 1:21), having borne the heavy cross of his office in health and in sickness with what can best be described today as a form of Alzheimer's disease. "His example of brotherhood and his dedication to the spiritual and physical welfare of his people will for years to come be a challenge to clergymen of all faiths," declared the editorial in *The Portland Press Herald*, on September 10, 1955. After the solemn obsequies in the Cathedral of the Immaculate Conception where Bishop Feeney, his successor, eulogized the late bishop for his efforts in preserving the church and recalled how twelve churches had been built and 110 priests were ordained during his years, the body of Bishop Joseph E. McCarthy was returned to his native Waterbury in Connecticut for its final resting place in the family lot at Calvary Cemetery.

Chapter 9

A Native Son as Bishop of Portland

Since Bishop Daniel J. Feeney (1894-1969), Administrator of the Diocese of Portland, had been named, on March 4, 1952, Coadjutor Bishop of Portland, consequently, on September 8, 1955, the day of the death of Bishop McCarthy, he succeeded him as the Ordinary and became the seventh Bishop of Portland. The son of Daniel J. and Mary (Quinn) Feeney, he was born in Portland, Maine, on September 12, 1894, and was a graduate of Portland High School (1913). Having attended the College of the Holy Cross (1913-15), he entered the Grand Seminary in Montreal where, in St. James Cathedral, he was ordained a priest, on May 21, 1921, by Coadjutor Archbishop Georges Gauthier (1871-1940).

Feeney had been consecrated Titular Bishop of Sita and Auxiliary Bishop of Portland in the Cathedral of the Immaculate Conception in Portland, on September 12, 1946, by Amleto Giovanni Cicognani (1883-1972), Apostolic Delegate to the United States, with the assistance of Bishop Matthew Francis Brady of Manchester, and Auxiliary Bishop Louis Francis Kelleher of Boston.

Relatively unknown outside of the Diocese of Portland, there are various explanations of Feeney's appointment. It is said that his name came to the attention of Rome because of Archbishop Francis J. Spellman of New York who, as Military Vicar of the United States, had been welcomed by Feeney to Presque Isle when the archbishop's plane had been forced to land there. While Father Daniel J. Hagerty (d. 1978), who was an eyewitness of that visit, spread the story (and the story sounds plausible given Cardinal Spellman's influence at the Vatican because of his friendship with Pope Pius XII), Feeney himself totally discounted it as nothing more than speculation. Another explanation is that Cicognani, who was the Apostolic Delegate at the time, had asked Archbishop Murray of St. Paul, a former Bishop

Bishop Daniel J. Feeney

of Portland, for a recommendation and the latter submitted Feeney's name because of his knowledge of him as his Superintendent of Schools (the two remained good friends in their years as bishops). In any case, it was Pope Pius XII (1939-58) who was mainly responsible for having a native son like Feeney appointed as Bishop of the Diocese of Portland for the first time.

Since it was not appropriate to mark the centennial of the diocese during the illness of his predecessor, Feeney did so two months after taking over as Bishop of Portland. The celebration, which was delayed for two years, corresponded more closely to the consecration of Bacon as the first Bishop of Portland. *The Portland Sunday Telegram* recognized the anniversary with a special supplement in its edition on November 6th. Then, on November 8th, Governor Edmund S. Muskie extended the state's greetings to Bishop Feeney. The religious celebration was held in Portland's Cathedral of the Immaculate Conception on the following day, with four archbishops and fifteen bishops from Canada and New England present.

Pectoral cross, Bishop Feeney

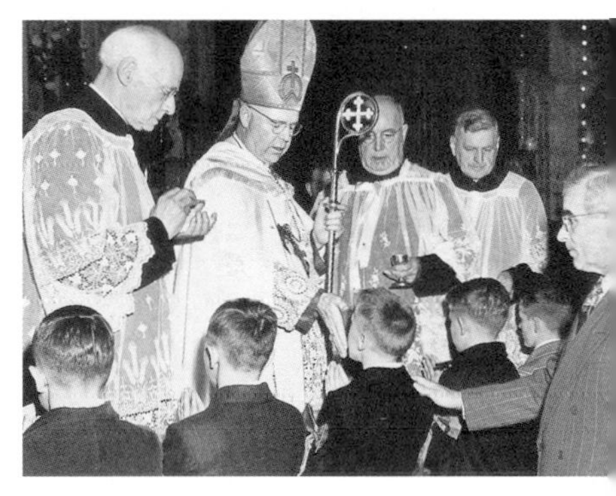

Bishop Feeney confirming

Coat of arms of Bishop Feeney

St. Theresa, Oakland

In succeeding McCarthy, Feeney was quite knowledgeable in the details of his office, having exercised the authority of a residential bishop for seven years during which he sought to revitalize the neglected administrative structure of the diocese when the health of his predecessor was declining. While he was responsible for at least 130 parish churches and 225 priests, not to mention the care for some sixty missions, forty chapels, and twenty stations, Bishop Feeney was able to expand the diocese even though the bond issue tended to restrict expansion by placing a limit on loans. He established St. Mary Star of the Sea, in York Beach in 1961, set up Our Lady of Ransom in Mechanic Falls as an independent parish in 1962, brought into being St. Pius X in Portland in 1962, and created St. Theresa's in Oakland in 1963. Next door to the new Parish of St. Pius X, the first one created in his episcopal city in thirty-eight years, Bishop Feeney opened up a new chancery office for the administration of his extensive diocese in 1963. What enabled the diocese to expand in this way was its reliance on its own deposit and loan program without resorting to external financing so that major programs could go forward. Thus, a new physical plant at St. John the Baptist in Winslow, for example, with a church, rectory, school, and convent became a reality.

While Catholic religious and social organizations like the Knights of Columbus, the Holy Name Society, the Legion of Mary, and the Daughters of Isabella continued to flourish during Feeney's tenure, his years saw the introduction of the Catholic Youth Organization. Organized in 1930 by Bishop Bernard J. Sheil (1886-1969) of Chicago, to promote spiritual, social, and athletic programs for youth within the parishes, the first C. Y. O. in the state was organized in Presque Isle in 1956 under Father Royal J. Parent (b. 1930). Spreading throughout Aroostook County, the C. Y. O. gradually spread throughout the Diocese of Portland reaching as far south as Old Orchard due to the efforts of Father Parent, its founder in Maine.

Given his tendency to speak his mind without mincing his words when the interests of Catholics were at risk, Bishop Feeney at times drew local, state, and even national attention. On June 3, 1955, as reported the next day in *The New York Times*, he publicly clashed with Rear Admiral William W. Warlick of the Maine Maritime Academy at Castine for not allowing

Chancery Building, 510 Ocean Avenue, Portland

Father John McVicar (d. 1990), Catholic pastor at Bucksport to minister to the Catholics on campus only to learn that it was the academy's tradition to have its students attend to their religious needs off campus, a policy that has somewhat changed. This controversy, which continued during the summer, was documented in Feeney's own column, "The Bishop Speaks," published in the diocesan newspaper. What the bishop found particularly annoying about the policy at the academy was that Catholic priests could celebrate Mass in state institutions like prisons and hospitals but they could not even hear confessions on the maritime campus.

Bishop Feeney's views with respect to other practices relating to religion occasioned other controversies. In March of 1958, the bishop unexpectedly drew national attention when he prohibited Catholics graduating from high school to take part in baccalaureates because they were, in his view, Congregational religious services that violated the consciences of Catholic students. Five year later, in March of 1963, the bishop adamantly fought the impending law to permit retailers to open their stores on Sundays because "Sunday should be preserved as a day of worship." However, by the spring of 1967, Feeney had modified his view about the baccalaureates in light of the ecumenical thrust of the Second Vatican Council.

Understandably, during his years as bishop, Feeney's major preoccupation was the dissolution of the $4,800,000.00 diocesan debt. When this was accomplished on November 1, 1963, he looked upon the date as "Independence Day" for the diocese. Since taking over the government of the diocese, on July 27, 1948, it remained his major contribution during his years as apostolic administrator, coadjutor, and bishop. "The credit for this belongs to the loyal priests and the people of the diocese," Feeney declared in an interview published in the city's major newspaper three years later. The clergy and the laity in the parishes of the diocese had shouldered the burden successfully. With that goal achieved during the first year of the Second Vatican Council, Bishop Feeney faced the future with confidence, ably assisted by Monsignor William G. Cunneen as his vicar general and Monsignors Edward C. O'Leary and Vincent A. Tatarczuk as his chancellors, not to mention the counsel of Judge Francis W. Sullivan (d. 1967) and Dr. Francis M. Dooley (d. 1972), chief of staff at Mercy Hospital.

Most ironically, given the financial burden on the diocese in those days before the reforms of the Second Vatican Council, there were pastors who administered their parishes as benefices. When Jesuit priests from their major house of studies in New England were sent to exercise their ministry on weekends, some were instructed to keep preaching at the mission chapels until the pastor arrived to take up the collection. In such a situation, the pastor appeared to be more interested in the donations, especially since he had absolute control over the disposal of the collections. Certainly, anyone familiar with the financial condition of the diocese during those years could not have been pleased about a pastor exercising so much authority over parish finances which were not as closely audited as they are today.

The Second Vatican Council was summoned by Blessed Pope John XXIII (1881-1963), to update the Catholic Church. It opened the first of its four sessions on October 11, 1962, and ended on December 8, 1965. Although Bishop Feeney was present at all four sessions of the council, one will not find his name in Xavier Rynne's history of that unusual gathering of prelates. Still he was one of more than two thousand bishops who gathered in Rome to help in the renovation of Catholicism under the leadership of Pope John and his successor, Pope Paul VI (1897-1978). While Bishop Ernest J. Primeau (1909-89), his contemporary in the Diocese of Manchester, made at least one intervention at the council, Bishop Feeney made none. In replying to Monsignor Vincent A. Yzermans, who was investigating the role of the American bishops after the first three session of the council, Bishop Feeney wrote: "For your records, I was and shall continue to be a 'silent observer' at the Council." While he was disappointed at the death of Pope John, Bishop Feeney was very pleased with Pope Paul's determination to carry on the work of the council and his stress on the

Msgr. George P. Johnson, Vicar General

Bishop Feeney attending the Second Vatican Council (Paolo Gloriani photograph)

collegiality of bishops by using the phrase, "fellow bishops," in the work of the Catholic Church. Like other American Bishops, Bishop Feeney was quite happy when Pope Paul VI, in a first visit by a pope to this country, came to the United States, on October 4, 1965, and addressed the General Assembly of the United Nations and celebrated Mass in New York's Yankee Stadium.

One person who created quite an impression at the Second Vatican Council as a correspondent for *The Brooklyn Tablet* was Frances Lee McGillicuddy (1904-92), a native of Portland. Having taught French in the public schools in New York City, she had pursued a career there and became involved with the United Nations and the rights of women. In fact, she was a leader of the American branch of St. Joan's International Alliance, a Catholic feminist organization. She continued to make a name for herself after the Second Vatican Council as a spokesperson for women's rights within the Catholic Church, leading Archbishop Leo Byrne of St. Paul, Minnesota, to refer to her as a "buzz saw," because of her determination.

First Grade, St. Joseph's School, Lewiston, 1957

Once the Second Vatican Council had ended, Bishop Feeney turned his attention with great confidence to implementing its decrees in the Diocese of Portland. "Now I have got to see that the decrees of the council are implemented in this diocese," he declared. And, he did so shortly after his return from the council by exercising collegiality on the local scene with three innovations: a senate elected by the priests to help the bishop in the government of the diocese, parish councils to involve the people in the operation of the parishes, and the updating of the work of at least one thousand religious men and women in the diocese.

In a period of change like the implementation of the decrees of the council, people used to the old ways were, not surprisingly, slow to change. Such resistance was understandably evident in the reluctance to take advantage of the new changes in the Eucharistic and Lenten fasts. One change, the abstinence from meat on Fridays throughout the year, was an innovation which, when it was announced at the end of 1965, was thought to be a threat to Portland's fishing industry. Interestingly enough, the bishop's progressive attitude in this matter was already exhibited when, on November 2, 1961, he had granted a dispensation to lumberjacks in view of their living conditions, "from the law of abstinence on all Fridays of the year, except Good Friday."

Nevertheless, there were other aspects of the changes that brought a breath of fresh air in relations between Catholics and other Christians. This was particularly true in relations with non-Catholics among whom Bishop Feeney was viewed as a staunch ecumenical leader in Maine. Speaking before the Greater Portland Ministerial Association in 1964, when the

First Holy Communion, St. Teresa's Church, Brewer, c. 1960.

Religious Profession, Sisters of St. Joseph, Sacred Heart Church, Auburn, c. 1957

Second Vatican Council was in recess, the bishop endorsed the cordiality that existed among Catholics, Jews, and Protestants in Maine. Later Feeney continued to make history as he entered St. Luke's Episcopal Cathedral to preach during the Church Unity Octave at which many Catholic as well as Protestant clergymen were present, including Bishop Oliver L. Loring of the Episcopal Diocese of Maine (1941-68) who officiated. Bishop Feeney's other engagements as guest speaker were at Immanuel Baptist Church in Portland and the First Congregational Church in South Portland. At all these gatherings, Feeney spoke eloquently in ecumenical accents as an apostle of cooperation and understanding. In fact, he was one of the first Catholic bishops in the country to allow an informal affiliation of his priests with the Maine Council of Churches, an ecumenical body of Protestant churches, even before the Second Vatican Council.

Prior to the Second Vatican Council, rarely did parish schools like Notre Dame in Skowhegan (1954) and Our Lady of Mt. Carmel in Lille (1962) close. However, back in September of 1966, Bishop Feeney had set up a school board to formulate policy regarding the parochial schools of the diocese. Subsequently, a relatively large number of elementary schools did close like Champlain School in Van Buren, St. Anthony's in Jackman, St. Joseph's in Hamlin, and St. Joseph's in Wallagrass in 1965; St. Agatha's in St. Agatha and St. Michael's in South Berwick in 1966; St. Thomas Aquinas in Madawaska in 1967; St. Mary's in Lewiston in 1968; and St. Joseph's in Old Town, in addition to three in Waterville, namely, St. Francis de Sales, Notre Dame, and Sacred Heart, all in 1969. Many of these schools closed when they could not operate with a majority of religious as teachers, especially when the nuns withdrew from teaching, or when the schools did not measure up to educational standards.

That development, of course, was not unrelated to the emphasis which Bishop Feeney gave to teaching of religion to adults and to children. In May of 1961, he provided spiritual help for adult Catholics by dedicating St. Francis de Sales Chapel at 13 Brown Street in the downtown Portland where there was also a library for Catholic discussion groups. For the children, he emphasized the Confraternity of Christian Doctrine in the parishes of the diocese. And, he advocated the ecumenical direction given by the Second Vatican Council for Catholics by reaching out to his separated Christian brethren and emphasizing their common religious roots.

St. Joseph College, Standish

St. Ignatius Chapel at Cheverus High School

Cheverus High School, Portland

■ *Little Franciscans of Mary, St. Louis School, Auburn, 1952*

■ *Mother Evangelist Ward, RSM, Superior General, Sisters of Mercy*

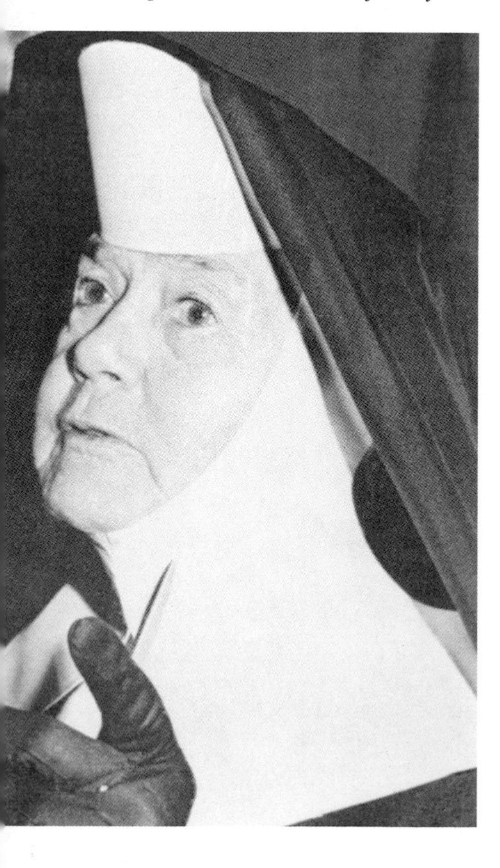

Despite all the changes, Bishop Feeney did not neglect the Catholic education of youth beyond the religious sphere. His annual gatherings of an institute for teachers held at the Cathedral Guild Hall in his episcopal city demonstrated this in providing for the updating of all teachers within the parochial school system. His commitment to them emerged even during the years of the Presidency of John F. Kennedy (1961-63), as the bishop did not hesitate to speak out against a federal aid to education bill designed to deny loans to parochial schools. More than ever, too, Bishop Feeney sought to involve the laity in the work of education by establishing an education board which included them, along with clergy and religious, in the diocesan department of education. In that connection, back in 1957, the Catholic laity in Augusta carried on a dispute which the majority of the public supported and led the city council to allot a token amount of money to transport some nine hundred Catholic school children to private schools. Although such concerns highlighted an issue of justice, they also foreshadowed the financial crisis which the Catholic Church was facing in trying to maintain its vast network of primary and secondary schools.

During his years as bishop, Feeney received some recognition in higher education. Institutions like the University of Maine, St. Francis College in Biddeford, St. Michael's College in Vermont, and the College of the Holy Cross in Worcester, Massachusetts, conferred upon him honorary degrees, an indication that the Bishop of Portland had some public standing as a leader. Like other bishops in the country, he was supportive of raising money for The Catholic University of American in Washington, D. C. And, in the case of his own region, Catholic college education was growing as St. Joseph's College, formerly Our Lady of Mercy College, moved from Deering to its present site on Sebago Lake in Standish in 1956.

Having taken as his motto the preaching of the Word of God (2 Tim. 4:2) "*Praedica Verbum*," Bishop Feeney fulfilled this mission as bishop through his sermons at religious services and his addresses at public gatherings. Although he was quite unlike Bishop Healy and Bishop Murray before him because he allowed the dignity of his office to stand in his way, he unhesitatingly preached the message of the Gospel and was not at all shy about what he expected of Catholics in the exercise of their religious beliefs and practices. That Bishop Feeney created, in taking over as Bishop of Portland, a diocesan office to take care of radio and television activities shows how sensitive he was to pubic relations as very important in the preaching of the word of God.

In 1966, on his twentieth anniversary as a bishop, Feeney indicated his concern with the decline of vocations to the priesthood. However, earlier, on June 4, 1955, a year when Catholics were celebrating the centennial of the Diocese of Portland, seventeen candidates had been ordained to the priesthood (fifteen diocesan and two religious priests), the largest class ever in Maine. That was the year when John R. Willis (1917-2001), a former Congregational minister and professor at Bates College, entered the Society of Jesus (after his ordination to the priesthood in 1962, he had a successful career at Boston College). Certainly, these various developments during Bishop Feeney's tenure of office were not entirely irrelevant to the status of vocations nor to the spiritual life of the diocese.

Still, at the same time, the decline in the number of priests was underscored by the deaths of a number of prominent ones such as Monsignors Arthur M. Décary, Pastor of St. André's in Biddeford, and Joseph A.

Laflamme, Pastor of St. Joseph's in that same city, in 1957; Clarence H. Coughlin, Pastor of Dominic's in Portland, and Clement M. Frazier, Pastor of St. Athanasius in Rumford, in 1959; Vital E. Noñorgues, Pastor of Holy Family in Lewiston, in 1961; Arthur J. Dubé, Pastor of Our Lady of Lourdes in Saco, George P. Johnson, Pastor of St. Joseph's in Portland, and Anthony E. Thibault, Pastor of St. John's in Rumford, in 1964; Michael F. Tierney, Pastor of St. Mary's in Houlton, in 1966; John J. Barrett, Pastor of Holy Cross in South Portland, in 1968; and Philippe E. Desjardins, Pastor of St. Hyacinth's in Westbrook, who was at ninety-two the oldest priest in the diocese, in 1969.

Sister of Mercy with infants at Holy Innocents Home, Portland (courtesy of Catholic Charities Maine)

Although the Second Vatican Council had set seventy-five years of age as the time for retirement for bishops, Bishop Feeney was facing that possibility not too long before his seventy-second birthday when Rome, on March 4, 1966, appointed Peter Leo Gerety as his coadjutor with the right of succession. Subsequently, Bishop Gerety ably assisted Bishop Feeney in carrying out the duties of his office just as the latter had done for Bishop McCarthy. Then, on February 18, 1967, as Feeney's health was declining, Rome elevated Bishop Gerety to Apostolic Administrator of the Diocese of Portland. Consequently, it is Bishop Gerety's hand that is seen, once he was installed, in such developments under Bishop Feeney as the establishment of the new parishes, the renovations in the Cathedral, and the launching of the Diocesan Bureau of Human Services and the Bishop's Campaign.

Of the parishes in which Bishop Feeney's coadjutor had a hand, they were Our Lady of Good Hope in Camden, St. Anne in Gorham, St. Gregory in Gray, and Our Lady of Wisdom in Orono which date from 1967; and Holy Martyrs in Falmouth, St. Andrew in Augusta, St. Bartholomew in Cape Elizabeth, St. Matthew in Hampden, and St. Philip in Auburn which date from 1968. The parish in Gray had evolved out of the property of Camp Gregory for Boys (1925-73).

While most older Catholics would not be upset with some of changes following the Second Vatican Council because they were not forced to break from their old ways, the innovations which were introduced by Feeney's coadjutor triggered opposition in Maine. These changes were in the fabric of the church such as turning the altar towards the people, removing the altar rail, and reducing the number of statues. When these were combined with the change of Latin to English in the liturgy itself, the reaction in the state was not unlike what developed throughout the nation even leading some Catholics to launch a conservative movement which still exists today. Yet, Bishop Feeney's tenure was setting an example for renovations within the churches themselves by introducing the innovations of the council into his own church. There the faithful would be able to participate actively in the liturgy there with the completion of the changes in 1969, the 100th anniversary of the Cathedral.

May Procession, Holy Martyrs Church, Falmouth, 1966

The Catholic Church, moreover, has always been active in providing social services for its people. In the Diocese of Portland, when Bishop Feeney had the authority of a residential bishop, bureaus for such a program were established in Bangor and Brewer, as well as in

■ *Stained glass window depicting President John F. Kennedy, St. Patrick's Church, Portland*

Auburn and Lewiston. However, with Neil D. Michaud as a catalyst, the bishop set up a district operation of the Bureau of Human Relations Services in the fall of 1966 with a budget of $50,000. While this was all preliminary to the development of an agency for the whole state, it was a major step in updating the services of the diocese for the role of the church in the modern world envisioned by the Second Vatican Council. Yet, in 1968, when the Diocese of Portland launched the Bishops' Campaign Fund Drive as an attempt to raise $4,250,000.00 to advance the social and other services of the diocese in making effective the Gospel message of caring for those most in need, this undertaking must also be considered as the work of his coadjutor bishop.

After spending his last months in Mercy Hospital, death came to Bishop Feeney on September 15, 1969, not too many days after his seventy-fifth birthday. "The death of the Most Rev. Daniel J. Feeney, seventh bishop of Portland, though not unexpected" declared the editorial in *The Portland Press Herald*, "is a profoundly sorrowful event to the more than a quarter of a million Catholics in Maine and countless friends of all faiths." Providentially, since the Cathedral was still undergoing renovations, the funeral was held in St. Dominic's, once the Pro-Cathedral of the diocese and Feeney's home parish where he was affectionately known as "Father Dan" in his early days as a priest. Like Bishop Healy, in whose memory he had dedicated a new residence hall at their alma mater in August of 1962, Bishop Feeney was buried in Calvary Cemetery in South Portland. The Knights of Columbus in Presque Isle have honored his memory by naming its Fourth Degree Assembly after him. Throughout his years in office, he had directed the helm of the Catholic Church in Maine with a firm and steady hand confirming its members in their faith.

■ *Grave of Bishop Feeney, Calvary Cemetery, South Portland*

Chapter 10

Portland's Most Progressive Catholic Bishop

On September 15, 1969, Bishop Peter Leo Gerety (b. 1912) became the eighth Bishop of the Diocese of Portland, Maine. Born in Shelton, Connecticut, on July 19, 1912, he was the son of Peter Leo and Charlotte Ursula (Daly) Gerety, and began his early studies for the priesthood at St. Thomas Seminary in Bloomfield, Connecticut. As a candidate of the Archdiocese of Hartford, Gerety continued them for five years at St. Sulpice, in Issy outside of Paris, and was ordained a priest in the Cathedral of Notre Dame, on June 29, 1939, by Sulpician Cardinal Jean Verdier (1864-1940). Having served as a curate at St. John the Evangelist in New Haven (1939-42) and as the director of Blessed Martin de Porres Interracial Center (1942-56) there, Gerety was appointed pastor of what became St. Martin de Porres Church (1956-66). In these years, he helped the blacks in the depressed area of New Haven, directed the Spanish-speaking apostolate, and represented the archdiocese on the state board on race and religion.

Ordained Titular Bishop of Crepedula and Coadjutor Bishop of Portland by Archbishop Henry J. O'Brien (1896-1976) of Hartford, who was assisted by Bishop Feeney of Portland and Auxiliary Bishop John Francis Hackett of Hartford in this city's Cathedral of St. Joseph, Gerety was the third Bishop of Portland to come from the Archdiocese of Hartford. As the leader of some 270,000 Catholics in the State of Maine, the new bishop had, like O'Connell and Murray before him, just about five solid years as bishop before leaving Portland due to a promotion to an archiepiscopal see. That such a development would take place was foreshadowed at the outset of his tenure when early in 1970, *The Critic*, a national Catholic magazine, recognized Gerety as one of the twelve top bishops in the country.

Before he assumed his new appointment by Pope Paul VI as Coadjutor Bishop of Portland in 1966, Monsignor Gerety had been recognized, for two years prior to his appointment to Portland, as the leader among priests of the Hartford Archdiocese on questions relating to interracial justice, in his office as head of the archbishop's committee on human rights. Thus, due to his experience with New Haven's Puerto Ricans at the interracial center, Gerety had acquired a reputation as a liberal and as an activist on social issues.

In coming to Portland, Gerety did not abandon his progressive social ideas as bishop. He supported Cesar Chavez (1927-95) and the United Farm Workers of America in their California boycotts, against grapes in Delano in 1969 and joined other bishops of the region of New England in 1973 on behalf of the same workers boycotting lettuce in the Selinas Valley. This same interest in the cause of social justice was simultaneously reflected in Gerety's work as a leader within the Diocese of Portland.

In focusing on the priests of the diocese, Bishop Gerety built on the initiatives of Bishop Feeney. He consolidated the Priests' Senate beyond its experimental stage and undertook to increase the involvement of the clergy and laity

Bishop Peter L. Gerety

Coat of arms of Coadjutor Bishop Peter Leo Gerety

Bishop Gerety meeting Pope Paul VI

■ *Mount St. Joseph, Waterville*

■ *St. Philip, Auburn*

by establishing the Diocesan Pastoral Council, the Priests' Personnel Board, and the Diocesan Hospital Chaplaincy Ministry. While such decisions were governed by the need at times for confidentiality, Gerety was once quite disturbed to find, at least on one occasion, a default in confidentiality which led him to request that the members of the Personnel Board submit their resignations in writing.

Moreover, to provide for the involvement of chaplains in higher education, Gerety had established the Newman Center of Our Lady of Wisdom as a personal parish at Orono (1967), and he set up for the first time the Diocesan Campus Ministry Apostolate with its own Vicar. This was further evidence that he was not afraid to make truly extraordinary decisions because this expanded the Newman Apostolate from eight institutions of higher education in the year when Bishop Gerety first arrived in Portland to twenty-eight in the year of his departure.

As for the colleges directly under Catholic auspices, there were only two in existence, St. Joseph's in North Windham and St. Francis in Biddeford Pool. That both had become coeducational, the latter in 1967 and the former in 1970, indicated that the changing trends in Catholic college education had reached into Maine. As the uncle of Thomas Gerety who later served as President of Trinity College and of Amherst College, the bishop was not unfamiliar with such trends in higher education.

In addition to the apostolate of higher education, the Diocese of Portland was involved in secondary schools. Catherine McAuley High School was added for girls by the Sisters of Mercy in Portland in 1969, replacing St. Joseph's Academy and Cathedral High School. By 1974, the Ursulines in Waterville reduced their high school, Mount Merici Academy, to a private Catholic elementary school after St. Joseph's closed. By that time, St. Anthony's High School, under the Lithuanian Franciscans at Kennebunkport, which was in existence when Bishop Gerety first came to Portland, was no longer operating. This was, likewise, true of the private high schools operated by Brothers of Christian Instruction in Alfred, the Sisters of the Presentation of Mary in Biddeford Pool, and the Sisters of St. Joseph in Jackman Station and South Berwick, in addition to parish high schools like St. Louis in Biddeford and St. Ignatius in Sanford. At the same time, Cheverus High School in Portland, John Bapst in Bangor, and St. Dominic's in Lewiston (from which the Dominicans withdrew in 1969) continued to be the major Catholic high schools within the Diocese of Portland.

While Bishop Gerety was expanding the ministry of the church's involvement in higher education, he had to deal with the closing of elementary schools in many parishes where it was too costly to support them, especially with a decline in the religious personnel to staff them. When, for example, it was announced in June of 1969 that St. Mary's in Bath, St. Teresa's in Brewer, Immaculate Heart of Mary in Fairfield, Sacred Heart in Portland, and St. Athanasius in Rumford were closing, the bishop had to take the heat from irate parishioners. That trend continued as other schools like St. Louis in Auburn in 1970, St. Ignatius and Holy Family in Sanford and St. Theresa's in Mexico in 1972; Holy Family in Lewiston, Notre Dame in Springvale and Holy Rosary in Caribou in 1973, and St. Anne's in Lisbon and St. Hyacinth's in Westbrook in 1974 all went out of existence. Given the United States Supreme Court decision in 1971 *(Lemon v. Kurtzman)* which prohibited the use of state funds to support parochial school teachers of secular subjects and to support secular educational services in those schools, it became impossible for the diocese to keep many of these schools open. And, to compensate for the closing of some schools, there was a new arrangement as the Consolidated School in Waterville (1969-74) and the St. Thomas School which consolidated the schools of Holy Family, Notre Dame, and St. Ignatius in Sanford in 1972.

Moreover, in the overall summary of statistics, Catholic elementary schools had declined from about sixty in 1966 to about twenty-five in 1974. Since this apostolate of education was primarily the work of women religious, Bishop Gerety was responsible for another first in establishing the Council for

Women Religious, as he restructured the organization of the Diocese of Portland, and sponsored the first national conference of women religious. This was held at Portland's *Eastland Hotel*, paving the way to the birth of the National Association of Women Religious.

As for new parishes within the Diocese of Portland, Gerety had already been responsible for helping to set up at least the last four parishes credited to Bishop Feeney's tenure of office. Although the Oblates had taken over St. Mary of Lourdes in Lincoln in 1968, Gerety, in his own years, established parishes like St. Mary's in Wells (1970) and St. Joseph's in Bridgton (1971) and paved the way for Our Lady of Perpetual Help in Windham (1974). However, what was becoming evident was the need to consolidate, rather than expand, parishes. That parishes had actually increased from 134 in the year of his appointment to Portland to 142 when the bishop left Maine should not distract from the merger of St. Athanasius and St. John in Rumford in 1970 as a warning about a trend that would become more explicit in the future. Among the parishes which constructed new churches dedicated during Gerety's time was St. Mary's in Eagle Lake where Joseph S. Marcoux (1850-1918) had been a pioneering pastor who had been very much involved in the social welfare of Catholics in that part of Aroostook County, especially in the founding of the hospital there.

Since Gerety was the bishop who handled the changes in the renovations of the Cathedral, he was not free from criticism. While he and Bishop Feeney had envisioned more involvement by the laity in the church's liturgical worship, the Cathedral took on a modern and simple appearance as the altar, pulpit, rail, and throne, all fashioned from Italian marble, were removed so that the sanctuary had a new and simple look compared to its former ornate and regal style. Understandably, these changes, which updated the liturgical environment in accord with the reforms of the Second Vatican Council, did not sit well with a number of the faithful. However, in assuming more responsibility as his predecessor's health was declining, Gerety gracefully bore the criticism for these decisions which he saw as basic to the renewal of liturgical life in the Catholic Church.

St. Joseph, Bridgton

On the tenth anniversary of Pope John XXIII's encyclical, *Pacem in Terris*, promulgated on April 7, 1963, Bishop Gerety published a pastoral letter in 1973 entitled "The Day of Peace Restored" and gained national attention by being interviewed on *Face the Nation* about his unique pastoral. Yet, anyone familiar with Gerety's strong opposition to the American involvement in Vietnam would find the pastoral quite characteristic of the Maine prelate. In the case of the outburst of protest over Vietnam in 1970, Gerety asked that President Richard M. Nixon listen to the students who were demonstrating against the war and the bishop himself supported those conscientious objectors who refused to serve in the war. In 1971, Gerety joined a group of other bishops in New England in condemning the bombings which were causing civilian deaths in North Vietnam. Actually, all these decisions were just further indications confirming why the Bishop of Portland had been recognized as one of the few bishops who was actually sensitive to measures required to renovate and strengthen the Catholic Church after the Second Vatican Council.

After the Bishop of Portland had been chosen by his fellow bishops to chair the American Catholic Bishops Ad Hoc Committee for Liason with the National Office of Black Catholics, Gerety supported the blacks who had requested that a central office be established granting black Catholics the power to assign, in consultation with bishops, black clergymen to parishes. And, in May of 1972, Gerety was one of five Americans who participated in an international gathering at Nemi, Italy, dealing with racial discrimination, a subject with which he had been involved for a quarter of a century.

■ *St. André's Adoption Agency, Biddeford*

■ *Central Services, Catholic Charities Maine, Falmouth*

■ *Bishop Gerety at Bishop Edward C. O'Leary's ordination, January 25, 1971*

In coming to Maine, Bishop Gerety had become familiar with the needs of the Native Americans. After the Association of Aroostook Indians was formed in 1969, he was instrumental in obtaining funds from the American Catholic Bishops' Campaign for Human Development in 1972 to care for their legal fees. Earlier in 1970, he had, like Bishop Healy, rejected the view that the Native Americans were wards of the state and emphasized that the tribal councils were the authoritative governing bodies for the reservations. To Gerety's credit, for the first time in a century, J. Stanley Bowe (1923-77), a Jesuit, was appointed to St. Ann's in Pleasant Point, thereby linking the Passamaquoddies once more with their historical roots in Catholicism. Though the mission had been staffed by diocesan priests (Thomas Coyne, Michael McGarrigle, and Coleman O'Toole among others), Bowe was the first Jesuit assigned to an Indian mission in Maine in more than a century.

A major development in the restructuring of the administration of the diocese was the expansion on a statewide basis of its social services. Under Bishop Feeney, Bishop Gerety, early in his work as coadjutor bishop, had spent one third of a year surveying the status of the social work of the Diocese of Portland. This was important in helping him to meet the people and the priests throughout the state and in understanding what had to be done in the reform of social structures within the state. Out of this experience with Maine's problems, it became clear to Gerety as the new bishop, in assessing the strengths and weaknesses of the church's social services, that a fundamental change was in order for the Catholic Church to be relevant to the challenges of society. Consequently, in exercising the powers he had as Bishop Feeney's health declined, Gerety overhauled the church's social services and established the Diocesan Bureau of Human Relations Services, Inc., now known as Catholic Charities Maine.

It was that work which marked Bishop Gerety as more than just a religious leader. That the Catholic Church was reaching out to the people of Maine through seven homes for the aged, including St. Joseph's Manor in Portland, six general hospitals, four day care centers, and providing a host of other programs, through the operation of at least a half dozen of district offices, indicates that Catholics, under the leadership of their bishop, were vigorously engaged in spreading a social gospel in today's world. In this way, with the charities of the Catholic Church no longer concentrated around the region of Portland, many people throughout the state were benefiting from its programs under an advisory board set up by the bishop to carry on the campaign for human development in the aftermath of the Second Vatican Council. This became evident when the first statewide appeal for Catholic Charities was launched by Gerety, on May 7, 1972, with a goal of $956,286.00. Thus, the way was opened for drives in the subsequent years when this campaign became known successively as the Catholic Charities Appeal, the Catholic Stewardship Appeal and, finally, the Annual Bishop's Appeal.

To help him in his work, Bishop Gerety obtained, on November 17, 1970, an auxiliary in Monsignor Edward Cornelius O'Leary, a favorite among the clergy, who wore the ring of Bishop Feeney at his ordination as bishop. In the reforms following the Second Vatican Council, Gerety had involved the priests as his partners in caring for the diocese. That he treated his priests well was foreshadowed in the five seminarians whom he ordained to the priesthood the following spring and in the twelve monsignors whom he installed early in 1971, including his chancellor, David K. Fitzpatrick.

Unfortunately, the Diocese of Portland continued to decline in its number of priests as giants went home to God. Among them were Monsignors James F. Savage, one of the major consultors of the diocese, in 1970; Felix Martin, a diocesan dean, in 1971; Daniel J. Honan, an expert on the Fathers of the Church, in 1972; and Edmond J. Haché, pastor in Auburn, and Emmanuel R. Grondin, pastor in Winslow, in 1973. From the 243 diocesan priests when Gerety came to Maine, they had declined to 203 at the end of his tenure in Portland.

If the priests had reason to have confidence in Gerety, so did the laity. Not only had he honored a number of them as he had with his priests, but the bishop authorized eighty-six of them in seventeen parishes to distribute the Holy Eucharist, and had gone on record, as early as the summer of 1971 in favor of women, in addition to men, as lectors. That lay persons in the state legislature did their part to help their church defend prolife issues was evident in the leadership of Representative Louis Jalbert (D), the prime opponent of an abortion bill which was defeated in the Maine House of Representative by a vote of eighty-nine to fifty-three in May of 1971.

Though brief audit reports of the diocese had been available as early as 1963, Gerety chose to share with all the faithful the financial status of the Diocese of Portland by publishing fuller reports in June of 1970 showing that it had taken in $8,261,535.00 in the previous fiscal year. This helped to build up the confidence of the faithful in the bishop's ability to care for the corporation of which he was in charge. That Gerety followed through on this in the next two years really placed the bishop and his diocese among the first in the nation to undertake such responsible stewardship.

For the first time in the history of the Diocese of Portland, statistics revealed a decline in the number of Catholics in Maine. From a total figure of closer to 270,000 at the end of Bishop Feeney's tenure, the statistics were closer to 260,000 at the end of Bishop Gerety's tenure. When one considers the number of baptisms and converts, the shortfall can be attributed, apart from deaths, to more sophisticated ways of collecting the census data of the parishes and to the greater accuracy in the recording of Catholics than in previous years, not to overlook the very large exodus of people from Aroostook County in the 1960s and the 1970s when many Americans of French ancestry went to work for Pratt-Whitney in Connecticut.

Moreover, as the media became more important, Bishop Gerety undertook a decision for the benefit of the diocese by purchasing *The Church World*. Ever since the time of Bishop

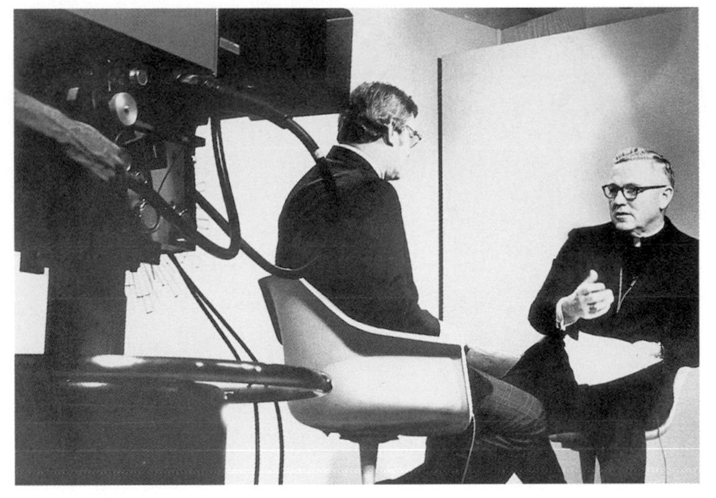

Bishop Gerety on television

Murray, it had been in the hands of the family of Thomas H. Fahey (d. 1978). As an important step in the restructuring of the Diocese of Portland, Bishop Gerety viewed the newspaper as a key way to spread the Gospel of Christ. At the same time, he moved its central office from Portland to Brunswick where it was placed under Henry Gosselin, editor. "If you don't tell me how to run the diocese of Portland," the bishop reportedly said to Gosselin in offering the job, "I won't tell you how to run the newspaper." With that assurance, the new editor proceeded to turn the weekly into one of the top diocesan newspapers in the country over the next quarter of a century by winning close to seventy awards before his retirement in 1994. In this way, the bishop, who had been concerned in other decisions to get the right person in the right place, succeeded beyond his fondest expectations.

On March 25, 1975, Gerety was appointed Archbishop of Newark, and one of those who spoke prior to the new archbishop's departure for Newark was Maine's Governor Kenneth M. Curtis (1967-75). Curtis was the only governor in the history of the state whose years corresponded with that of any Roman Catholic Bishop of Portland. That he and Gerety had a mutual respect for one another was evident, on June 24, 1974, at the Holiday Inn in Portland, when Curtis praised the departing bishop, on April 2, 1974, in these words: "He's been a leader of all the people of the State of Maine." The governor, whom the bishop had met at the annual Red Mass and at the funeral of Susan, Curtis's daughter, at St. Mary's in Augusta, was very much impressed by what the

Deering Pavilion, Portland

Immaculate Heart of Mary Church, Fairfield

bishop had done through the Diocesan Bureau of Human Relations Services, and especially in providing low-income housing for the elderly in Deering Pavilion (Diocesan Bureau of Housing) which opened in the summer of 1973 on the corner of Forest Avenue and Holly Street in Portland. Given the evidence of the large number of people present at that testimonial, it is clear that Bishop Peter Leo Gerety had lived up to his episcopal motto, "Christ in all things" ("*In omnibus Christus*") and made the message of the Gospel relevant to his times in Portland.

After Archbishop Gerety served the people of Newark for twelve years, he retired on June 1, 1986, and was spending his remaining years in service to the Catholic Church as Archbishop Emeritus, having celebrated his sixtieth anniversary as a priest in 1999. Reflecting on his calling to the priesthood, on June 7th of that year at the archdiocesan seminary in Newark, he recalled how Father Cornelius Buckley, a curate at his home parish of St. Joseph's in Shelton, Connecticut, had given him a "shove" towards the priesthood by challenging him one day when Gerety was wrestling with the idea of a vocation. "Peter Leo," the priest said looking the teenager straight in the eye, "if you had the guts you would go to the Seminary and become a priest." For that confrontation, the archbishop said, he blesses the memory of Father Buckley.

As Archbishop of Newark, Gerety had risen nationally as a progressive prelate. While Portland had provided a microcosm for his later work, what the archbishop accomplished in Newark was recognized as valuable to the whole church in the United States. This is a conclusion that one can derive from the book on the archiepiscopal office by Thomas J. Reece who provides a number of valuable reflections on Gerety's years after he left the Diocese of Portland.

Lastly, in all these years since leaving Portland, it can be said that Gerety remained true to his words on his departure when he declared: "I will never, never forget the State of Maine and the Diocese of Portland." His love of the sea, so evident in the sailboats, *Charlotte U. I* and *Charlotte U. II*, named after his mother, Charlotte Ursula Gerety, when he was Bishop of Portland, have made him return to Maine for his summer vacations even as an archbishop. And, as recently as May 27, 2001, he honored one of his former aides, Rev. Stephen F. Concannon, Pastor of St. Charles Borromeo in Brunswick, by concelebrating Mass, on May 27, 2001, at the new summer mission in memory of St. Katharine Drexel on Mountain Road in Harpswell, Maine, which replaced two missions closed in September of 2000, Precious Blood on Bailey Island and St. Mary Star of the Sea in South Harpswell. In the following year, when he celebrated his ninetieth birthday, he became the first of the diocese's bishops to achieve that milestone.

Chapter 11

A Bishop Loved by Priests and People

Edward C. O'Leary (1920-2002) succeeded to the See of Portland as its ninth Bishop, on October 22, 1974, having served as its Apostolic Administrator since June 28th of that year. Born in Bangor, Maine, on August 21, 1920, he was the son of Cornelius J. and Annabell Cecilia (McManus) O'Leary. A 1942 graduate of the College of the Holy Cross, he was influenced by the Jesuits, particularly Rev. Leo A. O'Connor, S. J., in his decision to study for the priesthood. Subsequently, he pursued his theological studies at St. Paul's Seminary in Ottawa, Canada, before he was ordained a priest in the Cathedral of the Immaculate Conception in Portland by Bishop Joseph E. McCarthy, on June 15, 1946.

Bishop Edward C. O'Leary with Speaker of the House John Martin at the University of Maine at Fort Kent

Bishop O'Leary was a caring and personable bishop who was loved by those to whom he ministered in the Catholic Church. His approachability had emerged in his priestly work at the Cathedral in Portland, at St. Margaret's in Old Orchard, and at St. Charles Borromeo in Brunswick. Having served as pastor in the last two parishes during the 1960s, he was appointed Titular Bishop of Moglena and Auxiliary Bishop of Portland by Pope Paul VI (1963-78), on November 17, 1970, and ordained bishop by Bishop Peter L. Gerety, on January 25, 1971, in the Cathedral of the Immaculate Conception, assisted by Bishop Bernard J. Flanagan of Worcester and Auxiliary Bishop Lawrence P. J. Graves of Little Rock.

When he was installed, on December 18, 1974, by Archbishop Jean Jadot, the Apostolic Delegate (1973-80), and Humberto Cardinal Medeiros (1915-83), Archbishop of Boston, Bishop O'Leary had a vast administrative background as vice chancellor (1950-52), chancellor (1952-65), and auxiliary bishop (1970-74) that prepared him to handle the problems of the Diocese of Portland. Pope Pius XII had made him a papal chamberlain (1954) and Blessed Pope John XXIII had elevated him to the rank of domestic prelate (1959), both with the title of monsignor. Like other Holy Cross men, Patrick J. Hayes (d. 1970) and Vincent A. Tatarczuk (b. 1925), who had served Bishop Feeney, O'Leary had attended at least one of the sessions of the Second Vatican Council and was tuned in on the challenges facing the church in the contemporary world.

In assuming leadership for the Diocese of Portland, Bishop O'Leary was responsible for a Catholic population which would expand by slightly more than two thousand from 264,538 to 266,638 of the faithful during his tenure. To accommodate this growth and the shifts in population less than a handful of new parishes were required at a time when there were fewer priests for the ministry. Among the parishes which the bishop established were St. Edmund's in Westbrook in 1975, St. Philip's in Lyman in 1981, and St. Maximilian Kolbe in Scarborough in 1988. This last parish was named for a Franciscan monk, a victim of the Nazis in World War II, who was canonized, on October 10, 1982, and was an excellent model for priests in modern society. Given O'Leary's belief that the

Bishop O'Leary's Episcopal ring

Coat of arms of Bishop Edward Cornelius O'Leary

success of a parish depended upon the depth of the spirituality of its priests, the name of the parish was an excellent choice. "In his mind," his successor said in speaking of the late bishop at O'Leary's funeral, "the vitality of the parish depended on the spirituality of the clergy."

While the total number of parishes rose from 143 to 146 during Bishop O'Leary's years, it is noteworthy that a change was evident in the contributions of the religious priests in the diocese. The Holy Cross Fathers had taken over the operation of Most Holy Trinity in Saco in 1973. The Jesuits, having assumed responsibility for the operation St. Dennis in North Whitefield in 1976 and for St. John's in Bangor in 1978, saw the bishop dedicate, on May 31, 1980, on the grounds of the Knights of Columbus in Augusta, a replica of the original chapel of the Assumption erected by Gabriel Druillettes in August of 1646. And the Franciscans, who had been in Portland with the Conventuals at St. Louis since 1959, took over two other parishes in the city, with the Capuchins going to St. Joseph's in 1977 and the Friars Minor to St. Peter's in 1983 where the bishop blessed a unique Chapel of the Saints, on January 17, 1988.

St John, Bangor

During the same period, the Dominicans turned over to the diocese their control of Our Lady of the Rosary in Sabattus in 1975 and a majestic Gothic church, Saints Peter and Paul in Lewiston, in 1986 for lack of personnel. That *The Church World* ran a series of articles on "The Parish of the Week" between the summers of 1981 and 1983 contributed to the appreciation of a sense of tradition within the individual parishes at a time when the consolidation of parishes had already been underway.

Meanwhile, the total number of priests in the diocese declined from 345 to 287 (in terms of active diocesan priests the number went from 203 to 156). Msgr. John T. Arsenault, Director of the Propagation of the Faith, died on August 26, 1974. Msgr. Teresio DiMingo, the Pastor of St. Peter's Church, Maine's Italian Parish, died on January 8, 1975. In 1976, Msgr. Aimé Giguere, Pastor of St. André in Biddeford, died on October 6th, and Msgr. Eli A. Hévey, Pastor of St. Joseph's in Biddeford, died on December 7th. And, in 1977, Msgr. Georges E. Cyr, Pastor of St. Athanasius' and St. John's in Rumford, died on August 27th, and Msgr. Albert E. Long, Pastor of St. Thomas Aquinas in Madawaska, died on November 23rd.

And, there were others. Msgr. Armand E. Cyr, Diocesan Superintendent of Schools (1957-67), died on May 28, 1978; Msgr. Michael P. Davis, Pastor of Sacred Heart in Portland and a former principal at Cheverus, died on November 23rd, 1979; Msgr. Robert J. White, the first naval chaplain with rank of commodore to serve on active duty (he had retired as a rear admiral and was honored by France for his service in World War II with the Chevalier of the Legion of Honor), died on December 3rd, 1984; and Msgr. Thomas N. Nelligan, Pastor of St. Mary's in Augusta, died on February 17th, 1985. To these, one can add Rev. Thomas F. Coyne who, having served as Diocesan Director of Sodalities, had a pastoral career which spread from the city, to the country and even to the reservation, before his death on August 25, 1984.

Bishop O'Leary's tenure saw a number of anniversaries that marked the history of the Diocese of Portland. After he had led a pilgrimage to Rome for the 1975 Holy Year, O'Leary dedicated, in Madison, on the eve of 250th anniversary of the martyrdom of Sebastian Râle, on August 22, 1974, the new church of St. Sebastian, the patron saint of the Jesuit martyr. The 150th anniversary of the establishment of St. Dominic's Parish was celebrated in 1980, recalling how Irish families like the Murphys, the O'Connells, O'Donnells, O'Tooles, Sheas, and others had deep roots in the city. President Jimmy Carter sent congratulations to the Slovaks, on May 12, 1977, for the conclusion of their golden anniversary celebration in Lisbon Falls. That same year the Maronites celebrated their golden jubilee as Lebanese Catholics in Waterville. On August 22, 1979. St. Hyacinth's in Westbrook celebrated its 100th anniversary. That year, too, the Daughters of Wisdom celebrated the seventy-fifth anniversary of their arrival in Maine. Two years later, the Sisters of Mercy, the largest group of women religious in the diocese, marked their 150th in the state in 1981. And, St. Bruno's in Van Buren celebrated its 150th anniversary, on July 10, 1988.

Bishop O'Leary meets Pope John Paul II on one of the ad limina visits (Photography by Felici.)

Some of the milestones in O'Leary's years were not without a touch of sadness. Though St. Mary's in Bangor, which had celebrated its centennial five years previously, was destroyed by fire in early February of 1978, the bishop had the joy of blessing a new church by mid-December of 1980. Benedicta, Maine, founded by Bishop Fenwick's as a colonization project, had rejoiced at the celebration of its sesquicentennial as a town from July 1st to 4th in 1984, but was disorganized as a civil entity in 1987.

Interior, St. Mary's Church, Bangor, destroyed by fire, February 1978 (Watler V. McHale photograph)

One of the stories of O'Leary's early days is typical of his extending himself to others. While at Holy Cross, where he had a reputation as a scholar, he was instrumental, because of his family's connection with Fred Allen at Old Orchard, where the O'Learys summered, in having the star invite Holy Cross students on his famous national radio program. This took place on CBS from eight to nine in the evening, on March 8, 1942, in a show sponsored by Texaco. In that opening Sunday night of Allen's new program, a number of collegians participated, including John J. McDonald, then a student and later a doctor, who starred for Holy Cross. Throughout his years as a priest and a bishop, Bishop O'Leary reflected that same concern for his alma mater and its graduates by his support for it and by his presence at alumni reunions at Holy Cross, and in Maine during the spring and in Florida during the winter. Recently, Father Thomas H. Maguire of the Archdiocese of Boston pointed out to the author that his father, Paul Maguire, a Boston College man, and the future bishop, a Holy Cross man, were Beano Callers, in those days when their families summered at Old Orchard.

That same spirit of generosity earned the love and respect of others. This was evident when O'Leary was in charge of the rehearsal in 1955 for a class of fifteen diocesan and two religious candidates who were to be ordained by Bishop Feeney. During that rehearsal, O'Leary kept on coming up with plans that were turned

Bishop Amédée W. Proulx giving Holy Communion to his father, Mr. Francis Proulx

down by the bishop when Richard A. O'Donnell (b. 1929), one of the ordinandi, whispered to one of his classmates: "If they don't canonize Msgr. O'Leary after this, there isn't any justice." Years later, when O'Leary was named Bishop of Portland in 1974, this news evoked joyous Alleluias among the Sisters of Mercy at their motherhouse in Portland.

In coming to leadership of the Diocese of Portland, Bishop O'Leary was very much concerned about his priests whom he regarded as his coworkers in fulfilling the mission of the Catholic Church in Maine. "I feel that he led by example, persuasion and consensus, rather than by mandating," declared Msgr. Paul D. Gleason (b. 1921), who was acquainted with O'Leary since their days at the College of the Holy Cross. In achieving that goal, the bishop saw to it that the desire of the Franco-American community in having one of its own a bishop was fulfilled.

Consequently, it was a dream come true for many priests of the diocese when Amédée Wilfred Proulx (1932-93), a Sanford native who had been named Titular Bishop of Clipia, on September 16, 1975, was ordained, on November 12, 1975, Auxiliary Bishop of Portland by Bishop O'Leary in the Cathedral of the Immaculate Conception, assisted by Bishop Odore J. Gendron of Manchester and Auxiliary Bishop Timothy J. Harrington of Worcester. Certainly, not since Bishop Healy's tenure had the Diocese of Portland witnessed such a change which underscored the Catholic Church's character of universality.

Moreover, there were other historical benchmarks in Bishop O'Leary's time that reaffirmed that characteristic of the church's universality. The ordination of Paulius Antanas Baltakis (b. 1925), a Lithuanian Franciscan, in the Cathedral of the Immaculate Conception in Portland, on September 14, 1984, was a first in the history of bishops in the United States. Ordained a priest, on August 24, 1952, Baltakis, who had resided in Kennebunkport, was named, on June 1, 1984, Titular Bishop of Egara with the responsibility for all the Lithuanian Catholics who had been dispersed after World War II.

Also, not entirely unrelated to the history of the diocese was the episcopal ordination, on May 6, 1986, of David Edmond Pelotte (b. 1945), a native of Waterville, Maine, as Coadjutor Bishop of Gallup, New Mexico. He had learned how to serve Mass at the Blessed Sacrament Convent in Waterville where two nuns, Sister Edna Mary Cardozo and Sister Marie Julien Fortin, were later killed by a deranged man near the end of January 1996. Having joined the Blessed Sacrament Fathers, Pelotte was ordained a priest, on September 2, 1972, and, having been named a bishop, on February 24, 1986, he was ordained, on May 6, 1986, and became the first Native American Catholic bishop. Four year later, when he succeeded as the Bishop of Gallup, New Mexico, on March 20, 1990, he became the first residential bishop of Native American background in the United States. As bishop, he returned for the funeral of those two nuns who had been so important in the development of his religious vocation.

In his work of administering the Sacrament of Confirmation in his extensive diocese, Bishop O'Leary invited Bishop Lawrence A. Burke (b. 1932) to assist him for a number of years. Bishop Burke had been ordained a priest of the Society of Jesus, on June 16, 1964, and Bishop of Nassau in the Bahamas, on October 11, 1981. Since the Sisters of Mercy in Portland had a mission within Bishop Burke's diocese, Bishop O'Leary was reaffirming the connection of his diocese with the broader mission of the church. Later, in the year 2000, Bishop Burke's diocese was elevated to the rank of an archdiocese by Pope John Paul II thereby elevating the native of Jamaica to the rank of archbishop.

As for the schools of the diocese, the trend of closing schools continued. Among the elementary schools which closed were St. Louis in Fort Kent in 1975, Saint Remy in Keegan in 1976, and Saint Gerard in Grand Isle in 1983, leaving just about twenty of them in the diocese. Therefore, it was no wonder, given the shift in Catholic education, that the Diocese of Portland was one of the five dioceses in the country chosen in July of 1987 for a development program regarding the importance of Catholic education and the way to keep its parochial schools in operation.

Understandably, some of the developments which were taking place in elementary education were related to the changes which women religious were facing after the Second Vatican Council. With fewer vocations and with changes in their lifestyles, the total number of sisters in the diocese had declined by at least 375 during Bishop O'Leary's years. In the case of the Sisters of Mercy, who bore responsibility for many of the elementary schools, there was a split between those who favored wearing religious garb and living within a religious community and those who wanted to be more modern and live outside the traditional cloister undertaking apostolates which some regarded as more relevant in their service to society.

On the high school level, the bishop saw his alma mater in Bangor, John Bapst High School (Class of 1938), where the Xaverian Brothers and the Sisters of Mercy had taught for many years, undergo a transformation. Changing the name to John Bapst Memorial High School in 1978, it became a private school totally removed from the control of the Diocese of Portland with its administration under sponsorship of the laity. This came about once the school could no longer depend on tuition provided by those neighboring towns which were sending their students to John Bapst. Since this practice had been ruled unconstitutional by the state's attorney general, the school was forced to reorganize as a secular institution without a religious connection to regain the loss of income. With that accomplished, the school continued under secular sponsorship.

St. Thomas School, Sanford

St. Joseph's Manor, Portland

Also, in 1978, a similar decline in religious vocations saw the Diocese of Portland lose another college with St. Francis in Biddeford Pool being sold to the University of New England. The Canadian Franciscans who had come from Montreal to open a high school and a college there many years previously just did not have the personnel to continue the operation. Consequently, St. Joseph's College, which was expanding with lay professors, became the only Catholic college in the state and an attractive option for some Catholics.

Catholic Charities Maine St. Louis Child Care Facility, Biddeford

St. John (detail), Brunswick

One of the decisions that singled out O'Leary as a leading reformer in the Catholic Church was his ecumenism which led him to join the Maine Council of Churches. Religious leaders like Portland's Rabbi Harry Sky and Rev. Edward N. Nelson admired the bishop for being so open by speaking in their houses of worship where O'Leary exhibited that warmth which helped him to be an effective leader. That he named Rev. James E. Connor (b. 1934) as the first representative of the Diocese of Portland to the Maine Council of Churches underscored the bishop's sincerity in attempting to reach common ground with other believers in facing the problems of society. Noteworthy, too, was the covenant of cooperation between neighboring churches signed on Pentecost Sunday in 1978 by Father Joseph E. Whitlock (b. 1929) of the Cathedral of the Immaculate Conception and by Father Harold A. McElwain (d. 2000) of St. Paul's Episcopal Church which both Bishop O'Leary and Episcopal Bishop Frederick Barton Wolf of Maine (1968-86) approved thereby acknowledging the need to work together in common efforts on the local level to advance ecumenism. All this was no surprise since Whitlock had already taken such ecumenical action at Francis Xavier in Brownville Junction in 1970.

On the local scene, too, Bishop O'Leary dealt with the consequences of developments in American society, especially with legislation regarding such issues as abortion, physician-assisted suicide, and pornography in the latter half of the 1970s. When a referendum to ban pornography came up in 1976, O'Leary spoke in favor of the ban only to learn that Maine voters defeated it by a margin of three to one. Later, in 1977, his opposition to abortion, capital punishment, and living wills voiced in a letter to Maine's legislators did not, however, result in any substantial changes in the laws. Abortion and capital punishment remained on the books and living wills became legal despite his fear that they would open the way to euthanasia. Nevertheless, Bishop O'Leary was not at all happy with politicians, whether Catholic or not, whose position was pro-choice rather than pro-life.

However, O'Leary's leadership did provide for the poor and the vulnerable through Catholic Charities of Maine which, under the direction of Neil D. Michaud from 1967 to 1988, expanded its programs statewide to provide for child care, home care for the elderly, and services for the visually handicapped. At the same time, the diocese broadened its counseling programs for those families where members were in need because of lack of jobs, poor health, their elderly condition, or were victims of alcohol or drugs. And, in 1987, O'Leary urged that Catholics respond to the AIDS epidemic with care and understanding by extending to them the various services of the diocese. Much of this was done, it should not be forgotten, when his episcopal city was undergoing an economic revival as one of the more attractive cities of the northeastern section of the country.

In the case of the victims of alcoholism, the diocese went out of its way to provide for them in Portland. When a twenty-four hour detoxification shelter was to close for lack of funds in the late summer and early fall of 1986, Catholic Charities took it over to keep it in operation. And, in June of the following year, it undertook to provide a half-way house exclusively for women who were victims of alcoholism. Thus, at the end of Bishop O'Leary's tenure, the Arnie Hanson Center was in operation on India Street and Evodia House on Cedar Street in Portland.

One of the more controversial issues that faced the Catholic Church during the period of Bishop O'Leary's tenure was the position of women. Early in 1975, six churches in the diocese already had girls serving at the altar in a service that had been exclusively for boys. At the same time, his auxiliary, Bishop Proulx was making a favorable national impression by his concern for the place of women in the church, both religious and lay, who found him very supportive. However, in 1984, Bishop O'Leary, fearing that the proposed amendment on equal rights for women would lead to the funding of abortions by taxpayers, withdrew support for it and, in the election of November of that year, sixty-four percent of the voters supported his position by voting against the equal rights amendment.

Yet, that did not mean that O'Leary was opposed to a role for women in the church. Quite the contrary since, during his years as bishop, some milestones achieved by Catholic women were noteworthy. There was the remarkable Sister Elizabeth Cyr (1920-77) who, before a fatal automobile accident, pioneered in the care of unwed mothers and the adoption of children at St. André's Home in Biddeford where the Good Shepherd Sisters of Quebec had been working since 1935. There was Bernadette Gilbert Cyr (b. 1933) whose healing, on June 25th, 1978, from a medically diagnosed incurable condition led her to launch the Little House of Prayer on River Road in her native Saco. And, there was Sister Mary Leona Burke (1886-1988), who was, before her death, the oldest living Bates College (A. B. 1908) graduate and the oldest living Sister of Mercy in Maine at 101.

More directly, as far as women's equality in the church was concerned, Bishop O'Leary made historic decisions. In May of 1978, there was his appointment of Sister M. Gemma Connelly as Superintendent of Catholic Schools, a position which has, subsequently, been filled by a woman religious. And, in February of 1987, Sr. Rita-Mae Bissonnette , R. S. R., joined Father J. Joseph Ford, chancellor, as vice chancellor of the diocese, a move making her one of the first Catholic women in the country to hold such a high office in the Catholic Church. In the case of this religious sister, O'Leary had already broken tradition by obtaining a dispensation from the Vatican, on May 5, 1976, for her to become a defender of the bond on the marriage tribunal, thereby making Sr. Bissonnette the first women ever to serve in that capacity in the history of the Catholic Church in the whole country if not in the whole world. If any proof were needed to show that O'Leary was not at all opposed to the equality of women, those appointments demonstrated that.

In O'Leary's early years as bishop, seventy percent of the elderly in Maine were in the lower income level and the diocese had already provided in Deering Pavilion, a low income facility in which the elderly could live with dignity in Portland. During O'Leary's years as bishop, Seton Village, Inc., another facility for the elderly, was built in Waterville. And, St. Marguerite d'Youville Pavilion, sponsored by St. Mary's Hospital in Lewiston, was dedicated in 1983 as "the largest nursing home in Maine, and the largest nonprofit home in New England."

In the case of the Native Americans, the original residents of the state, Bishop O'Leary had to cope with changes that affected relations between church and state. By 1973, the Maliseets in the Houlton area and the Micmacs in the Aroostook area, in addition to the Passamaquoddies and the Penobscots, had been recognized as tribes by the state. Before President Jimmy Carter signed the Maine Indian Land Claims Settlement Act for $81.5 million dollars in 1980, the State of Maine acted unilaterally. After providing services guaranteeing to the Native Americans the free exercise of religion for 200 years, from 1777 to 1977, it put an end to the practice of providing salaries for chaplains on the reservations, much to the disappointment of the diocese. While most of the federal money went to purchase 305,000 acres of land, the rest was held in trust. However, the State of Maine's action had left the tribes much more on their own, while the Catholic Church, by default, sought to compensate for the state's abandonment of those subsidies dating from the American Revolution.

St. André's Health Care Facility, Biddeford

Under Bishop O'Leary, moreover, the Catholic Church in the State of Maine achieved a high level of maturity. Its political pattern historically was not at all monolithic having been open to political leaders of the two major parties and to independents. In fact, during his years as Bishop of Portland, O'Leary saw two Catholics serve as Governors of Maine, one James B. Longley, Sr. (1975-79), an Independent, and the other, Joseph E. Brennan (1979-87), a Democrat who had been raised in the Cathedral Parish.

In the movement of immigrants from Europe to this country, the social program of the Catholic Church and the development of its own school system remained essential aspects of the Church's ministry in a nation that had been hostile to Catholics. Today its emphasis on the

Mount Saint Joseph Nursing Home, Waterville

Catholic Scouting Award Ceremony, Cathedral, Portland, April 29, 1979 (J.R. Messmer photograph)

US Route 1, Verona Bridge

Americanization of the immigrant from Asia, Africa, and Latin America carries on the earlier tradition of what it did for the immigrants from Europe. Consequently, one finds in the time of Bishop O'Leary, at least since the changes of his immediate predecessor, the Catholic Church in the role of a social activist and reformer, as evidenced in its work on behalf of refugees from Vietnam when O'Leary was bishop. That the Human Relations Services of the Diocese of Portland received funding for that purpose in 1979, was operating a transit house for those refugees in Portland in 1982, and opened a center for refugee donations at Sacred Heart Church in 1986 are actions that show new approaches to the Church's mission.

Catholic Charities Maine, as a strong arm of the diocese, has been helping the bishop carry out the church's mission which extends not only to the older residents of the state but also to the newer ones. Certainly, the changes that came over the Diocese of Portland during O'Leary's years were not unlike the changes taking place in other parts of the Catholic Church in the United States. "The issues at stake," according to Msgr. George A. Kelly, author of *The Battle for the American Church* (1979), "are the correctness of Catholic doctrine and the survival of the Catholic Church as a significant influence in the life of her own communicants." At heart, it is the clash between those who view the Catholic Church as more an instrument for social reform than for personal conversion. In the case of Bishop O'Leary, he believed that the mission of the church, as indicated by his own motto, "One Who Serves," was to embrace both aspects. If the legacy of his predecessor was to broaden the strategies for achieving the church's mission in Maine, O'Leary's legacy has been the consolidation of those strategies in preparation for the future.

After Bishop O'Leary retired, on September 27, 1988, for reasons of health, he enjoyed the status of Bishop Emeritus and helped his successor whenever he could. Then, in July of 2000, he moved into St. Joseph's Manor where he died around 9:30 P. M., on Tuesday, April 2, 2002, having endured a number of strokes after his initial setback with a heart condition in 1981. His funeral was celebrated by Bernard Cardinal Law (1984-2002) of Boston, head of the ecclesiastical province which includes Maine, on April 9th, 2002, assisted by two retired archbishops and at least thirty other bishops and almost 100 priests joined by 900 invited guests in the Cathedral of the Immaculate Conception. He was later buried in the family plot in Bangor's Mount Pleasant Cemetery.

Speaking of his love for Maine, O'Leary, said early in his years as bishop: "It has always been my State, its people have always been my people." The bishop who visited the hospitals every Christmas Day truly loved his priests and his people. His enduring affability, his genuine humility, his joyful laugh, his fabulous memory, and his ready wit made Bishop Edward C. O'Leary a person, who was regarded as "a holy man" at the time of his death and who sought to improve the quality of life of those whom he met during his eighty-one years on this earth. Such characteristics had earned him respect among his brother bishops who had appointed him to chair at least one national committee and to membership of one national task force just as they led St. Joseph's College, the only Catholic college in the state, to award him an honorary Doctor of Humane Letters (1975), and Bowdoin College, the oldest college in the state, to award him an honorary Doctor of Laws (1979). Significantly, he was the only Bishop of Portland who did not put his motto in Latin on his coat of arms.

Chapter 12

A Benedictine As Bishop of Portland

Joseph John Gerry was named Bishop of Portland, on December 21, 1988. Born in Millinocket, Maine, on September 12, 1928, he was the son of Bernard Eugene and Blanche Agnes (McManemon) Gerry. Professed as a member of the Benedictine Order, on July 2, 1948, he received a bachelor's degree from St. Anselm College in 1950, a master's degree from Toronto University in 1955, and a doctorate from Fordham University in 1959. Ordained a priest, on June 12, 1954, by Bishop Matthew F. Brady (1893-1959) of Manchester, Gerry was associated with St. Anselm's for most of his adult life rising to the position of abbot in 1972. Named by Pope John Paul II as Titular Bishop of Praecausa, on February 4, 1986, he was ordained bishop, on April 21, 1986, in the Cathedral of St. Joseph, in Manchester, by Bishop Odore Joseph Gendron (b. 1921) of Manchester with Bishop Emeritus Ernest John Primeau of Manchester and Bishop Robert Edward Mulvee of Wilmington as co-consecrators.

Bishop Joseph J. Gerry, O .S.B., Tenth Bishop of Portland

Having served as Auxiliary Bishop of Manchester, Gerry came to Portland when Archbishop Pio Laghi was the Apostolic Pro-Nuncio (1984-90) to the United States. Having once remarked, in reply to an inquiry about how bishops were chosen, Laghi said: "We choose the saint to fill the niche." That this is not entirely irrelevant to the selection of Bishop Joseph, as he came to be known, can be derived from his formal involvement in the work of sanctification as superior (1953-63) and prior and novice master (1963-71) of the Benedictines at St. Anselm Abbey where he was effective in implementing the reforms of the Second Vatican Council.

With his installation as tenth Bishop of Portland, on February 21, 1989, Joseph was very fortunate because, unlike his predecessors, he had two experienced bishops in Bishop O'Leary and Bishop Proulx to assist him, in addition to about 225 priests active in the diocese (156 diocesan and seventy-five religious). Later, to fill the vacuum left by the death of Bishop Proulx in 1993, Pope John Paul II appointed, on May 9, 1995, Michael Richard Coté (b. 1949), a native of Sanford, Titular Bishop of Cebarades and Auxiliary Bishop of Portland. Coté had been ordained to the priesthood by Pope Paul VI, on June 29, 1975, and his ordination as bishop took place on July 27, 1995. Bishop Coté's responsibilities were centered primarily in those northern parts of the state with his principal residence at Holy Family Rectory in Old Town. In the bishop's office, Coté joined the team of co-chancellors which Bishop Joseph appointed in July of 1991, with Sr. Rita-Mae Bissonnette and Fr. (now Msgr.) Michael J. Henchal who has been succeeded by Msgr. Marc B. Caron. Meanwhile, Bishop Gerry continued to have the help of two bishops, at least until Bishop O'Leary's health forced him to retire to St. Joseph's Manor in July of 2000.

Coat of arms of Bishop Joseph J. Gerry, O.S.B.

Coming to Portland, Bishop Joseph had a background that was not devoid of national and international recognition. He had been given a presidential appointment on the National Advisory Council on Equality of Educational Opportunity (1973-76) while serving at St. Anselm College as chancellor (1972-86), and his preaching of the Word of God gained attention not only in his published sermons, *Ever Present Lord* (1989), but, as this later became evident, in his homilies published in *The Church World* as well as in his exposition of Catholic doctrine in his numerous pastoral letters during his years as Bishop of Portland. With such a background, it did not come as a surprise when Pope John Paul II named him in early 1990 to the Pontifical Council for Interreligious Dialogue, a role that complemented his role as a member of the Committee for Ecumenical and Interreligious Affairs for the National Conference of Catholic Bishops which he has moderated for most of his years as Bishop of Portland. A highlight of the pontifical assignment was his role in the Gethsemani Encounter of 1996 that brought together monks from both the Buddhist and Catholic traditions.

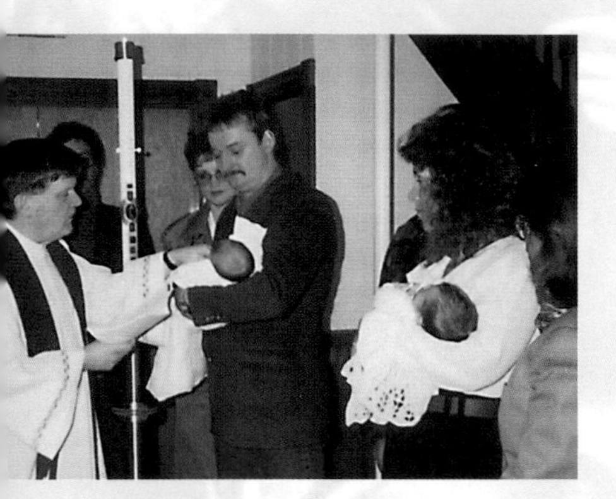

Fr. Tom Lequin baptizing Caitlyn Marie and Cristine Anne Dionne, St. Peter's Church, Bingham

As a religious leader, Bishop Joseph strengthened the religious and spiritual life of the diocese through preaching the word of God and administering the sacraments, particularly the Sacrament of Confirmation which brought him around the state. On September 21, 1997, the bishop issued a pastoral letter entitled *Confirmation: A Sacrament of Initiation,* in which he stated his decision to allow the administration of Confirmation at the age of seven along with the Sacrament of the Eucharist. Consequently, starting in 1998, the bishop placed the Diocese of Portland in the forefront of those dioceses in the United States restoring the administration of the Sacrament of Confirmation to as early an age as seven, a practice more in accord with the tradition of the Catholic Church.

Bishop Michael R. Cote presents the 1998 Catholic Charities Maine Bishop Proulx Award to Dot Sanchas of Rumford (Courtesy of Catholic Charities Maine)

Moreover, in his tenure, the bishop allowed Masses in Latin according to the Missal of St. Pius V in his Cathedral, starting on September 15, 1991, and he granted a similar concession for a Latin Mass once a month at St. Patrick's in Newcastle in 1998. As for other languages, the bishop initiated a weekly Mass at Portland's Sacred Heart Church in 1994 for Hispanics who have grown to number about 10,000 in Maine by 2000.

While the religious and spiritual aspects of the lives of Catholics in Maine were emphasized by Joseph Gerry as a bishop, he also had to cope with the needs of the various parishes. That declining populations or buildings in need of repair forced the closing or conjoining of certain churches were challenging decisions. Although many of these changes affected the English-speaking Catholics, the effects were also deeply felt in the French-speaking parishes. The decline of the French-speaking population was particularly evident in the federal census of 2000 which showed a drop among them in Maine by almost 45,000 compared to the 1990 census. Such centers of Roman Catholic strength as Biddeford, Lewiston, the St. John Valley, and Waterville saw a decline which varied anywhere from ten to twenty percent. In northern Aroostook County alone, the decline in population in such towns as Frenchville, Madawaska, and St. Agatha was at least by fifteen percent during the 1990s. Therefore, the bishop was forced to undertake a policy that would not please everyone because it resulted in the closing of some churches and the reduction of Sunday Masses.

Consequently, the effects of Bishop Joseph's actions were evident in various parts of the diocese during that decade of decline. The merging of St. Bruno's in Van Buren and St. Remy in Keegan in 1991, the twinning of Saints Peter & Paul and St. Patrick's in Lewiston in 1992, and the merging of St. Mary's in Wilton with St. Joseph in Farmington in 1995 are clear examples of a realistic policy. Though the bishop did establish new parishes like Holy Trinity in Lisbon Falls in 1995 by consolidating St. Anne, Holy Family, and Saints Cyril and Methodius there, he also consolidated St. Joseph's and St. Mary's in Old Town by establishing there Holy Family in 1992. He merged Notre Dame, Sacred Heart, and St. Francis de Sales in Waterville to set up there the Parish of the Holy Spirit in 1996. He was constrained to close St. Dominic's in Portland, the oldest parish in the

St. James School, Biddeford

Conrad W. L'Heureux, former pastor of Sacred Heart in Auburn, died on June 30, 1995. Msgr. David K. Fitzpatrick, a former chancellor of the diocese, died on August 12, 1996. Msgr. Edward F. Ward, at ninety-six the oldest priest in the diocese, died on February 18, 1997. Rev. Henry F. H. Sims, a very active ecumenist, died on October 5, 1999. Rev. Joseph Romani, former pastor of St. Peter's Church in Portland, died on May 16, 2001. And, Rev. Patrick J. Barrett, former pastor of St. Mary's in Westbrook, died on April 14, 2002.

All Saints School (St. John's Campus), Bangor

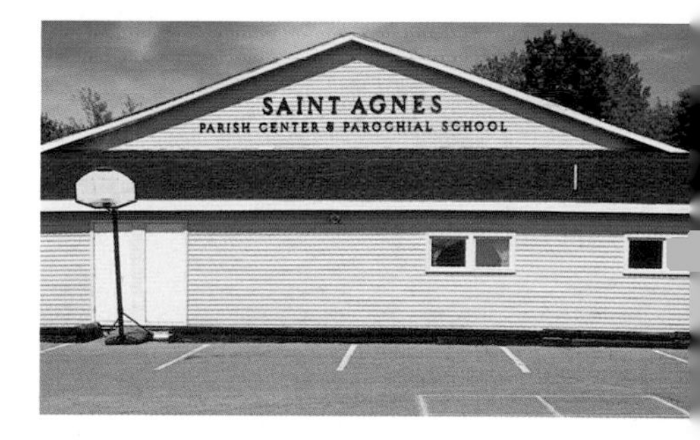

St. Agnes School, Pittsfield

While Bishop Joseph appreciated how important the parishes are as the centers of the religious and spiritual life for all Catholics, he also realized that he had to be strongly supportive of Catholic schools in his diocese because of their role in developing and shaping the religious beliefs, character, and practices of the youth. Of the twenty-four elementary schools in existence at the start of Joseph's tenure as Bishop of Portland, there were only eighteen twelve years later. In Biddeford, to compensate for the closing of St. André's, St. Joseph's and St. Mary's in 1992, St. James School was opened in that city in that same year. In Pittsfield, St. Agnes School was opened in 1993. Another, St. Patrick's in Portland, celebrated its seventy-fifth anniversary with Bishop Joseph, on October 17, 1997. Though a survey had been taken in 1998 about the feasibility of opening up another school in the Scarborough area, this has not yet materialized. In the case of St. Mary's and St. John's in Bangor, they were consolidated into All Saints School in 2000. Though fewer Catholic schools existed in the diocese, they continued to remain popular enrolling at least four thousand students in the state.

Another problem for the diocese in education had to do with measuring up to government standards. When the family of Matthew Denger, a youngster at St. James School in Biddeford, sought to have the diocese make the school accessible for their handicapped son, the diocese announced in April of 2000 that Matthew could not attend the school in September of the next academic year, a decision based on the boy's educational needs. By Columbus Day 2001, the Maine Human Rights Commission had ruled that the diocese was guilty of discrimination. Consequently, by November 1, 2001, the diocese changed its

Aerial view of the new St. Dominic Regional High School under construction in Auburn, 2000, (Photograph by the Lewiston Sun-Journal, used with permission)

mind and indicated that it would install the facilities to make the school accessible for the handicapped. By the end of that same year, it was ready to make a financial arrangement, thus avoiding a federal law suit. With the diocese adopting a policy of nondiscrimination on disabilities and apologizing to the family, in addition to awarding it a financial settlement, the matter ended.

As the trend towards coeducation increased among Jesuit schools, Cheverus High School, which had considered the possibility of accepting girls for some years, began a determined drive early in the summer of 1998 to open up the school to girls. This led to an announcement shortly before the Christmas vacation that year, by Rev. John W. Keegan, S. J., President of Cheverus, saying that he was asking his Jesuit superiors for permission for the school to convert to a coeducational institution. Operating with 390 male students at the time, the Jesuit had hoped to boost the school's enrollment in the future upward to at least 675 to 700 students.

While Bishop Joseph appeared somewhat tentative in coming to a decision that would affect both the high school operated by the Sisters of Mercy and the one by the Jesuits in his episcopal city, he had the best interest of the Catholic Church in mind. Not wanting to hinder the development of Catherine McAuley and desirous of continuing and fostering the Catholic character of Cheverus with so few Jesuits available for teaching, the bishop engaged in his usual style of consulting widely and listening carefully in facing such a problem. In the end, with the Jesuit superiors in favor of the change, the bishop did not veto it. Thus, the school went ahead and brought off coeducation successfully by admitting about fifty girls for the academic year which began in the fall of 2000.

During Bishop Joseph's time, moreover, St. Dominic's Regional High School moved out of Lewiston and into Auburn. In the winter of 1998-99, it became clear that the diocese was blessed with of a gift by John H. and Lynn Schiavi of almost seventy acres valued at some $770,000.00. At the same time, the diocese was the beneficiary of a substantial gift from John E. Callahan, a late Lewiston millionaire, which could subsidize the new physical plant. In this way, in January of 2002, the bishop was able to dedicate a new thirteen million dollar school for St. Dominic's totally free from debt.

A few years after he had taken over Diocese of Portland, Bishop Joseph began to meet annually with the state legislators at the end of January. This usually took place at the St. Paul Conference Center in Augusta, at the former Governor Hill Mansion, which had been used as a retreat center before the diocese acquired it from the Oblates in early November of 1997. Here the bishop hosted a luncheon at which he voiced his concerns over upcoming legislation. In 2001, at their annual luncheon, the bishop reminded the legislators that "you are your brother's keeper," in his key message. And, at the end of January in 2002, the bishop asked the legislators not to cut deeply into the budget lest those in the lower income brackets suffer from such reductions, a position that he repeated at the tenth annual luncheon on January 28, 2003.

Bishop Joseph's objective was clearly to sensitize the lawmakers to moral and social issues related to economic and social justice and to their obligation to help others. Particularly concerned that the legislators uphold the dignity of the human person in the laws which they passed, the bishop clarified his position on a number of issues other than abortion which he, like his brother bishops in the country, continued to oppose. These included such questions as gay rights and physician assisted suicide so that by the end of April 1997, it was clear that the Catholic Church in Maine was involving itself much more in social activism on a number of issues as evident from its presence at hearings, in press conferences, and through letter writing.

On the question of abortion, the fight focused on partial-birth measures. Near mid-March of 1997, the bishop had urged legislators to enact legislation against "partial-birth" abortions and, at the end of April of 1998, the diocese announced that it was joining a coalition of those opposing such late-term abortions. Subsequently, the issue was first among the referenda placed on the ballot, on November 2, 1999, and it was opposed by the Maine Choice Coalition which included such groups as the League of Women Voters, Maine State Nurses Association, Maine Civil Liberties Union, and Planned Parenthood of Northern New England. The November outcome showed that eleven out of twenty voters went against the ban so that the Yes for Life Coalition and the Maine Christian Civic League, both supported by the diocese, were defeated in that campaign. On the national scene, *The Daily Catholic*, a watchdog agency on abortion, sought to have Bishop Joseph and Theodore Cardinal McCarrick of Washington in recent years come out publicly against Roman Catholic politicians for their pro-abortionist stands. Like Bishop O'Leary, Bishop Joseph did not look kindly on those politicians who took a pro-choice stand rather than one that was pro-life.

On the question of gay rights, the Maine State Legislature in 1997 passed a bill against discrimination on the basis of sexual orientation which Governor Angus King (1995-2003) signed, only to have it overturned by a special election of February 10, 1998. Prior to this election, the diocese took a neutral stand which was stated in *The Church World* (January 22, 1998) making it clear that it was not urging a vote in favor of repeal. Subsequently, when a third statewide vote on gay rights came up in 2000, the Catholic Church did not remain neutral. In fact, it had reached an understanding with the supporters of the bill that allowed it to tolerate the referendum in favor of gay rights. This led a Grass Roots Coalition, about a month before the election, to openly protest the Church's stand at the chancery. In the end, on November 7, 2000, the referendum was defeated despite the Church's position. While at least ten Maine communities in 2003 had ordinances against such discrimination, there was still no statewide law prohibiting it.

Holy Martyrs, Falmouth

St. John (detail), Brunswick

On the question of physician-assisted suicide, the diocese won a major victory. In 1998, when the legislature rejected a bill calling for doctor-assisted suicide, Mainers for Death with Dignity began a campaign to get the issue on the ballot for November 2000. The diocese, ever sensitive to issues involving morality and religion, started as early as late September 1999 to shape its opposition to the right-to-die campaign. Since 1992, the state legislature had defeated such a bill at least four times and was about to do so again in 2000. With a nine to nothing vote by the Legislature's Judiciary Committee, in February of that year 2000, against a bill to allow such suicide, the issue would again go to voters with supporters of such suicide gaining national support. However, in the campaign, aided by the diocese with a video of seventeen minutes sent out to the parishes, the coalition was able to defeat the referendum favoring physician-assisted suicide, on November 7, 2000. As a consequence, the coalition thanked the bishop and diocese with a plaque which now hangs on the wall in the Roman Catholic Chancery in Portland.

Since the diocese was involved in social services that involved insurance benefits, Bishop Joseph was sensitive to laws and policies relating to the same. He issued a statement in the latter half of January of 1997 against a managed health-care plan by Blue Cross / Blue Shield because their changes would put Catholic hospitals like St. Mary's Medical Center in Lewiston at a grave disadvantage with their managed-care for profit decisions. Consequently, a month later matters had improved for the diocesan health-care services since Mercy Hospital was allowed to join the partnership arranged between Maine Medical Center and Blue Cross / Blue Shield. However, when the legislature passed a bill in spring 1999 requiring health insurance to cover birth-control pills and other contraceptive devices, the diocese, understandably, registered its opposition.

Ever since Bishop Gerety's time, the Diocese of Portland had been involved in providing health care and low-cost housing for the elderly and Bishop Joseph continued this policy. With St. Xavier Home in Bangor, Deering Pavilion and St. Joseph's Manor in Portland, and Seton Village in Waterville as components of its structure in such housing, the diocese, in July 1997, joined with the state to provide, out of the former St. André School, thirty-five units in the St. André Housing, Inc., for low income elderly in York County. This project of three million dollars, which opened in July of 1998, helped to expand the work of the diocese for the elderly and is a distinct operation from St. André Home, Inc. (The latter was established for pregnant mothers in Biddeford in 1940 by the Good Shepherd Sisters. One of its congregation, Sister Theresa Therrien (b. 1932), was honored by the United States Congress with the *Angel in Adoption Award*, on September 26, 2000.)

Bishop Joseph faced a number of other problems during his fifteen years in Portland. When a suit was brought against him that he was bound by a civil law of employment in the case of a priest who had a relationship with a woman of his parish, the Maine Supreme Judicial Court ruled four to two in early April 1997, in *Swanson v. the Roman Catholic Bishop of Portland*, that the bishop was not liable and reaffirmed this as recently as July 9, 2002, thereby making it very difficult to sue any church in the state for the abusive actions of its clergy. However, if those decisions were any consolation to the bishop, the revelations of the sexual abuse of children and young people by priests, which swept over the Catholic Church in the United States throughout 2002, certainly were not since they marked the time as an *Annus Horribilis* for him and his brother bishops. Unfortunately, the subject of sexual abuse by the clergy had come up as early as mid-April of 1998 when the Diocese of Portland had issued a public apology through an advertisement in the major newspaper of the secular press in Maine. And, the bishop himself had held in his own Cathedral a "Healing and Reconciliation Service" for the victims of sexual abuse with 200 attending. Then, Bishop Joseph had apologetically declared: "Some of our priests have abused minors and that is wrong."

Bishop Joseph having lunch with the participants of the 2003 Christian Leadership Institute in Farmington

Understandably, those revelations of past abuses by priests in the Diocese of Portland shocked the faithful in that first half of 2002. There was the case of the director of St. Joseph the Provider, a thrift store in Portland sponsored by the diocese, who pleaded guilty to tampering with a witness in 1985. There was the case of the two priests in the St. John River Valley, one in Madawaska and the other in St. Agatha who could no longer serve as priests after Bishop Joseph's decision of March 9, 2002. There was the case of the two Jesuits which focused on Cheverus High School and Boston College High School. And, there was the case of the pastor at St. Joseph's in Ellsworth where allegations of misconduct led to his removal on April 25, 2002.

At the annual Chrism Mass in the Cathedral, on March 26, 2002, before 700 present, Bishop Joseph again expressed sorrow for the victims of sexual abuse. Advertisements in Sunday papers in Portland and Bangor and Lewiston, on April 28, 2002, spoke to Mainers of sexual abuse. Then, Stephanie Anderson, District Attorney of Cumberland County revealed, on May 29, 2002, that accusations of sexual abuse have been made over the past 75 years against thirty-three other priests who were either inactive or retired (eight of them members of religious orders) and eighteen who were dead. By the time the bishops met at their national conference in Dallas that year, Joseph and his fellow bishops were so driven by the revelations that, on June 14, 2002, they approved a charter condemning the sexual abuse of children and young people by a vote of 239 to 13.

However, the scandal continues to haunt the Catholic Church and its fallout, in addition to other causes, was apparently affecting the Annual Bishop's Appeal, the major fund drive for the Diocese of Portland. In 2000, for example, it exceeded its goal of $3,266,000.00 with close to $3.3 million coming from 23,000 Catholic families. Yet, in light of recent dissatisfaction with the church and its priests over the sexual abuse scandal and over the sponsorship of refugees in the state by Catholic Charities Maine, the appeal was falling short of its goal by at least $225,000.00 in the closing year of Bishop Joseph's episcopacy, as he pointed out to the members of the Bishop's Guild in Orono, on November 19, 2002. Still, at the same time, one cannot overlook the impact which the apparent decline of Catholics by close to 55,000 during the bishop's tenure of office might have had on that same annual appeal.

Understandably, Bishop Joseph reflected a different style in the administration of his diocese. His motto that it was greater to serve than to rule ("*Magis Prodesse Quam Praeesse.*") reflected a style that became more evident over his fifteen years in Portland through his broad consultation and his careful listening to others,

Neil Michaud and Gloria Dugan, past Executive Directors of Catholic Charities Maine (Catholic Charities Maine photograph)

St. Patrick, Portland

St. Xavier's Home, Bangor

as evident in the victims of sexual abuse. Much of this, furthermore, was manifested in his participation in the annual Red Mass for judges and lawyers and the annual White Mass for health care ministers like aides, doctors, and nurses. This was also evident in his conferring of the Sacrament of Confirmation in the visits to his parishes, not to mention his participation in the Jubilee of the Millennium in 2000 and of the Diocese of Portland in 2003.

What is exceptional in his years as Bishop of Portland has been the exercise of Gerry's priestly role so evident not only in his model pastoral letters on such topics as worship, youth, and the diaconate, but in the way he has handled a number of challenges, including the sexual abuse scandal. At the same time, he has been supportive of Catholic education at a time when it has experienced a widespread decline on the elementary level and he has compensated for the lack of priests by introducing creative changes in parish structures and staffing while not overlooking the need to oppose civil legislation that is not in accord with the moral order. In all this, like other bishops, he has been forced to cut budgets, eliminate debts, and raise funds in order to convey the message of the Gospel more effectively.

Conclusion

While this history covers four hundred years, there has been no attempt to cover every detail of that history. In itself, it is an impossible task, especially since it would require omniscience. But, as everyone knows, only God is omniscient and knows everything about what really happened in history and why it happened. The best that one can expect in a survey of this type is a fair picture of what has happened in the structuring of Catholicism in a part of the United States and an explanation of why it happened.

In his column in *The Church World*, on November 16, 2000, Father Richard P. McBrien informed his readers how Blessed Pope John XXIII, an historian himself, reminded people that history is the great teacher of life (an axiom of Marcus Tullius Cicero) and how George Santayana, the philosopher, warned that those who do not learn the lessons of the past are condemned to repeat them. In light of those truths, what, then, are the important lessons to be derived from this history of the Diocese of Portland?

In general, there are the lessons that show how the Catholic Church in the Diocese of Portland, as elsewhere in this country, has contributed to the health of society. In a nation devoted to religious freedom, it has fought against bigotry throughout its history from the explicit anti-Catholicism of the colonial period down to the concealed anti-Catholicism among the higher levels of today's power elites. In a land of opportunity, it has helped to Americanize the immigrant so as to adjust the newcomer to American society and ways of living while not neglecting one's ancestral roots. In the field of education, it has supported a vast complex of schools from the elementary level to the college level that has enabled the children of the first generation and their descendants to gain respectable positions in various professional fields like business, education, law, medicine, religion, and science. In the area of social justice, it has established hospitals, housing, nursing homes, orphanages, shelters, and other facilities and programs to care for society's neediest. And, in relations with non-Catholics, it has emphasized what unites them with Catholics rather than what divides them in order to build a world based on the love of God and love of neighbor.

While that last development has come about because of the teachings of the Second Vatican Council, it was also coincidental with the time when it was becoming financially impossible for Catholics to continue to live separately in isolation from the rest of American society with its vast network of social institutions like schools and hospitals as well as organizations for men and women. Although the Catholic Church of the twentieth century with the influence, money, power, vocations, and wealth, which made that separation possible, has been disappearing, another image of the Catholic Church was coming into existence as it was approaching a new millennium.

However, there is also the evidence from history that the United States is not free from the process of secularization through which Europe has already passed leaving it today with a very low percentage of people who consider themselves church members. In this country, since the religious and cultural revolutions that marked the 1960s, there has been a similar development in the isolation of religion and morality from public and even private life as the country has become more suburbanized. While this may be manifest in the way in which people will go out of their way to avoid reference to the religious aspects of Christmas and Easter in conveying greetings to one another, it is also evident in the growing practice among Catholics to avoid a religious burial for a family member.

In fact, the consequences of such a process of secularization is underscored in the number of laws passed on the local, state, and national levels. These give legal sanction to actions that are objectively immoral while swerving away from directives which affirm that the legal order is part of the moral order. Clearly, the fundamental outcome of such an approach to the legal structure of any society becomes evident in the way in which a low value is placed on human life and its meaning. Therefore, the warning of Pope John Paul II, issued in his encyclical *Evangelium Vitae* (March 25, 1995), against a culture of death dominating a culture of life must be taken seriously if civilization is to survive.

Moreover, there is the lesson that it is the People of God who are important in this history. They were the Native Americans of colonial days, they were the immigrants of the emerging diocese, and they are the descendants of those who were the backbone of the parishes which emerged in the nineteenth and the twentieth centuries.

In the case of the Native Americans, they have demonstrated an incredible fidelity to Catholicism. Since their ancestors were the ones who first received the faith in Maine, they constitute a unique heritage in the history of the Diocese of Portland as the oldest group of Catholics. Understandably, they have been regarded with special concern by those ecclesiastical leaders who have exercised jurisdiction over the area even though they have been among the smallest group of Catholics in the state.

On the other hand, Americans of French background have constituted for some time the largest group in the Diocese of Portland. While the original French settlers had brought the faith to Maine and their descendants became the backbone of the diocese in the industries of Biddeford, Lewiston, Waterville, and the farms of the St. John River Valley, recognition of them was long in coming, whether they were the descendants of the Acadians who were driven by the English out of the Maritime Provinces of New Brunswick, Nova Scotia, and Prince Edward Island or of the Franco-Americans who came down from Quebec seeking economic opportunity in the United States. Not until the diocese was almost 125 years old were they properly recognized as a force in the development of Catholicism in Maine. This came about with the appointment of Amédée W. Proulx as auxiliary bishop in 1975, a lesson which was not forgotten even with the decline of the state's population of French ancestry in the last decade, as was evident with the appointment of Michael R. Coté to succeed him in 1995.

Certainly, another lesson from the history of the diocese is that the road to assimilation and adaptation for Catholics in Maine has not been a failure. That emerges in the way in which the Diocese of Portland, through Catholic Charities Maine, one of the largest agency for social services in the state, is doing so much to help the people of Maine. In conjunction with organizations on the local, state, and national levels, it builds communities, fights poverty, and supports families that are in need of its human relations services in today's multicultural society when the cultural climate, for example, differs dramatically from what it was in the last quarter of the nineteenth century.

Long before Catholic Charities Maine came into existence, the record of the religious communities of sisters in helping the people of Maine, especially in their schools and hospitals, is another lesson from the past. In the undertakings of religious, brothers and sisters, the latter in particular cannot be overlooked, not only because of their work in the schools, but especially because of the hospitals which religious women have staffed across the state in response to the health needs of the local communities. Even though these institutions were independent of diocesan control, they operated in cooperation with the diocese by carrying on a mission of charity which made the Catholic Church present in the lives of many citizens in an era when religious vocations flourished. In many ways, it was the devotion of these sisters that reflected a charism and a vitality which had an impact in transforming the lives of Mainers.

Finally, there is the lesson that each of the ten bishops in this history had his own special charism during his tenure as Bishop of Portland. Bishop Bacon has been responsible for launching the Diocese of Portland with more churches and schools. Bishop Healy has been responsible for extending the church into cities and towns which did not have a Catholic parish. Bishop O'Connell has been responsible for opening up civil society to Catholics by improving the public image of the church in Maine. Bishop Walsh has been responsible for spreading the Catholic school system. Bishop Murray has been responsible for strengthening the faith among immigrant groups. Bishop McCarthy has been responsible for helping to dissolve the debt of the diocese. Bishop Feeney has been responsible for launching the reforms of the Second Vatican Council. Bishop Gerety has been responsible for updating the diocese with progressive changes. Bishop O'Leary has been responsible for giving the church a more ecumenical and universal image and for demonstrating that it is composed of the People of God. And, Bishop Gerry has been responsible for emphasizing the pastoral work of the church through his homilies and pastoral letters as he coped with the decline in the number of priests and the need to consolidate parishes. In all of these bishops, there are lessons that can serve to guide the diocese in the present and to prepare it for the future.

A reflection of God's peace in Maine

Historic Sites and Places of Interest in the Diocese of Portland

St. Mark, Ashland

ASHLAND

St. Mark's Parish, centered in Sheridan in 1902, was founded for the French Canadians in the lumber industry. Under its first pastor, Joseph Drolet (d. 1922), it grew from 61 families to about 300 shortly before the new church in Ashland was built and dedicated in 1980 under Ernest L'Heureux (b. 1929) as pastor (1975-82). The parish, which had its centennial in 2002, includes the missions of Our Lady of the Lakes in Portage and St. Catherine's in Washburn.

Former St. Anne, Ashland

St. Louis, Auburn

AUBURN

1. In 1891, **St. Louis** had a chapel opened for the Canadians who came to build the railroads and to work in the shoe and textile industries. In 1892, the parish opened a school under the Daughters of Our Lady of Sion before it was established as a parish in 1902. Though it flourished with a new church in 1916, a general fire in 1933 destroyed the school which was later rebuilt so that in 1960 its enrollment was about 600. Paul S. Bührer (d. 1962) was one of its key pastors (1936-56).

2. In 1923, when **Sacred Heart** was established, a converted stable was used until a new church was opened under Father Armand Chabot (d. 1970) in 1938. Initially composed of 215 families of "Old Auburn," the parish grew to 600 families by the end of World War II. Under Father Emmanuel R. Grodin (d. 1973), known as "The Bulldozer," the parish began its own school in 1952. Staffed by the Sisters of St. Joseph, the school was educating 600 students a year by 1960.

Sacred Heart, Auburn

3. In 1968, **St. Philip's** was established as a parish under Msgr. Edmond J. Haché (d. 1973) because Sacred Heart in Auburn was overcrowded and St. Joseph in Lewiston was too far away. In its opening years, services were held in the United Methodist Church until the new church was built on Turner Road, on land given by Gilbert Hathaway a generous non-Catholic. Overlooking Lake Auburn, this church was dedicated on August 29, 1971.

4. **St. Dominic Regional High School,** now located in this town, was originally founded in Lewiston by Father Hervé Drouin, O. P., Pastor of Saints Peter and Paul Parish, in 1941. It had evolved out of St. Dominic's High School for Boys (1941) and St. Dominic's High School for Girls (1946), both previously located in Lewiston where they became a coeducational institution in 1968. In 1969, the school ceased to be a parish high school and came under the sponsorship of the diocese as a regional high school.

AUGUSTA

St. Mary of the Assumption, Augusta

1. **St. Mary of the Assumption,** established in 1834, derived its name from the mission set up by the Jesuit Gabriel Druillettes (1610-81) at Gilley's Point in 1646 (a model of this chapel can be found on the local grounds of the Knights of Columbus). The first parish on the Kennebec River after American independence, it served Catholics who fled Ireland and came to work on the river dam and to build the city as the center of the state government in the nineteenth century. Of its pastors (a stone tablet lists its pastors), Charles W. Doherty (d. 1910) served the longest (1896-1910). Its English Gothic church, dedicated in 1927, was placed on the National Register of Historic Places in 1987, and restored in 1993. When the city marked its 200th anniversary in 1997, the parish had some 1200 families. Roland C. Reny (d. 1991), a military chaplain at the Nuremberg Trials after World War II, was one of its parishioners.

2. **St. Augustine's** was founded in 1887 under Télesphore Plante as pastor (1887-89) with 218 families and 1,250 parishioners of French Canadian descent. A school, opened under the Ursulines in 1892, was taken over by the Sisters of the Presentation of Mary in 1904. The parish had acquired its own cemetery in 1894 and a the new church in 1916. Of its pastors, Joseph O. Casavant (d. 1960) had the longest tenure (1919-60).

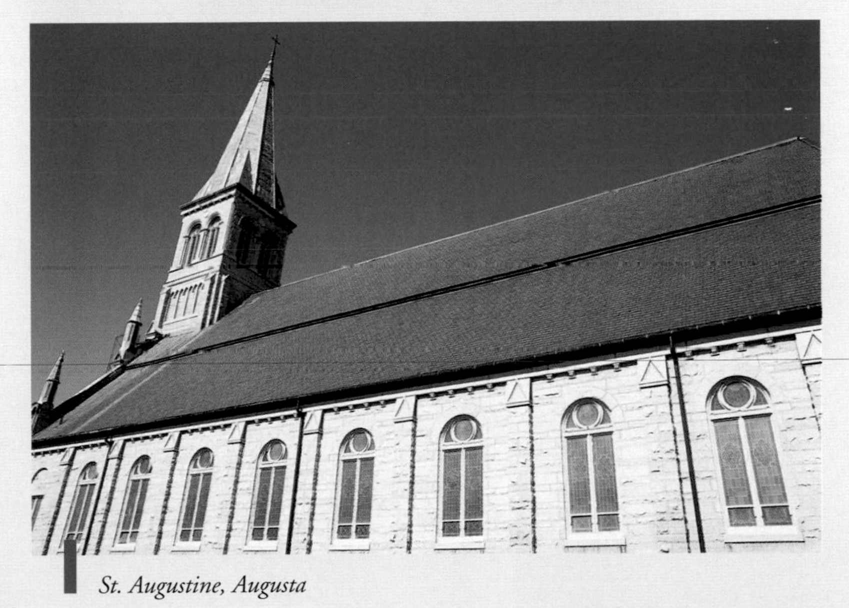

St. Augustine, Augusta

3. **St. Andrew's,** organized in 1968, had its First Mass in St. Barnabas Episcopal Church before parishioners gathered for Mass in a former store at Cony Circle until a new church was constructed. This came about under Father Louis J. Fortier (d. 1988) as pastor and it was dedicated, in 1970, with a bell donated by the Bates Manufacturing Company in memory of the immigrants who came there to work in that firm.

St. Andrew, Augusta

4. **St. Paul's Center,** originally the Governor John F. Hill Mansion, it was taken over by the Oblates as a retreat center in 1948. Added to the National Register of Historic Places in 1977, it has recently come under Catholic Charities Maine.

Catholic Charities Maine, St. Paul's Center, Augusta

Christmas decorations, St. James the Greater, Baileyville (Woodland), 1926

BAILEYVILLE

St. James the Greater, originally a mission of Immaculate Conception in Calais, dates from 1905. It served the immigrants who came to work in the St. Croix Paper Company which gave the land for the church that opened in 1907. This church is also noted for Patricia Phillips, the first lay parish coordinator of the diocese (1995-2001).

Interior, St. John, Bangor, view toward the organ loft

St. Mary's Church, Bangor

BANGOR

1. **St. John's** had Rev. Patrick M. McNamee as its first resident pastor when it was established as St. Michael's in 1832. The present church, designed by the architect Patrick C. Keeley, was built in 1854 under Father John Bapst (d. 1887) and dedicated in 1856. Placed on the National Register of Historic Places in 1973, it contains some rare stained glass windows by Franz Xavier Pernlochner of Austria dating from 1888 about which Franz Josef Van Beeck, a Jesuit, wrote *Meditations in Glass* (1981), and an historic organ by E. and G. G. Hook of Boston which was restored in 1981.

2. **St. Mary's**, dating from 1872, served Irish Catholics on the west side of the Kenduskeag River and the adjoining towns. The home parish of Bishop O'Leary, it had many religious vocations cultivated in its parish school which opened in 1896. In the late 1970s, when it experienced fires which destroyed the rectory in 1977 and the church in 1978, it had some 1,140 families and 3,800 parishioners. Today, with its new parish complex dedicated in 1980, the parish is more ethnically diverse. Msgr. Edward F. Ward (1900-97) who served the diocese in various positions, was a pastor (1950-71) here.

3. **John Bapst High School** which was founded by the diocese in 1928 and of which Bishop O'Leary was an alumnus (class of 1938), underwent a transformation after the Xaverian Brothers and Sisters of Mercy had taught there for many years. Ceased being sponsored by the diocese in 1978, it assumed a new name, John Bapst Memorial High School, as a private school.

4. **St. Joseph's Hospital**, originally the Paine Private Hospital, was taken over by the Felician Sisters of St. Francis in 1947 as one of a handful of Catholic hospitals in the state and renamed for St. Joseph.

5. **Mount Pleasant Cemetery** is a Catholic cemetery and the burial site of Bishop O'Leary.

St. Mary's Church, Bangor

BAR HARBOR

1. **Hulls Cove** is the burial site of Marie Thérèse de Grégoire (d.1811) and Barthélemy (d. 1810), her husband. A renowned Catholic woman, she was the grand-daughter of Sieur Antoine de la Mothe Cadillac (1658-1750) to whom, in 1688, King Louis XIV had granted Mt. Desert Island. A plaque marks the site of the De Grégoire Residence in the eastern part of the island which she had reclaimed in 1787.

2. The site of **Holy Redeemer Church**, Catholicism here on Mount Desert Island dates from the early mission (Saint-Sauveur) established in 1613 under the Jesuits. St. Sylvia's, founded in 1883, was the original parish dedicated to a saint to whom the church's benefactors, the DeGrasse Fox Family, had a devotion. However, it was renamed in 1913 at the dedication of the stone church commemorating the 300th anniversary of the early Jesuit mission (for which St. Saviour's Episcopal Church had been named in 1878). This town, where James Cardinal Gibbons (1834-1921) visited in 1890 and where Catholics once increased from 350 in winter to 4,000 in summer, attracted St. Katharine Drexel (1858-1955). She was the guest of her sister (Louise) and her brother-in-law (Edward de V. Morrell).

3. **St. Edward's**, a former school and convent of which the Morrells were the benefactors (their images are on the chapel's stained glass windows) was completed in 1918. Now the home of the Bar Harbor Historical Society, it was added to the National Register of Historic Places in 1998. Father James M. Gower (b. 1922), who celebrated his golden jubilee as a priest in 2003, graduated from this school.

4. **Oblate College and Seminary**, which was opened here in 1944 on the former Byrne Estate, had a Shrine of Our Lady of Fatima dedicated after the great fire of 1947. Although it had ceased to exist in 1967, the institution was under the sponsorship of the Oblates of Mary Immaculate.

5. On the summit of the mountain named for the Jesuit mission here on Mount Desert Island, Mrs. Winthrop Sargent (1839-1913) of Boston had hoped to set up a cross of granite before death intervened to prevent the realization of that dream early in the twentieth century.

St. Mary, Bath

BATH

Initially called Immaculate Conception at its founding in 1849, **St. Mary's** served the Irish who came here to build ships. For its services, the parish leased the old South Church (now a famous site on the city's historic tour), which the Know-Nothings burned down, on July 6, 1854, and which is portrayed by the artist John Hilling (1822-94) in a painting in the National Gallery. Though it had 145 families and 700 parishioners in 1860, by 1910 St. Mary's included 135 families and 675 parishioners. The present church, dating from 1969, was constructed after an expanding Morse High School purchased the old property. By 1985, the parish was serving almost a thousand families.

Holy Redeemer, Bar Harbor

BELFAST

In 1832, long before the present church was named for **St. Francis of Assisi** in 1891, Bishop Fenwick found about 150 Catholics in his visit here. Then, William S. Brannigan (1810-1901), an immigrant from Ireland in 1835, provided the land and the building on Prince Street for the first Catholic church in 1851. This parish, where Thomas F. Coyne (d. 1984) had served as one of its more notable pastors (1959-83), dedicated a new center in 1986 and marked its centennial in 1991. The parish also cares for the mission of St. Mary of the Isles in Islesboro.

St. Francis of Assisi, Belfast

St. Benedict, Benedicta

BENEDICTA

Founded in 1834 by Bishop Fenwick as a settlement for the pioneering Irish families of the Brodericks, Browns, Burkes, Caseys, Millmores, and Rushes, **St. Benedict's** grew to some 135 families and 535 parishioners within a year or so of its origin. While the town never had more than 500 residents, it declined to about 225 at the time of its 150th anniversary. Msgr. Joseph E. Houlihan (d. 1994) served as one of its pastors (1955-59). Today, Benedicta is an unincorporated town with the parish caring for the mission station of St. Joseph's in Sherman.

Our Lady of Peace, Berwick

BERWICK

Originally a mission of St. Michael's in South Berwick, **Our Lady of Peace (Notre Dame de la Paix**, as it was known) was established in 1927 with Henry L. Semery (d. 1945) as its first pastor (1927-42). Centered on the old Lord Estate, its first church had been converted from a barn and it was serving 200 families, mostly Franco-Americans, by 1955. Before it celebrated its seventy-fifth anniversary in 2002, the church was enlarged and renovated.

St. Mary's Cemetery, Biddeford

BIDDEFORD

1. **St. Mary's**, the first Biddeford parish in 1855, ministered to all Catholics of the area until French parishes were formed, and thereafter was know as the "Irish Church". The pastor was Fr. Kennedy, the first priest ordained by Bishop Bacon. St. Mary's church and cemetery were open within a year and the present rectory in 1886. St. Mary's school (1892-1992) and convent (demolished 2001) were staffed by the Sisters of Mercy. The old church was replaced by a new Gothic church (opened 1924). It has spectacular stained glass windows. The parish formed missions at Old Orchard Beach (1897) and Saco (1915) to later become separate parishes, and maintains St. Brendan's (1916) as a summer chapel at Biddeford Pool. St. Mary's church was extensively renovated in 2001 and ministers to 650 families.

2. **St. Joseph's**, the city's first French parish, came about in good part because of the efforts of Daniel Côté, a grocer, in the spring of 1870. The present church was dedicated in 1883 under Pierre Emmanuel Dupont (d. 1915), its second pastor (1877-1915). This parish, which opened St. Louis (de Gonzague) High School in 1929, was known for its religious vocations and had its first native son, Msgr. Elie A. Hévey (d. 1976), as pastor in 1953. Its Stations of the Cross, are from old St. Dominic's Church in Portland. It was the largest and the highest church in the diocese until 1960. A second Catholic cemetery in Biddeford is also named for St. Joseph.

St. Joseph , Biddeford

St. André, Biddeford

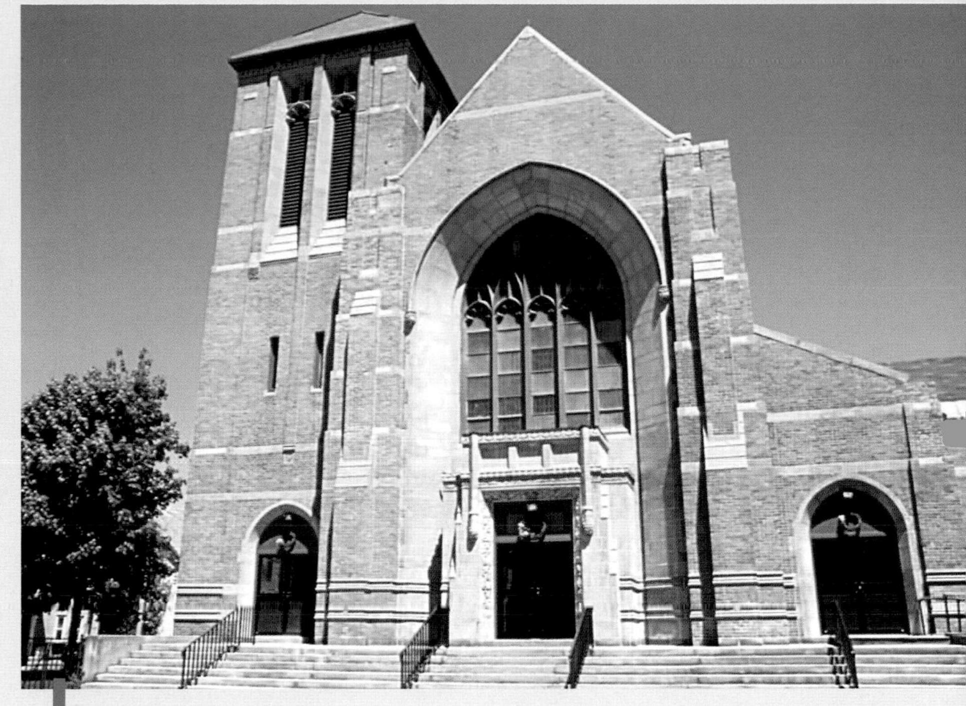

St. Mary, Biddeford

3. **St. André's** was established in 1899 as a second parish in the city for the French Canadians. Within a decade, the new parish had 830 families and 4,300 parishioners and, by the time of its centennial in 1999, it had 1,900 families and 7,000 parishioners. With the help of religious like the Sisters of the Presentation of Mary and the Brothers of the Sacred Heart, it paved the way for social services like a credit union, housing for the aged, and schools. The present church, which was dedicated in 1910, had Msgr. Arthur M. Décary (d. 1957) as one of its illustrious pastors (1919-51).

4. **Sisters of the Good Shepherd** have been deeply involved in the city's charitable works since they had established St. André's in 1940. Although their central office is in Biddeford on Elm Street, the Sisters have also been active in Bangor and Lewiston.

5. **Marie Joseph Spiritual Center** is a retreat house under the Sisters of the Presentation of Mary.

Good Shepherd Sisters, St. Joseph's Convent, Biddeford

St. André's Group Home, Biddeford

Our Lady Queen of Peace, Boothbay Harbor

BOOTHBAY HARBOR

Originally a mission of St. Dennis in Whitefield, **Our Lady Queen of Peace** had twelve families when it became a parish in 1928. Although the present church dates from 1917, it has undergone subsequent renovations. It is the first Catholic church in Maine in which an American President has worshipped (John F. Kennedy did so on August 12, 1962) and it is near the local memorial to some 230 fishermen lost at sea. Francis A. Mannette (d. 1985) was one of its famous pastors (1949-71) and, subsequently, in the last quarter of the twentieth century, the Blessing of the Fishing Fleet became an annual event.

BINGHAM

St. Peter's, previously a mission of Notre Dame de Lourdes in Skowhegan, was not established as a parish until 1920. Its present church dates from 1916 and was intended to serve Catholics who were helping to construct the Wyman Dam and to work in the Allen Quimby Veneer Company. The parish, which had embraced some 125 families by 1955, grew to 203 families, mostly of Irish and French background, by 1995. Among its noteworthy pastors was Napoleon J. Madore (d. 1976) who served its people for sixteen years (1936-52).

BRADLEY

Initially served by St. Joseph's in Old Town, **St. Ann's** became a parish in 1934 and the present church was dedicated in 1935. When the parish began to celebrate its fiftieth anniversary in 1984, it numbered some 225 families and 600 parishioners.

St. Peter, Bingham (courtesy of Fr. Maurice Morin)

St. Ann, Bradley

BREWER

1. Once a part of St. John's in Bangor, **St. Teresa's** was established in 1896 as a parish in honor of St. Teresa of Avila (1515-82). Matthew W. Reilley (d. 1926) was the pastor (1915-26) when Matthew V. Mutty helped to open a parish school in memory of his parents in 1926. Though the parish started with 100 families, it numbered at least 500 families as it neared its centennial in 1996.

2. Having been a mission of St. John's in Bangor, **St. Joseph's** became a parish in 1926 under Thomas H. Moriarty (d. 1969) as its pastor (1926-63). Its first church was dedicated in 1926 and served the parish until a new church was dedicated in 1975 under Richard E. Harvey (b. 1920), as its pastor (1970-95). By 2000, the parish had about 725 families and 2000 parishioners.

St. Teresa, Brewer

St. Joseph, Brewer

BRIDGTON

St. Joseph's had been a mission of St. Catherine of Siena in Norway before it was established as a parish in 1971 when the present church was dedicated. Gilbert A. Patenaude (b. 1919), its founding pastor (1971-74), was in charge of about 175 families. In the parish is St. Elizabeth Ann Seton, a mission in Fryeburg, not too far from the headwaters of the Saco River where there was once an old Jesuit mission for the Pequawkets.

BROWNVILLE JUNCTION

Catholics began here in the 1880s with about ten families and increased to 230 by 1979. Set up as a parish in 1929, **St. Francis Xavier** had been under St. Joseph's in Old Town (until 1893), St. Anne's in Dexter (until 1899), St. Martin's in Millinocket (until 1912), and St. Thomas' in Dover-Foxcroft (until 1926). In 1892, the Canadian Pacific Railway gave the land for the first church which served until 1916 when the present church was dedicated. Today the parish also cares for St. Paul's, a mission in Milo.

St. Francis Xavier, Brownville Junction

BRUNSWICK

1. **St. John the Baptist** was established as a parish in 1877 with 667 Catholics, the majority of whom were French Canadians. The parish grew to 1,500 families and 8,000 parishioners in 1955 only to see these numbers decline to 834 families and 3,271 parishioners by 1962. The present church, having replaced the one destroyed by fire in 1912, was dedicated in 1927 and, by this time, the Marists had taken over the parish. Prior to the centennial of the parish in 1977, the interior of the church was restored and, prior to its 125th in 2002, its exterior was renewed. Since 1882, the parish school has been educating its students (Ursulines staffed it, 1915-98). Its parish, which has ministered to the neighboring naval air station, today also cares of the mission of St. Andrew in Pejepscot.

2. **St. Charles Borromeo**, which began as a parish, under Thomas W. Dunnagan its first pastor (1930-39), with more than fifty families in 1930, grew to 500 families by 1967. While John L. Doherty (d. 1955) holds the record for the pastor with the longest term (1939-55), the parish also prides itself on having Bishop O'Leary as one of its pastors (1967-71). The original church, which was used since 1931, was replaced by the present one in 1975. Today it is also responsible for the new chapel, dedicated to St. Katharine Drexel in Harpswell, which replaced the former ones, Precious Blood on Bailey Island and St. Mary's in South Harpswell.

Interior, St. John the Baptist, Brunswick

St. John's School, Brunswick

St. Charles Borromeo, Brunswick

BUCKSPORT

St. Vincent de Paul was established as a parish in 1892 in a town where John Bapst, a Jesuit missionary, once served the French Canadians who had come into the area in 1835 and the Irish who had come in 1840. The property of Ruth Burgess was the site of the first place of worship for Catholics until the first church was dedicated in 1891. John McVicar (d. 1990), one of its pastors (1943-63), began the present church in 1950 and nourished Catholicism at the maritime academy in neighboring Castine. Fishing, lumbering, and shipbuilding fueled the town's economy as Catholics grew to number 350 families by 1981.

St. Vincent de Paul, Bucksport

Our Lady of Good Hope, Camden

CALAIS

Established in 1864 as a parish, **Immaculate Conception** had a new church in 1896 to replace the former town hall which had been remodeled and decorated with a bell tower to serve as a church. The Sisters of Mercy opened a school there in 1885 and there were 700 Catholics by 1896. One of its early pastors was James T. Durnin (d. 1873), a native of Eastport, who, in serving the parish for three years before his death, was responsible for the parish's first sodality and the town's first temperance society. The present church dates from the last decade of the twentieth century.

CAMDEN

Our Lady of Good Hope became a parish in 1967 under Arthur H. St. Pierre (d. 1995) as its first pastor (1967-72). It had been a mission since 1909, when the Chatfields from Cincinnati, Ohio, summer residents, were generous in building the church for their Irish domestics, one of whom, Mary Molly, died about that time. The parish, which had about 300 families in 1992, also includes a mission in North Haven and a station in Vinalhaven, both named Our Lady of Peace.

Immaculate Conception, Calais

St. Bartholomew, Cape Elizabeth

Interior, St. Bartholomew, Cape Elizabeth (Robert Anastasoff photograph)

CAPE ELIZABETH

St. Bartholomew's, established in 1968, was one of the first parishes in the diocese designed to accommodate Catholics who had moved from the city to the suburbs. The present church, dedicated in 1971, has been recently reconstructed and remodeled.

CARIBOU

1. **Sacred Heart** was established as a parish (originally Our Lady of the Sacred Heart) in the northern part of town in 1881. Located in the center of Aroostook County, it was the first Catholic parish in an area which is located 300 miles from the headquarters of the Diocese of Portland. A parish school was opened there in 1946.

Sacred Heart, North Caribou

2. Fifteen years after Sacred Heart was founded, **Holy Rosary** was opened as the second parish in Caribou in 1896. Its first church was dedicated in 1886, the second one in 1935, and the third one in 1961. From 350 families and 1,500 parishioners in 1920, the parish had grown to 1,300 families and some 3,571 parishioners by the opening of this century.

Holy Rosary, Caribou

CASCO

Established here in 1991, the **Community of the Resurrection**, is a handful of Catholic nuns living in accord with Dominican spirituality. Situated in an old farm house on the top of a hill overlooking many acres, the nuns are inspired by the ideals of Jean Joseph Lataste (1832-1869), a French Dominican priest known as "The Apostle of Prisoners." Thus, their major work consists in caring for women in difficulties, especially in prisons.

CASTINE

This historic town, visited by Jesuit Pierre Biard (1567-1622) in 1611, was the location of the old fort Pentagoet which had a chapel dedicated to St. Peter. This was constructed by the French of timber and mud with a bell in 1635 when the Capuchins ministered in the area. In 1648, a cornerstone was set for a more substantial chapel, under the title of **Our Lady of Holy Hope**, at this center of colonial Catholic life on the Penobscot River before the Jesuits later took over the missionary work. The chapel here today under the same title is in the area of the old fort and is a mission of the Catholic parish in Stonington. This archeological district was placed on the National Register of Historic Places in 1993.

DAIGLE

In 1906, **Holy Family**, formerly a mission of Fort Kent, became the first parish established by Bishop Walsh. The parish church was in a town named for Vital Daigle, Sr. (d. 1901), whose grandfather was one of the original Catholic settlers of Madawaska. From eighty-three families and 492 parishioners in 1908, it had eighty-eight families and 443 parishioners in 1955. Although the first church was destroyed by fire, on May 24, 1909, a new church was built. On July 14, 2002, a monument was dedicated marking the site of the church, the parish having closed in July of 2000.

DEXTER

Before **St. Anne's** was established in 1893, Eugene Vetromile (1819-81), a Jesuit later incardinated into the diocese, celebrated the First Mass here and the first church was constructed in 1871. Under John W. Houlihan (d. 1945), its first pastor (1893-1909), the parish, by 1895, was caring for about 600 Catholics, many of whom were from families which had migrated from Quebec to work in the woolen mills of the region after the Civil War. The present church on Free Street dates from 1901.

St. Anne, Dexter

St. Thomas Aquinas, Dover-Foxcroft

DOVER-FOXCROFT

St. Thomas Aquinas, a parish established in 1898, is centered in a church which was dedicated in 1899. The parish, which nourished a number of religious vocations, established a scholarship to the priesthood in memory of Maurice B. Boland (d. 1971), one of its pastors (1926-42). The parish once embraced Charleston Air Force Station within its boundaries and still serves Holy Family Mission in Sangerville.

50th Anniversary of Holy Family, Daigle, August 29, 1957

St. Mary, Eagle Lake

EAGLE LAKE

Although **St. Mary's** was not officially established as a parish until 1907, when Joseph S. Marcoux (1850-1918) became its first pastor (1907-18), it claims its origin when it became a mission of St. Joseph's in Wallagrass in 1892. Starting with 278 families, it had, within a year, grown to 410 families when its church opened in 1908. The present church, which dates from 1972, was the site of its centennial celebrations in 1992 when the parish numbered 320 families. Father Marcoux was also noted for founding the first hospital in the region.

EAST MILLINOCKET

St. Peter's, which was established as a separate parish in 1912, had Thomas J. O'Dowd (d. 1968) as its first resident pastor (1912-26). The present church was dedicated in 1966.

St. Peter, East Millinocket

EASTPORT

With families like the Barrys, Gilligans, and Sherlocks, Father Charles Ffrench (d. 1851) founded **St. Joseph's** in 1828 when there were 300 Catholics in the area. With 100 families in 1982, the parish has grown to about 120 families during the administration (1991-2003) of Paul M. Sullivan, S. J. (b. 1951), especially by the time it began celebrating its 175th anniversary in 2002 with the commemoration of Bishop Fenwick's five-day visit there in mid-July of 1827. Though the parish hall is the structure of the original church, the present church, dating from 1874, is noteworthy for its windows of stained glass. This parish is also responsible for St. John the Evangelist, a mission in Pembroke.

St. Joseph, Ellsworth

ELLSWORTH

St. Joseph's was established as a parish in 1862, less than ten years after town bigots in 1854 bombed the school, damaged the church, and tarred and feathered Father John Bapst, S.J., only to continue their violence by destroying the church by fire in 1856. Though the present church was dedicated in 1940, the parish embraces the missions of Our Lady of the Lake in Green Lake, and St. Margaret's at Grindstone Neck in Winter Harbor. This last chapel, which marked its centennial in 2002, a year when the naval base in Winter Harbor closed, was due to the generosity of the family of James G. Moore (1847-99) and had Richard MacDonough, a Sulpician, as a summer assistant priest there since 1964.

FAIRFIELD

After 104 French Canadians came to this town in 1882, **Immaculate Heart of Mary** was established as a parish in 1891 with 104 families which grew to 580 families by the time of its centennial in 1991. The parochial school, which was opened by the Ursulines in 1911 and was continued by the Sisters of Mercy in 1934, was closed in 1969.

Immaculate Heart of Mary, Fairfield

FALMOUTH

This parish was established in 1968 to honor the **Holy Martyrs of North America** and to cope with the move of Catholics from the city to the suburbs. The first church, which was constructed as a mission chapel under Edward F. Walsh (d. 1962), Pastor of Sacred Heart in Yarmouth from 1937 to 1954, was regarded as the first one in the country dedicated to the Jesuit martyrs of North America. The present church, which opened under its first pastor (1969-79), Raymond F. Begin (b. 1928), was dedicated in 1971 and has the first stained glass of the Native American Madonna (1991). The parish had about 725 families by 2000.

Stained glass window, Holy Martyrs of North America, Falmouth

FARMINGTON

1. **Anmesokkanti Mission** on the Sandy River was the location of a Jesuit mission established about 1694, the year in which Lydia Longley (1674-1758) of Groton, MA, was taken here as a captive on her way to Montreal where she became the first native of New England to become a Catholic nun. This was also the area of Pierpole (baptized Pierre Paul), the last surviving Native American Catholic here in the last quarter of the eighteenth century.

2. **St. Joseph's** was founded in 1885 for French Canadians drawn here by the construction of the railroad. In the twentieth century, the paper mill in nearby Chisholm drew Italians, Poles, and other immigrants. Famous among its parishioner was Cornelia T. Crosby (1854-1946), also known as "Flyrod," who converted to Catholicism due to the example of Nicholas J. Horan (d. 1933), a pastor (1893-97) and a devoted priest. A plaque was dedicated here in 1983 by the Order of Alhambra within the church to commemorate the Jesuit missions on the rivers of the region in colonial times.

St. Joseph, Farmington

St. Louis, Fort Kent

St. Denis, Fort Fairfield

FORT FAIRFIELD

Established in 1894 as a parish for Irish Catholics who came into the area from New Brunswick during the 1830s and 1840s, **St. Denis** began as a mission of Benedicta in 1842 and had three churches in its history (one on the South Caribou Road, 1842-72; another on Lower Main Street, 1872-1930; and a third, a brick one, since 1931, replacing one which burned in 1930). From 100 families at its birth, it grew to 300 families by 1955 only to decline to about 250 families by 1994. Stephen J. Rice (d. 1981) was the pastor with the longest tenure (1954-79).

FORT KENT

Though **St. Louis** was set up for French-speaking Catholics in 1870, its first resident pastor was Cleophas Demers (1875-82). The first church (1882 to 1907) was destroyed by fire and replaced by the present one in 1911. While this church was damaged by fire in 1949, it was repaired by 1951. François X. Burque (d. 1923) was the pastor with the longest tenure (1882-1904). As early as 1939, Aimé Giguere, at that time pastor at this parish, had expressed a vision that inspired what is today the Northern Maine Medical Center. On its 125th anniversary in 1995, St. Louis Parish numbered 1,289 households.

FRENCHVILLE

1. **St. Luce's** (the original church, built under Jean Elie Sirois, pastor of St. Basil's in New Brunswick and, dating from 1826, was named St. Emilie's) regarded by some as the mother parish of St. John River Valley, was established for Canadian lumbermen in 1843 under Father Henri Dionne. From about 140 households that year, it grew rapidly during the pastorate (1860-1908) of Charles Sweron (d. 1908) to number more than 2000 parishioners. At least two of its churches were destroyed by fire before the present one was opened in 1908 and renovated in 1993. Many Sisters of Our Lady of the Rosary served its people with the establishment of the Bailey School (1899), a state school, until the last part of the twentieth century. According to the census of 2000, the population in this area had declined by at least twenty percent during the 1990s.

2. **Christian Life Center** is a retreat house located in this section of the St. John River Valley.

St. Luce, Frenchville

Interior, St. Luce, Frenchville

Christian Life Center, Frenchville

St. Elizabeth Ann Seton, Fryeburg

FRYEBURG

The location of the mission of **St. Elizabeth Ann Seton**. Near the headwaters of the Saco River in colonial times there existed a Jesuit mission among the Pequawkets where Nescambiouit (d. 1727), known as the "Prince of the Abenakis,'" resided (he was honored by King Louis XIV at Versailles in 1705). Molly Ockett (174?-1816), also a Catholic Pequawket, resided in the area and was known for helping to heal others.

GARDINER

St. Joseph's was established in 1863 for a town which was perhaps the first one in New England to have a Catholic church on its town common. As early as 1832, this was a favorite stop for Bishop Fenwick, a friend of Martin Esmond, a merchant on Water Street. Here this Catholic family, especially Jean Stuart Esmond (1777-1867), Martin's wife, was instrumental in building the first church in 1858. A second church, dedicated in 1916, during the pastorate (1900-32) of Patrick H. Reardon (d. 1932), replaced the original wooden church for a parish which grew from a few Irish immigrants at its start to 2,434 parishioners in 1974.

St. Joseph, Gardiner

St. Anne, Gorham

St. Gregory, Gray

GORHAM

St. Anne's was established in 1967 under Roland E. Normandeau as its founding pastor (1967-75). Originally a part of St. Mary's in Westbrook, the First Mass here was offered in Gorham's Grange Hall by Rev. William K. McDonough (d. 1982) in 1944. Today the parish has grown to 1200 families covering the surrounding towns of Buxton, Standish and part of Windam. Rev. Lawrence J. Conley is undertaking a historic compaign to expand the present facilities.

St. Gerard/ Mount Carmel, Grand Isle

GRAND ISLE

St. Gerard's was established in 1930 with 150 families. Albert Charette (d. 1960), its first pastor (1930-43), built the school, rectory, and convent for the parish. Before it merged in 1977, some of the parishioners from Our Lady of Mt. Carmel in Lille had engaged in a legal battle with the bishop over preserving their identity in a parish now known as St. Gerard & Mt. Carmel.

GRAY

On Crystal Lake, once the site of a boy's camp (1925-73), a church of rustic style stands as the center of **St. Gregory's**, a parish established in 1967. By 1980, the parish had some 400 families whose breadwinners were working either in Lewiston or in Portland. Within this region, Camp Pesquassawassis for girls was opened at Dry Mills in 1927 and Our Lady of the Lake Camp for underprivileged children on Sabbath Day Lake in 1938.

GREENE

Here, north of Lewiston, was the site of the first monastery (St. Francis) of the Lithuanian Franciscans in the United States. Having fled the Soviet invasion of their country in June of 1940, they purchased for $5,000.00 in 1943 a farm of 100 acres. Here the monastery was dedicated by Msgr. George P. Johnson (d. 1964) on the Feast of the Transfiguration, August 6, 1944. It included **St. Francis**, a chapel on the property which became a mission of Our Lady of the Rosary in Sabattus by 1976.

GREENVILLE

Previously served from Jackman and Old Town, **Holy Family** was established as a parish in 1912 with John A. Driscoll (d. 1952), its first pastor in residence (1912-14). The present church, which opened in 1928 under Henry A. Sloan (d. 1949), as its pastor (1923-33), replaced one which went back to 1894. With its church and rectory located at the southern end of Moosehead Lake in the early 1980s, the parish had some 250 families. Today it is also responsible for St. Joseph's, a mission in Rockwood.

Holy Family, Greenville

GUERETTE

St. Eutrope became a mission of Daigle in 1910 before it was attached to St. Joseph's, a new parish established for Sinclair, in 1936.

HALLOWELL

Although the baptismal records for **Sacred Heart** date back to the early part of the nineteenth century when the future Bishop Cheverus visited the area, the parish was not established until 1889 under Peter E. Bradley as its first pastor (1889-91). The church is more than a hundred years old and was providing for 220 families in 1978, after it had been opened to provide services for immigrants of French, Irish, and Italian descent. Wilfrid J. Bernard (d. 1960) was the pastor here with the longest tenure (1934-60).

Sacred Heart, Hallowell

Dedication of the organ, Sacred Heart Hallowell, June 4, 1979

HAMLIN

Detached from St. Bruno's Parish in Van Buren, **St. Joseph's** was set up as a separate parish in 1920 under Vincent Bardin, who retired to France in 1933, as its first resident pastor (1920-23). The Good Shepherd Sisters opened a public school there in 1944. The first church, which went back to 1887, was destroyed by fire in 1950 and then rebuilt that same year.

St. Joseph, Hamlin

St. Matthew, Hampden

HAMPDEN

The parish, dedicated to **St. Matthew**, was founded in 1968, and the present church, was dedicated in 1971. By its twenty-fifth anniversary in 1993, it had some 550 parishioners.

HEBRON

Christ the King was established here in 1929 under John F. Conoley (d. 1960) to care for the patients and staff of the Western Maine Sanitorium until the institution closed in 1956.

St. Mary of the Visitation, Houlton

HOULTON

St. Mary of the Visitation, which was founded as a parish with about thirty families in 1839, grew to some 600 households by the end of the twentieth century. Though a fire destroyed the old church on January 12, 1958, it was replaced by the present church on Easter Sunday in 1960. Fr. Patrick M. Silke (d. 1953), one of its pastor (1910-33), Msgr. Michael F. Tierney (d. 1966), a later pastor (1943-66), and John B. Madigan (1917-89), one of its parishioners, were among the exceptional people in the parish. When Silke, who founded the academy in 1911 and Madigan Memorial Hospital in 1912, left Houlton to become Pastor of St. Dominic's (1933-53) in Portland, "so many tears were shed by the parishioners," a Mrs. Hogan recalled, "that a boat could be floated down Military Street."

St. Leo the Great, Howland

HOWLAND

Adolphe V. Anciaux (d. 1955) was the first resident pastor (1929-33) of **St. Leo the Great** established in 1929. Although the first church went back to 1897, the current one was dedicated in 1945. In 1955, about twenty-five years after its establishment, the parish had 145 families. A shrine on the parish grounds, dating from 1993, is dedicated to Our Lady of the Eucharist.

INDIAN ISLAND

St. Ann's, located on Indian Island in the Penobscot River, is at the center of the Penobscot Reservation with the oldest Catholic cemetery in New England dating from 1688. The Sisters of Mercy opened a state school for the Indians here in 1878. The grave of Louis F. Sockalexis (1871-1913), famous Penobscot baseball player, is also located in the cemetery in this town. The church, which dates from the time of Bishop Fenwick, was placed on the National Register of Historic Places in 1973 since it is one of the three oldest Catholic churches in New England. Here, on the wall behind the altar, instead of a crucifix, there is an old (perhaps at least 200 years) painting of the Crucifixion by a Native American portraying Christ and Mary with Penobscot features. Although the Penobscot population had declined to about 350 in the 1950s, there are now about 580 in the parish.

Interior, St. Ann's Church, Indian Island

ISLAND FALLS

St. Agnes, established in 1920 with some forty-five families, grew to at least sixty families and 225 parishioners in five years under Clement Frazier (d. 1959) as its first pastor (1920-25). Today the parish also is responsible for St. Paul's, a mission in Patten.

St. Agnes, Island Falls

ISLESFORD

Site of **Our Lady, Star of the Sea**, a mission cared for by Bar Harbor and Northeast Harbor in the past. Although it had no more than a dozen regular families, the Catholic population increases during the summer. Irene Bartlett, whose husband built the chapel, was affectionately known as the "Bishop of Islesford" for caring for it throughout the year.

Our Lady Star of the Sea Chapel, Islesford

JACKMAN

St. Anthony was established in 1892 under Joseph A. Forrest (d. 1940), its first pastor (1892-1940), who remained in office until his death and was responsible for its first church in 1893 and its parochial school in 1912, not to mention the present stone church which dates from 1928. When it celebrated its centennial in 1992, the parish had about 250 families. The parish also embraces Saints Philip and James, a mission at West Forks where a chapel was built in 1921 for Catholics who worked at the plywood mill in Bingham.

JAY

St. Rose of Lima was originally established as a mission with about twenty-five families in 1881 before it was set up as a parish in 1894. Its first church, which dated from the early 1880s, lasted until it was destroyed by fire on April 4, 1948, and the present one, dedicated in 1949, replaced it. The parish also had a school which it opened in 1923.

St. Rose of Lima, Jay

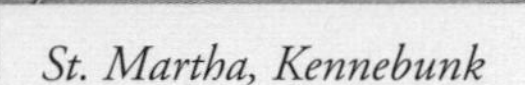

St. Martha, Kennebunk

Interior, St. Martha's Church, Kennebunk

KEEGAN

St. Remy was established as a parish here in 1923 under the Marist Fathers. It was independent until it was merged with St. Bruno's in Van Buren in 1991.

KENNEBUNK

Originally a mission of St. Mary's in Biddeford, the First Mass in this town, where some Irish and Canadian Catholics had settled in the nineteenth century, is believed to have been celebrated in the home of Thomas Casey in 1845. However, the parish dedicated to **St. Martha's**, was not established until 1909 under Charles W. Collins (d. 1920) as its first pastor (1909-13) with twenty-four families and 145 parishioners. He was succeeded by Michael Kenely (d. 1956) whose pastorate (1913-56) was truly exceptional. The present church was dedicated in 1999. The parish once cared for the mission of St. Monica's in Kennebunkport.

St. Raphael, Kittery

KENNEBUNKPORT

Site of **St. Anthony's Monastery**, which was purchased, on September 8, 1947, by the Lithuanian Franciscans who fled their country. Blessed by Bishop Feeney, on August 15, 1948, it was also the site of the short-lived St. Anthony's High School. Situated on historic property which evolved from Sir William Pepperrell in the eighteenth century down to William A. Rogers and William N. Campbell in the twentieth century, it is now a center of pilgrimage and retreat, enhanced by genuine monuments of Lithuanian art in its buildings, grounds, and shrines.

KITTERY

This was not exactly a Catholic area when **St. Raphael's** was established as the first Catholic parish in 1916 with seventy-seven Catholics for the neighboring seacoast towns. James J. Rice (d. 1935) was its founding pastor (1916-35). The present church, which was on the site of a stable, was dedicated in 1934. Most of its parishioners were connected with the shipyard in Kittery and they numbered at least 860 families in 1984.

St. Joseph, Lewiston

LEWISTON

1. **Joseph's** was established as a parish for Irish and Franco-American Catholics in 1857 after the Know-Nothings had damaged and burned down the first Catholic church in 1855. The church was built on land made available to Catholics by Captain Albert H. Kelsey (d. 1901), a Protestant who had employed the Irish in the construction of the canal, much to the displeasure of people like Benjamin E. Bates who had financed the textile mills. Catherine Mangan O'Donnell (1826-1913), a pioneer of the Catholic church in this town, had opened her home as the original center of the Catholic community here before the first church was constructed. The parish church claims to be the location of the city's first parochial school system beginning in 1881. On May 27, 1926, a carillon of twelve bells, each reflecting a phase of Maine's Catholic history, was dedicated. The church was placed on the National Register of Historic Places in 1989.

2. **Saints Peter & Paul**, originally St. Peter's, was the first French church in the city. When the parish was established in 1870, Pierre Hévey became its famous pastor (1871-81). He began with a small wooden building on Lincoln Street and had 5,000 parishioners when the Dominican Fathers (Alexandre Louis Mothon was their First Prior) took it over in 1881. Then, with their own corporation, the Dominicans developed the largest church in the state which was dedicated in 1938. This church, placed on the National Register of Historic Places in 1983 and now operated by the diocese, is the jewel in the crown of the Catholic Church in Maine.

SS Peter and Paul Lewiston

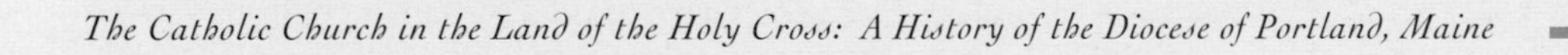

St. Patrick, Lewiston

3. **St. Patrick's**, which was originally established in 1887 as a parish for the Irish who were overflowing in St. Joseph's. Located on the corner of Bates and Walnut Streets, it had 450 families and 2,300 parishioners in 1902 and outstanding pastors like Matthew E. Curran (1933-54) and Paul D. Gleason (1971-91).

4. **St. Mary's**, in "Little Canada," was established as a parish in 1907 on the banks of the Androscoggin River for the French Canadians who came to work in the textile mills and shoe factories. However, after it was closed in 2000, the stone Gothic church was converted into a Franco-American Heritage Center after it was purchased for a dollar from the diocese. Timothy G. O'Connell, who designed a number of buildings in the diocese, including St. David's Church in Madawaska and St. Joseph's Convent in Portland, was the architect of this Norman Gothic structure.

5. **Holy Cross**, located in West Rose Hill, was established for Franco-Americans in 1923. Over the years, the parish had 345 families in 1940, 1,400 in 1952, and 2,000 in 1982 when its school, which opened in 1927, had one of the larger enrollments in the diocese with almost 550 students. The present church was opened in 1948 when Msgr. Felix Martin (d. 1971) was its pastor (1939-70).

6. **Holy Family** was established in 1923 under Msgr. Vital E. Noñorgues (1888-1961) as pastor (1923-61) with 203 families, mainly French Canadians from Saints Peter & Paul. The church, which is distinguished for its spacious sanctuary and a lack of pillars, was dedicated in 1960. Though the parish had grown to 2025 families by 1973, the number declined to about 1900 families by 1998 when it marked its seventy-fifth anniversary.

Holy Cross, Lewiston

7. The Dominican Block was a religious and cultural center on Lincoln Street for the Franco-Americans. Here, in 1883, was also located the parochial school for St. Peter's under the Grey Nuns (*Les Soeurs Grises*) who were replaced by the Daughters of Our Lady of Sion in 1892 before the Dominican Sisters took over in 1904. The site was placed on the National Register of Historic Places in 1980.

8. **St. Mary's Regional Medical Center**, the largest Catholic hospital in Maine, had evolved from the pioneering efforts of the Grey Nuns who obtained the charter in 1888 for the hospital on the property of Mrs. Sara J. Golder's estate which they had purchased. The hospital was placed on the National Register of Historic Places in 1987.

9. **St. Marguerite d'Youville Pavilion**, an undertaking sponsored by St. Mary's Hospital, is one of the largest nursing facilities in Maine. It was named for St. Marguerite d'Youville (1701-71) who founded the Grey Nuns and was the first native of Canada to be canonized a saint.

10. **Maison Marcotte**, an independent living facility for the elderly and the handicapped, dates from 1926 with a gift of $120,000.00 from F. X. Marcotte and is also sponsored by St. Mary's Hospital. It was placed on the National Register of Historic Places in 1985.

11. Before **St. Peter's Cemetery** was established as a Catholic cemetery on July 1, 1876, there were 172 persons interred in it. It was administered by the Dominican Fathers for more than a century (1881-1994). Located on the Switzerland Road, it is the largest Catholic cemetery in the state.

St. Joseph's School, Lewiston

St. Marguerite D'Youville Pavilion, Lewiston

St. Mary's Regional Medical Center, Lewiston

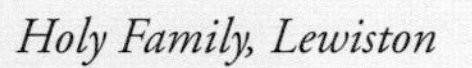

Holy Family, Lewiston

St. Louis, Limestone

LILLE

In 1884, when **Our Lady of Mt. Carmel** was established as a parish, it had been a mission of St. Basil in New Brunswick, the mother church of the region. In 1840, Bishop Fenwick had chosen the base of Mt. Carmel as the site for the mission chapel and, in 1884, Bishop Healy had established the parish under the title of *Notre Dame du Mont-Carmel.* The parish, which had numbered 292 families in 1913, had declined to seventy-five families in 1977 when it merged with St. Gerard in Grand Isle after the town had celebrated its centennial in 1969. The village school, which was situated on church land in 1913, was operated under the direction of the Daughters of Wisdom. The church in Lille was designed by the French architect Theophile Daoust and placed on the National Register of Historic Places in 1973. Since it closed in 1977, the church, also known as "Our Lady of Lille," has been undergoing renovations to preserve it as an historical landmark.

St. Matthew, Limerick

LIMERICK

St. Matthew's was established as a parish in 1921 under Francis J. McLaughlin as its first pastor (1921-35) in a town with a yarn mill. Cornelius A. Burke (d. 1985) was the pastor with the longest tenure (1938-55). Unfortunately, the church was only three years old when fire destroyed it in 1989. However, the Catholic community survived that tragedy and celebrated its seventy-fifth anniversary in 1996.

LIMESTONE

St. Louis was established in 1919 as a parish for Catholics engaged in potato farming and lumbering. It is in a town famous for its military air base in World War II and for its production of clapboards. From 132 families under Paul S. Bührer (d. 1962), its founding pastor, the parish grew to 362 families by end of the pastorate of Theodore A. Bouthot (d. 1971), its longest tenured pastor (1941-53). Its historic cemetery dates from early in the last century and has number of headstones in English and French.

LINCOLN

The first Catholics of this area were Penobscots whom John Bapst had served long before **St. Mary of Lourdes** was established as a parish in 1902. Its church was dedicated in 1903 and, when it celebrated its 100th anniversary in 2002, it had been enlarged and renovated. By this time, from some 420 families in 1977, it had declined to some 250 families. Still St. Mary's was the center of a parish which extended to the missions of St. Ann in Danforth, St. James in Kingman, Guardian Angel in Vanceboro, and Sacred Heart in Winn. Among those who served the parish were the Oblates who have been in charge of it since 1968.

Holy Trinity, Lisbon

Groundbreaking for Holy Trinity Church, Lisbon, March 29, 1999

St. Mary of Lourdes, Lincoln

LISBON FALLS

1. **Saints Cyril & Methodius** was founded with 300 families and 1500 parishioners, on September 8, 1923. However, it dates its anniversary from the dedication of the church, on September 19, 1926. By 1976, the parish had increased to about 150 families and 450 parishioners. Franciscan Conventuals were in charge from 1949 until 1977 when the Vincentian Fathers took over. The church was placed on the National Register of Historic Places in 1977.

2. **Holy Family** was founded as a mission of St. Anne's (known as St. Patrick's) in 1888 and became a parish in 1914. Originally, it was a parish for French, German, Irish, Italian, and Slovak Catholics who worked in the mills.

St. Cyril & Methodius, Lisbon Falls

Holy Family Church, Lisbon Falls

LISBON

St. Anne's, which had been founded as a parish in 1885, numbered 900 parishioners when it celebrated its 100th anniversary in 1985. Leo J. Bourque (d. 1980) was one of its illustrious pastors (1938-65) before the parish was merged with the other churches in Lisbon Falls (Holy Family and Saints Cyril & Methodius) to form the Catholic community of the **Holy Trinity** in 1995.

St. Anne, Lisbon

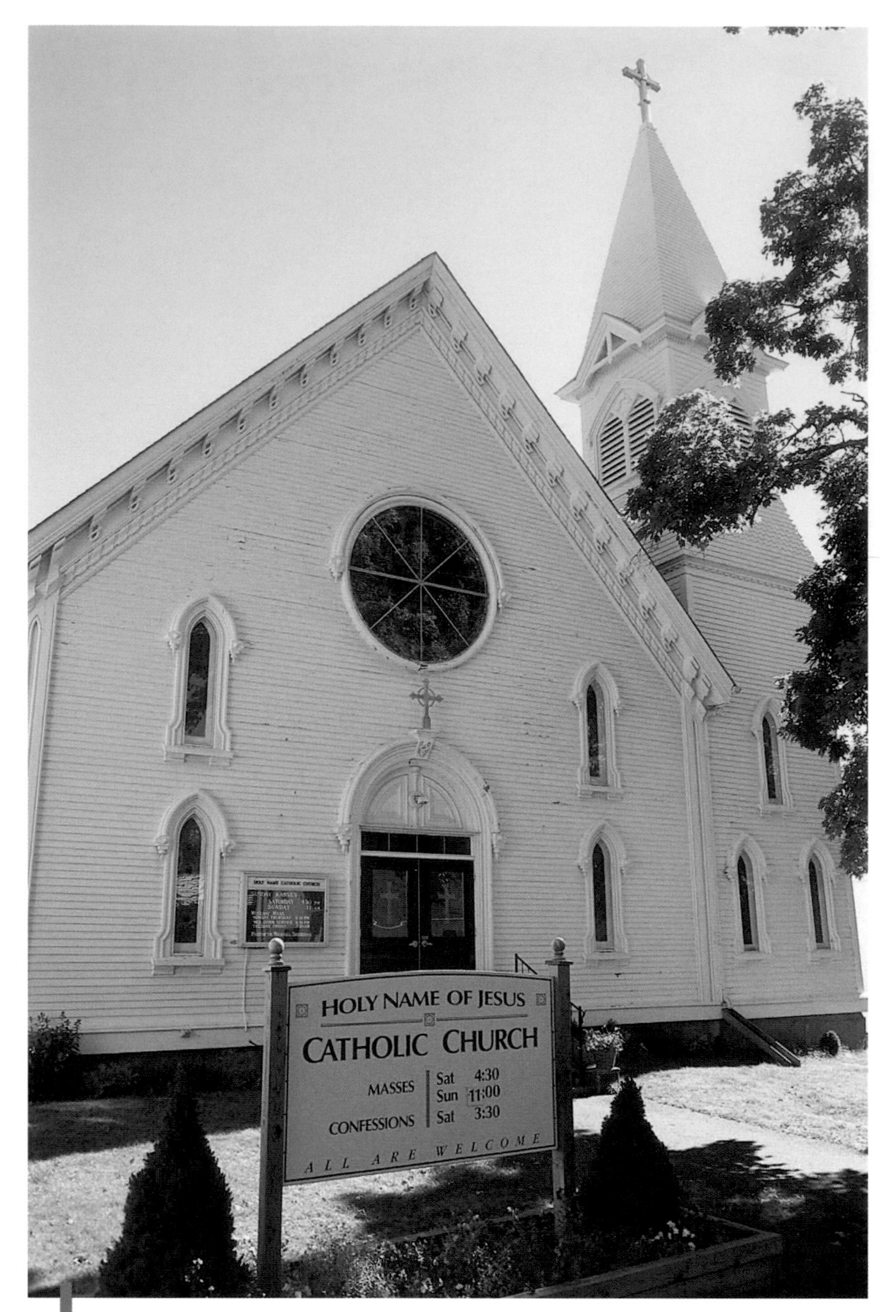

Holy Name of Jesus, Machias

LUBEC

Catholics had been in the area as early as 1815 and grew from about fifty families and 175 members in what was a mission of Machias to about seventy families and 200 parishioners by the end of the nineteenth century. However, it was not until 1913 that **Sacred Heart** was established as a parish for Catholics who were being drawn there by a growing fishing industry. Maurice Griffin (d. 1936) was one of its noteworthy pastors (1918-33). Today its pastor is also responsible for St. Timothy's over the international bridge on Campobello Island in New Brunswick, Canada.

Sacred Heart, Lubec

St. Philip, Lyman

LYMAN

This parish, dedicated to **St. Philip the Apostle**, was established in 1981 with 360 families under Philip A. Tracy (b. 1962), a former Trappist monk, as its first pastor (1981-85). The First Mass of the parish was offered in the United Methodist Church of Goodwin's Mills.

MACHIAS

Holy Name of Jesus, one of the parishes established for Irish immigrants in 1828, long before the Diocese of Portland came into existence, was served by the Jesuits in the period before the American Civil War. Cornelius O'Sullivan (1886-1924), one of its famous pastors, had spent about forty of his fifty years as a priest in the region. Today the parish includes St. Michael's Mission in Cherryfield, one of a number of towns in which the Jesuits had been active as missionaries in the 1850s.

St. Thomas Aquinas, Madawaska

Adoration of the Shepherds, St. David Church, Madawaska

MADAWASKA

1. **St. David's** was established in 1871 and the church has a cross and a plaque dedicated in 1934 which recalls how the early Catholic Acadians crossed over the St. John River from Canada to form the origins of the Catholic community here in 1785 as the descendants of those driven out by the British in 1755. The parish, which was named for the patron saint of Bishop Bacon, grew because of the opportunity for Catholics to work in the mills of the Fraser Paper Company. In 1973, the church was placed on the National Register of Historic Places as was the Acadia Landing Site east of the town on the St. John River off U. S. Route One.

2. **St. Thomas Aquinas** was established in 1929 and next to the church in this parish was a public school (1930-82) named for its patron. From at least 275 families in 1930 the parish grew to more than a thousand by 1982.

3. Local public schools like **Acadia School and Evangeline School** were staffed by the Daughters of Wisdom starting in 1949, and **Madawaska High School** by the Brothers of the Sacred Heart starting in 1952.

Mass, Fr. Râle Days, St. Sebastian's Parish, Madison (Photograph courtesy of Fr. Georges Plante.)

MADISON

St. Sebastian's was established in 1907 to honor the patron saint of Sebastian Râle, pastor (1694-1724) of the region in colonial times. The present church, dedicated in 1974, was constructed under Roland H. Rancourt (d. 1989), one of its pastor (1966-87), to help perpetuate the memory of the Jesuit martyr. "It never rains on Father Râle's Day," has become a saying regarding the annual commemoration on August 23rd of the martyred Jesuit missionary. A plaque was dedicated by the Order of Alhambra in the vestibule of the church in 1999 to commemorate the 275th anniversary of Râle's martyrdom.

Acadian Monument, St. David, Maine

MARS HILL

St. Joseph's celebrated its seventy-fifth as a parish in 2002. It was founded in 1927 under Garrett Burke as pastor (1927-30) for people who came mainly from Canada and from Ireland. The present church was dedicated in 1928.

St. Joseph, Mars Hill

MECHANIC FALLS

Our Lady of Ransom, which came about after the closing of Christ the King in Hebron, was established under Peter J. Flanagan (d. 1994) in 1956 as its founding pastor (1956-62). In the 1980s, this parish doubled in size with 327 registered families under John Dougher (d. 1998) as pastor (1982-91). Today the parish includes St. Mary's, a mission in Oxford.

Our Lady of Ransom, Mechanic Falls

MEXICO

Established in 1926 for Catholics of French Canadian descent, **St. Theresa of the Infant Jesus** had Aimé Giguère (d. 1976) as its first pastor (1926-34). Today its pastor also cares for St. Joseph's, a mission in Dixfield.

St. Theresa of the Infant Jesus Church, Mexico

MILLINOCKET

Although Patrick H. Reardon (d. 1932) offered the First Mass here in Union Hall, in a town known as "the magic city of Maine's wilderness," it was Martin A. Clary (d. 1927) who established **St. Martin of Tours** as a parish in 1899 for Catholics of French, Italian, and English backgrounds as its first pastor (1899-1907). The native parish of Bishop Joseph, it had a school which opened in 1939 and included the primary and secondary levels. The present church, which dates from 1970, when Antonio M. Girardin (d. 1974) was its pastor (1967-72), overlooks Mt. Kathadin in the distance. In 1975, the parish had about a thousand households in an area dominated by the Great Northern Paper Company.

Original St. Martin of Tours, Millinocket

St. Martin of Tours, Millinocket

Nineteenth century interior, St. Patrick's Church, Newcastle

NEWCASTLE

1. The origins of **St. Patrick's** as a parish go back to 1798 with the construction of St. Mary's of the Mills, a small chapel in Damariscotta, not too far away. By 1804, there were about 200 Catholics living within a twenty-mile radius of the old church. The present church is the oldest Catholic one in New England dating from 1808 when it was blessed by Cheverus, later Bishop of Boston (1808-23), whom the parish claims as its first pastor since he started his regular visits there in 1798. The historic church, which has a bell cast by Paul Revere, was placed on the National Register of Historic Places in 1973.

2. **St. Patrick's Cemetery** nearby the church contains the graves of many of the original parishioners, including Edward Kavanagh, first Catholic to serve as Governor of Maine, in addition to his sister, Winifred. More an historic than a large parish, St. Patrick's had about 425 households in 2000.

3. **Kavanagh Mansion** which dates from 1800 was the home of Maine's First Catholic Governor and it was placed on the National Register of Historic Places in 1974.

NORRIDGEWOCK

The archaeological site of the mission, which was one in a defensive perimeter on the rivers of Maine separating New England from New France, was placed on the National Register of Historic Places in 1993. The spring from the nearby waters was regarded by the Native Americans as having healing powers.

NORTHEAST HARBOR

Named for **St. Ignatius Loyola**, founder of the Jesuits, this parish was established in 1929. The monument depicting the landing of the Jesuits on Mt. Desert Island in 1613 was done by Walter Widener, a sculptor, at the request of Captain John J. O'Brien, a summer visitor from Grosse Point Farms, Michigan. The parish embraces the missions of Our Lady Star of the Sea in Islesford and St. Peter's in Manset (named for the patron of Jesuit Pierre Biard, the first priest to visit there).

N

St. Catherine of Siena, Norway

NORTH HAVEN

On August 30, 1918, Bishop Walsh dedicated **Our Lady of Peace Chapel** here (its name is a reflection of the concern for peace during World War I). Originally a mission of Rockland, it was for the Irish and Scotch Catholics who served as boatmen, chauffeurs, cooks, and maids for the wealthy summer residents on the island. A number of its furnishings (altar, organ, and pews) came from the chapel which had existed on Hurricane Island before that Catholic mission was demolished.

St. Margaret's, Old Orchard Beach

NORTH VASSALBORO

St. Bridget's, which was established as a parish in 1911, had its first church in this town as far back as 1874 before fire destroyed it in 1925. The present church dates from 1955 and the chapel at St. Peter's on China Lake was dedicated in 1962 to serve as a summer mission. Peter W. Hamel (d. 1957) was one its illustrious pastors (1941-57).

NORWAY

Although the original church of **St. Catherine of Siena** was built in 1911, the parish was not canonically established until 1914. However, Catholics had grown in that region and had a church in South Paris where the Dominicans from Lewiston offered Mass during 1890s. Philip J. Boivin (d. 1953) was its first pastor (1914-18) and J. Francis Brady (d. 1976) was the pastor with longest tenure (1929-68). The new church dates from 1977, and the parish also includes Our Lady of the Snows, a chapel in Bethel.

OAKLAND

St. Theresa's Parish, once a mission station of North Vassalboro, was established in 1963. The First Mass was celebrated in this town as far back as 1878 by Father Narcisse R. Charland (1848-1923). The parish, which includes St. Helena's, a mission in Belgrade Lakes, had at least 350 families and 1300 parishioners in 1978.

Holy Family Old Town

OQUOSSOC

Our Lady of the Lakes was founded in 1927 under N. J. Boucher (1927-37) as its pastor. Starting with fifty families, it had decreased by eleven in 1955. The parish also includes missions such as St. Luke's in Rangley, St. John's in Stratton, and the Richard H. Bell Memorial Chapel in Sugarloaf U. S. A.

St Mary, Old Town

OLD ORCHARD BEACH

St. Margaret's was established in 1926 with James J. Mullen (d. 1954) as its first pastor (1926-54). John J. Clancy (d. 1991), its fourth pastor (1967-78), was responsible for rebuilding a new chapel at the parish mission of St. Luke's by the sea in Old Orchard in 1969. The parish, which had grown from twenty families in 1926 to about 500 by 1954, celebrated its seventy-fifth year in 2001.

OLD TOWN

1. **St. Joseph's,** which dates from 1848, was established as a parish in 1862 and continued until 1992. The Jesuits, especially Father Bapst, had come here to care for the Irish and the French in the 1850s.

2. **St. Mary's** existed for more than sixty years from 1928 to 1992 as the English-speaking parish before it was merged with St. Joseph's.

3. **Holy Family** was created by merging St. Joseph's and St. Mary's in 1992.

ORONO

1. **St. Mary of the Assumption** was established as a parish in 1888. The town was named for the Penobscot Chief Joseph Orono (d. 1801, age 112) in whose memory a monument, originally intended for the town park, stands on the church property. The stone church, which was the first one dedicated by Louis S. Walsh as bishop in 1906, was built during the pastorate (1899-1926) of James M. Harrington (d. 1926). St. Mary's, which had its first high school graduation in 1920, was regarded as an exception among the Catholic schools in the state with record high enrollments (700 in the mid-1960s) due in part to the air force base at Dow Field near Bangor.

2. **Our Lady of Wisdom** is the Newman Center which was founded in 1946 and was established as the campus parish for the educational system of the University of Maine in 1967. Recently, both parishes have been twinned.

St. Mary, Orono

Our Lady of Wisdom/ The Newman Center, University of Maine, Orono

St. Christopher, Peaks Island

PEAKS ISLAND

1. **St. Christopher's** became the first parish in Casco Bay when it was established in 1923. Samuel M. Donovan (1881-1955), a former Franciscan, was pastor (1928-43) when the Sisters of Notre Dame de Namur opened their convent in 1941. Its pastor also cares for Our Lady Star of the Sea, a mission on Long Island.

2. **Mother of the Good Shepherd Monastery** By the Sea was established in 2000 on Pleasant Avenue with Seamus Kuebler, O. A. S., for monks who wish to follow the rule of St. Augustine. It was the former convent, St. Joseph by-the-Sea, of the Sisters of Notre Dame de Namur.

St. John the Evangelist, Pembroke

PEMBROKE

St. John the Evangelist is a mission of sixty families under the care of St. Joseph's in Eastport. Dating from 1854 when the Jesuits had a store there converted into a church, it is noted for its old pews.

PERRY

1. Although **St. Ann's** had one of eight churches in Maine when Bishop Bacon took over the diocese in 1855, a parish was not established at Pleasant Point until 1907. Meanwhile, a short-lived private school had been opened there by Virgil Barber in 1828 and a public school by the Sisters of Mercy in 1879. While the first church in the township was opened in 1804, the present one dates from 1928. During the 1950s, the Passamaquoddies had numbered about 400 compared to about 650 today. On October 1, 1979, a delegation from the reservation with Joseph E. Mullen (b. 1919), their Jesuit chaplain, led the procession received by Pope John Paul II on Boston Common in the first visit by a pope to New England during a very rainy evening.

2. **The Beatrice Rafferty School** is named for the only Sister of Mercy buried in the tribal cemetery. Known as "Mother of Pleasant Point," Sister Mary Beatrice Rafferty (1877-1955) spent thirty years of her life there.

St. Ann, Perry

First Communion, St. Agnes, Pittsfield

PITTSFIELD

St. Agnes, which was established as a parish in 1927, serves at least a dozen towns. The First Mass was offered in the Monahan Home here in 1893 before the town became a mission in 1894. Beginning with less than forty families, the parish grew to about 200 families in 1965 and was serving about 500 households by 1994 when its new parochial school was already a year in operation under the Sisters of the Presentation of Mary. Its longest tenured pastor (1928-48) was Leo R. Carey (d. 1954).

St. Agnes, Pittsfield

Cathedral of the Immaculate Conception, Portland

Interior, Cathedral of the Immaculate Conception, Portland

PORTLAND

1. **Cathedral of the Immaculate Conception** was established as a parish in 1856. The Gothic church itself, which dominates the skyline, as one rides on the highway which passes through the city, was designed by Patrick C. Keeley. In addition to its stained glass windows, the Cathedral is the site of the crypt with the vaults of the Bishop Bacon, Bishop Walsh, and Thomas Kenny (d. 1857), first priest ordained in the new diocese (August 15, 1855). The sacristy has a bust of St. Pius X which arrived here, on March 12, 1910, for Bishop Walsh from the pope himself. In 1985, the Cathedral was placed on the National Register of Historic Places.

2. **St. Dominic's**, which was established as the city's first parish in 1830, had a church in the Gothic style whose steeple once dominated the city's skyline and whose historic bell was consecrated by Bishop Healy in 1892. While it is the native parish of Bishop Feeney, Josue Maria Young (1808-66), who converted to Catholicism in 1828, was really the first native of the parish to be ordained a Catholic bishop since he was among the original members of its congregation. From 300 parishioners at its founding, the parish grew to at least 3,500 by its centennial only to decline to 1,358 by its 150th. When the parish merged with Sacred Heart in 1997, the parish had 268 households. Following the merger, the church was sold to the city by the diocese for $50,000.00, and it later became the Irish Heritage Center.

Former St. Dominic's Church and School, Portland

3. **Sacred Heart** was established as a parish in 1896 under John O'Dowd (d.1919) as its first pastor (1896-1919) under whom the present Baroque church was completed in 1914 (it was modeled on Notre Dame de la Garde in Marseilles). James A. Carey (1874-1953) was pastor from 1919 to 1950 and Michael P. David (d. 1979) was pastor from 1950 to 1968. Emily Baxter, sister of Governor Baxter and a convert to Catholicism, was a member of the parish and the organist of the church. When it was merged with St. Dominic's in 1997, the parish had about 382 households. It is now known as Sacred Heart / St. Dominic Parish.

Sacred Heart/St. Dominic, Portland

St. Joseph, Portland

4. **St. Joseph's** was established as a parish in 1909 with seventy-five families. It grew to more than 1,500 families by 1977 when the Capuchins assumed responsibility for the church and the school. In the pastorate (1909-45) of Msgr. John W. Houlihan (d. 1945), the church evolved from a chapel on Walton Street to a stone Gothic church on Stevens Avenue in 1931.

5. **St. Peter's** was established as a parish for Italian Catholics in 1911 and the original church, a converted stable, was dedicated just in time for Christmas in 1911. As early as 1903, Bartolomeo Montrucchio was assigned to minister to the Italians in Portland. Of its different pastors (Edmund Ansaloni, Bruce Czapla, Teresio DiMingo, Kieran Monahan, Antonio J. Petillo,

St. Peter, Portland

Roland Petinge, Joseph Romani, and Agnello Santagnello), Msgr. DiMingo (d. 1975), under whom the present church was dedicated in 1929, had the longest tenure (1927-67). Now under the Franciscans, the parish had about 500 families in 2002. The center of the Italian community in Maine, the church is noted for its Chapel of the Saints and its art work on the life of St. Peter.

6. **St. Louis** was established for Polish Catholics in 1915. Founded under John J. Sciskalski, C. M., Peter M. Pojnar (d. 1959) became the pastor with the longest tenure (1918-59). Then, the Conventual Franciscans took over the parish under Valerian Czywil (1959-76) until the end of the century when, in 1999, Irenaeusz Chodakowski, M. I. C., arrived as pastor. From 250 families at its birth, the parish had about 125 households at the end of the twentieth century.

7. **St. Patrick's** was founded in 1922 under Timothy H. Houlihan as its pastor (1922-27) with a church-school combination typical of Bishop Walsh's times. With the flight to the suburbs in the 1950s, a new church building was required and it was dedicated in 1964. Significantly, in this period, the parish grew from 500 families in 1957 to 800 in 1981. The church contains historic stained glass windows, among them perhaps the first in the nation of President John F. Kennedy.

St. Louis, Portland

St. Patrick's School, Portland

St. Pius X, Portland

8. **St. Pius X**, now a parish of about 800 families under the Jesuits, was established in 1962 under Peter J. Flanagan (d. 1994) as its first pastor (1962-84), mostly with families from St. Peter's and from St. Joseph's.

9. **St. Aloysius School**, located on the corner of Congress and Sheridan Streets, was a wooden structure with four classrooms which opened in 1864 as the first parochial school in the Diocese of Portland. It had a hall on the second floor, the Children's Chapel, which was the site for Sunday Mass on Munjoy Hill to care for the overflow from the Cathedral.

10. **The Kavanagh School** was opened in 1877 for the education of girls due to the generosity of Winifred Kavanagh (1805-83). Today a stone tablet with the name of the school can be seen in the parking lot near the Cathedral.

11. **Motherhouse of the Sisters of Mercy of the Americas** was established after the separation of the diocese from New Hampshire for the Sisters of Mercy who came to Portland in 1873. Sister Mary Evangelist Ward (1889-1980), sister of Msgr. Ward and Mother General of the Sisters of Mercy (1949-67) in Portland, was one of their more forceful leaders. While the sisters have been the backbone to many apostolates in the Diocese of Portland, some have also served on Andros Island in the Archdiocese of Nassau, Bahamas.

12. **Cheverus High School** established as the Catholic Institute in 1917 with Clarence H. Coughlin as its first principal (renamed Cheverus Classical High School in 1925 with Samuel M. Donovan as its second principal), it was operated by the priests of the diocese until the Jesuits took it over in 1942 when it was located on Free Street, next to the old Jefferson Theater. In 1952, a new physical plant opened on Ocean Avenue with a new school and later a chapel. A granite memorial established by the Order of Alhambra in 1986 and blessed by Bishop Proulx commemorates the 375th anniversary of the coming of the Jesuits to Maine. On October 12th, 2002, under Father John W. Keegan, the Jesuit who has served the longest as its president, the school marked the eighty-fifth anniversary of its founding, the sixtieth of its Jesuit presence, and the fiftieth of its campus on Ocean Avenue. While

the campus chapel has historic stained glass windows of their history, the Jesuits have a famous painting of the martyrdom of Sebastian Râle by Mother Margaret Mary Nealis, R.S.C.J. (1876-1957) in the Sebastian Râle Chapel at their private residence and the school has a copy of a painting of Bishop Cheverus by the renowned artist Gilbert Stuart (1755-1828).

13. **Monastery of the Precious Blood** was established in 1934 under the Sisters Adorers of the Precious Blood. Jesuit Nicholas J. McNeil (1916-99) served as chaplain here for at least thirty-five years.

14. **Mercy Hospital** replaced in 1943 the old Queen's Hospital which had opened in 1918 during the influenza epidemic.

15. **Catherine McAuley High School** opened in 1969 on Stevens Avenue to replace the Kavanagh School, St. Joseph's Academy, and Cathedral High School, schools previously operated by the Sisters of Mercy.

Cathedral School, Portland

16. **Deering Pavilion**, which opened in the summer of 1973, provides low-income housing for the elderly.

17. The growth of the church in Bishop O'Leary's own career can be seen in the expansion of the Chancery from a handful of people in the **Cathedral Guild Hall** in 1950 when he began his career as an official of the diocese to at least fifty people in 1988 when he dedicated a new wing of the present building (Ocean Avenue) financed by the John P. Dunworth Fund.

Cathedral Chapel, Portland

18. **Maine Historical Society** has the bell and strong box taken from the mission of Sebastian Râle in a raid on Norridgewock during the winter of 1721-22.

19. Memorials on at least two buildings on India Street near the corner of Commercial Street (from Jordan's to the old railroad building) recall the site of the 1690 attack on Fort Royall near Casco Bay by Indians from the Jesuit missions in Canada who had joined the French in the struggle against New England.

20. Before Catholics had their own cemetery, **Western Cemetery** had a section where the Irish buried their dead. This was memorialized by the Ancient Order of Hibernians with a memorial as "The Catholic Ground" towards the end of the twentieth century.

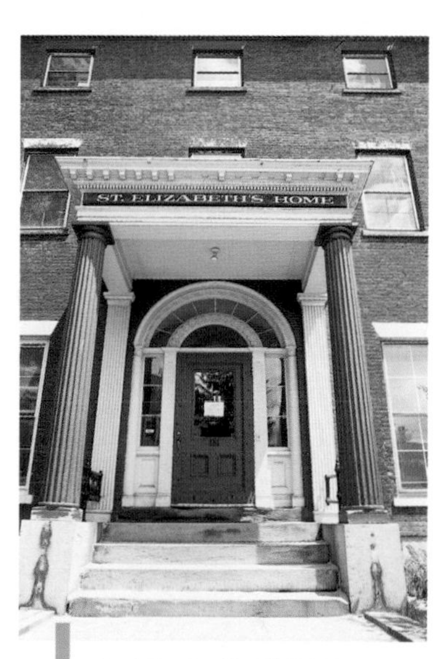

St. Elizabeth's Child Care Center, Catholic Charities Maine, Portland

St. Bernard, Rockland

PRESQUE ISLE

Once a mission of Fort Fairfield, it was founded in 1893 for Canadians from Madawaska under the title of **The Nativity of the Blessed Virgin Mary** before it became known as St. Mary's. Among its pastors have been Daniel J. Feeney (1929-46) and John J. Harris (1946-61).

St. Anne, Princeton

PRINCETON

After the reservation was established as a Catholic community at Peter Dana Point (once described as "the only purely Indian Township in all the New England States") around 1836, the Sisters of Mercy opened a state school in 1879 for the Passamaquoddies whose present **St. Ann's** Church dates from 1929. **St. Theresa's**, once a mission in the Indian Township, was under its jurisdiction. On May 21, 2002, the tribe, which here numbers about 675 today, rejoiced with the return to it of Gordon's Island where many of its ancestors had died of small pox and were buried 150 years previously.

RICHMOND

Established with ten families as a mission of Gardiner in 1889, **St. Ambrose's** was founded as a parish in 1928 under Charles P. Biglin (d. 1962) as its first pastor (1928-35). One of the early Catholics of the area, before the Catholic community was established here, was Samuel Bishop (1770-1837), a lawyer from Dresden, who received the Sacraments of Baptism, Confirmation, and Holy Eucharist from Bishop Cheverus, on August 4, 1816.

ROCKLAND

Established as a parish in 1857, the first church was dedicated in 1858 as St. David's during the pastorate of Andrew Barron (1857-66). That church lasted until a fire destroyed it in 1889 and that year the new church, which replaced it, was named **St. Bernard's**. Cornelius Hanrahan, a friend of Anthony F. Ciampi (1816-93), then a Jesuit missionary in Rockland, helped to finance both churches. James A. Flynn (d. 1939) was the pastor with the longest tenure (1907-39). The present church was dedicated in 1975 for this parish which embraces the Mission of St. James in Thomaston.

RUMFORD

The First Mass in this town took place in 1892, not too long before the establishment of **St. Athanasius** in 1902, for English-speaking Catholics, and of **St. John** in 1905, for French-speaking Catholics. With Joseph A. Laflamme (d. 1957) as the founding pastor of the first (1902-05) and the second (1905-20) of these churches, the Catholic community grew from about 200 families to 700 for St. Athanasius and 900 for St. John. After a lower court, in October

St. Mary (Nativity of the Blessed Virgin Mary), Presque Isle

St. Ambrose, Richmond

of 1919, had convicted Mykolas X. Mockus (d. 1939), a visiting speaker of Lithuanian background, for blasphemy in directly ridiculing the beliefs and practices of Catholics in September of 1919 (by this time there were at least 400 Lithuanian Catholics in the town), the conviction was upheld by a higher court in March of 1921. Edmund S. Muskie (1914-96), the first Roman Catholic elected Governor of Maine, was a native of this town. Although there were 1,600 families when the parishes merged in 1970, that number has declined to about 1000 households. The parish also includes St. Mary's, a mission chapel in Roxbury Pond.

Notre Dame de Lourdes Church, Saco

St. Athanasius/St. John, Rumford

SABATTUS

Our Lady of the Rosary Parish, which includes St. Francis, a mission in Greene, was established in 1975 after the Dominicans, who had cared for the mission here from 1905 to 1975, transferred it to the diocese. The present church was completed in 1916 but the school, which opened there in 1928, was closed in 1986. In 2000, the parish numbered about 500 households.

Our Lady of the Rosary, Sabattus

SACO

1. Although **Holy Trinity** was not established until 1916 under Timothy J. Mahoney (d. 1938) as its founding pastor (1916-38), the First Mass was celebrated here in 1827 by Bishop Fenwick at the home of Dr. Henry B. C. Greene (d. 1848) at what is now 374 Main Street. Its first church, dedicated in 1918, was a transformed theater before the present church was dedicated in 1993 under the Holy Cross Fathers who took over the administration of the parish in 1973 and celebrated its seventy-fifth anniversary in 1991. The rectory was the family home of Charles Eugene Woodman (1852-1924), a convert who became a Paulist Father and achieved fame as an orator and writer. James A. Daly (d. 1987), one of its later pastors (1967-73), began the reforms of Vatican II here.

2. **Notre Dame de Lourdes** was founded in 1929 as a parish under Joseph A. Fredette as its first pastor (1929-33). He was responsible for its famous Lourdes Grotto dating from 1929.

3. Bay View Villa, Guest & Retreat House is a ministry of the Good Shepherd Sisters.

Former Most Holy Trinity Church, Saco

Most Holy Trinity Church, Saco

St. Agatha, St. Agatha

ST. AGATHA

St. Agatha's, a parish established in 1889 has its church located on Long Lake. From a population of about 300 in 1888, the parish grew to some 1500 parishioners by 1955. Investing in themselves, the people founded the St. Agatha Federal Credit Union in 1952. However, like other towns in the St. John Valley, this one experienced a significant decline in population during the 1990s. Today the parish includes St. Michael's, a mission chapel in Madawaska.

STE. CROIX ISLAND

This is the site of the First Mass offered in Maine in a chapel dedicated to the **Holy Cross** in the summer of 1604. Today a national historical monument, which was placed on the National Register of Historic Places in 1966, stands on this island which is at the international boundary of the Ste. Croix River where Catholicism in the Diocese of Portland was born. The Maine State Knights of Columbus, of which there have been at least eighty councils established in the state, erected an historical memorial on September 30, 1971, on Red Beach, indicating that the First Mass was offered on June 26, 1604.

St. Charles Borromeo, St. Francis

St. Paul, Allagash

ST. FRANCIS

Named for **St. Charles Borromeo**, this parish was established for Catholics in the lumber camps in the northern part of Aroostook County in 1894. Although Charles Sweron was important in its early days when it was a mission of Frenchville, the parish was founded under Philippe A. Jovin (d. 1910) as its first resident pastor (1894-99) when there were at least 125 families and 800 parishioners. The present church was dedicated in 1981 when G. Albert Roux (b. 1937) was pastor (1977-85). The parish, which merged with the parish in St. John in 2002, is also responsible for St. Paul's, a mission in Allagash Plantation.

ST. JOHN

A mission of St. Charles Borromeo in St. Francis since 1909, **St. John the Baptist** was established in 1930 under Gerard P. Dugal (d. 1962) as its first pastor (1930-37). Originally, it served a community of sixty farming families between St. Francis and Fort Kent. The town's schools were staffed by the Sisters of the Presentation of Mary starting in 1945. In 2002, the parish merged with St. Charles Borromeo in St. Francis.

SANFORD

1. The parish established here in 1892 was in honor of the martyr, **St. Ignatius of Antioch**. Fathers John J. McGinnis (d. 1924) and Joseph H. Kalen (d. 1947) were two prominent pastors in the parish history. In the pastorate of McGinnis, the parish grew form 100 to 1,000 families. The parish had a parochial school which started in 1903 and eventually evolved into a two-year high school by 1923 and a four-year high school by 1941 (this lasted until 1969 with Brothers of Christian Instruction teaching the boys and the Ursulines teaching the girls). Eighteen acres for the parish cemetery was donated by the Sanford Mills.

2. **Holy Family** was founded in 1923 for French Canadians working in the shoe and textile factories of this town. From 1,000 families at its founding, it had declined to about 750 households by 1972. The present church

Holy Family, Sanford

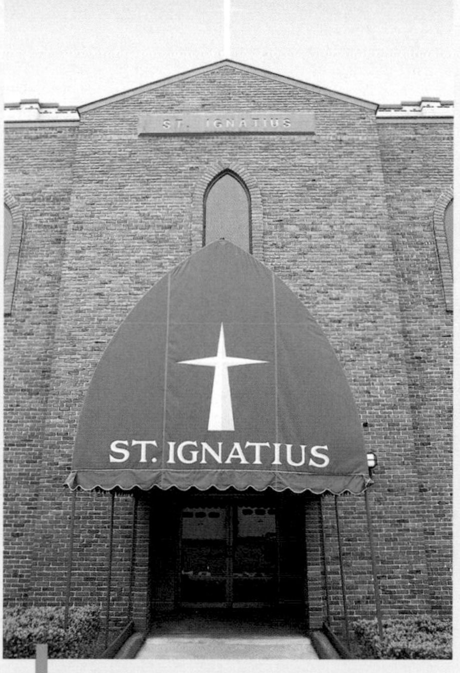

St. Ignatius, Sanford

was opened in 1962 before Roland N. Patenaude (d. 1983) took over as its pastor (1969-83) and became known for his compassion and understanding. This is the home parish of Bishop Amédée Proulx.

SCARBOROUGH

St. Maximilian Kolbe Parish, which includes St. Jude's, a mission in Pine Point, was established in 1988 (835 families were taken from St. John the Evangelist in South Portland) under Stephen F. Concannon as its first pastor (1988-97).

SEAL HARBOR

Here, on August 25, 1912, Bishop Walsh blessed **Holy Family Mission** which remained under the diocese until the early 1980s. The land and building cost $7,000.00 and it was made debt free ("a unique condition of a chapel without debt," Walsh wrote in his diary) through the generosity of a non-Catholic, who gave the bishop a check for $2,650.00. The donor was Mrs. Mark Hanna, the wife of the famous leader of the Republican Party at the turn of the twentieth century.

SINCLAIR

St. Joseph's was established in 1936 with 126 families and celebrated its fiftieth anniversary in 1986. Its first church was dedicated in 1941 and the present one was dedicated in 1952. J. Wilfrid Soucy (d. 2000) was its founding pastor (1936-52).

SKOWHEGAN

Notre Dame de Lourdes was established as a parish for French Canadians in 1881. John Bapst offered the First Mass ever recorded in the area which had been a mission of Waterville. United States Senator Margaret Chase Smith (1897-1995), a native of this town, had Catholic roots here through Carrie Murray (Caroline Morin), her Franco-American mother. While the present church was dedicated in 1952 and has historic windows of the early Capuchin and Jesuit missionaries who ministered in the area, two of its previous churches were destroyed by fire, one in 1881 and the other in 1946. J. Louis Renard (d. 1936) was the pastor with the longest tenure (1916-35).

St. Maximilian Kolbe, Scarborough

St. Joseph, Sinclair

Notre Dame de Lourdes, Skowhegan

Holy Cross Church, South Portland

St. John the Evangelist, South Portland

SOUTH PORTLAND

1. **Holy Cross** , which was established in 1911, was named for the first Holy Cross Church which was built in 1604 on St. Croix Island in what is now the Diocese of Portland. Its founding pastor (1911-14) was John B. Sekenger (d. 1919) who said the First Mass at Union Hall in Ferry Village. Under Frederick H. Karpe (d. 1952) as pastor (1914-52), the school opened (1922) and the parish grew from 145 families and 658 parishioners to 891 families and 2,961 parishioners. The present church, unique for the mural on its tower, was opened in 1963 during the pastorate of John J. Barrett (1952-68). Roland C. Reny (d. 1991), having retired as a full colonel in the Air Force, also served as its pastor (1969-81).

2. **St. John the Evangelist** was set off from Holy Cross as a parish with about 100 families in 1926 under Dennis A. McCabe (d. 1941) as its founding pastor (1926-38). Known as Mt. Calvary, the chapel in Calvary Cemetery served as the parish church until 1940 (the chapel was closed in 1970 and demolished in 1988). John R. Ryan (d. 1974) was the founding pastor (1940-70) of the new church. With the increase in housing projects, the parish grew to about 500 families by 1950 and reached a peak of 1,935 families by 1988 when a number of these were taken for the new parish created for the Catholics in Scarborough. Today Holy Cross and St. John's are both are under the same pastor.

3. **Calvary Cemetery**, which is the site of the graves of Bishops Healy, Feeney, and Proulx, and many priests and Sisters of Mercy associated with the Diocese of Portland, now includes a new section.

4. Diocesan **Sisters of Mercy**, established, on July 22, 1991, as an independent religious group, are separate from the Sisters of Mercy of the Americas and have at least four houses in Maine, including Our Lady of Mercy Convent here on Cottage Road.

St. Joseph, Soldier Pond

SOLDIER POND

St. Joseph's in Wallagrass has recently been transferred to this township. For many years, the parish cared for Sacred Heart, a mission chapel on Soldier Pond which had been converted in its early days from Michaud's General Store.

Interior, St. Michael's Church, South Berwick

SOUTH BERWICK

St. Michael's was established in 1886 and set off from Salmon Falls, New Hampshire, for French-speaking Catholics. With 209 families and 1389 parishioners in 1908, it expanded to 325 families and 1340 parishioners by 1955. Denis J. O'Brien (d. 1924) was one of its pastors (1903-22) and William Lem (d. 1966) was another (1933-52). The Cotters, James (1837-1905) and Rose (1834-1906), were among its benefactors.

SOUTHWEST HARBOR

The location of **Fernald Point** (variously known as *Jesuit Field*, *Jesuit Meadow*, or *Jesuit Point*) near the mouth of Somes Sound was the site of the first Jesuit mission in New England, according to American historians Francis Parkman and Samuel Eliot Morison (Jesuit historians Lucien Campeau and Antonio Dragon hold that it was more on the mainland at Lamoine rather than on Mount Desert Island). This is also the area of *Jesuit Spring* which after the tide of salt water recedes, bubbles up with fresh water.

St. Peter, Manset

St. Thérèse, Stockholm

SPRINGVALE

Notre Dame de Lourdes was established as a parish in 1887 for a community of predominantly French-speaking Catholics who worked in the cotton mills of this town. Growing from forty families in 1890, it had about sixty families in 1992. The Ursulines had been involved in its parish school from 1919 to 1954, before it closed in 1973. The present church, which opened in 1963, shares the same pastors with the two parishes in Sanford. Notre Dame is the home parish of Bishop Michael Coté.

STANDISH

The site of **St. Joseph's College** (once known as the College of Our Lady of Mercy) was established as a college for young women in 1912 (it received its civil charter in 1915) under the Sisters of Mercy, especially Sister Mary Xaveria Toohey (1869-1938). Like many colleges, it has become coeducational, and is the only Catholic college in Maine. Having expanded significantly since its move to this town in 1956, it recently named its new residence hall in memory of Bishop Feeney.

STOCKHOLM

Originally a mission of Caribou for the French Canadians, **St. Thérèse** Parish was founded in 1928 by Eugene Louis Cramillon (d. 1948), the son of a designer of submarines for the Tsar of Russia, as its first pastor (1928-35). This parish, which began with 200 families, did not see its church completed until 1950 due to lack of funds.

STONINGTON

Although the First Mass was said in the new church here in 1931, **St. Mary Star of the Sea**, which was originally served from St. Ignatius Loyola in Northeast Harbor, was founded in 1934 under Cornelius A. Burke as its first pastor (1934-38) with twenty-four families and ninety-six parishioners in 1934. It is responsible for Our Lady of Holy Hope, a mission in Castine.

Notre Dame de Lourdes Church/School, Springvale

St. Mary Star of the Sea, Stonington

St. James, Thomaston

THOMASTON

Although this is the site of **St. James** Mission, it is also the site of Fort St. George which the Penobscots had attacked in 1723 during the French and Indian War when at least one Jesuit (Étienne Lauverjat) was present. This town, instead of St. George with its village of Tenants Harbor, where the Gilchrests, a Baptist family, resided, is usually cited as the native town of Lillius Gilchrest. There, on September 11, 1859, she married William Russell Grace (1832-1904) who, in 1880, became the first Roman Catholic elected as Mayor of New York City. Now, on the site of the old Congregational Church in this town, stands the Catholic mission of St. James.

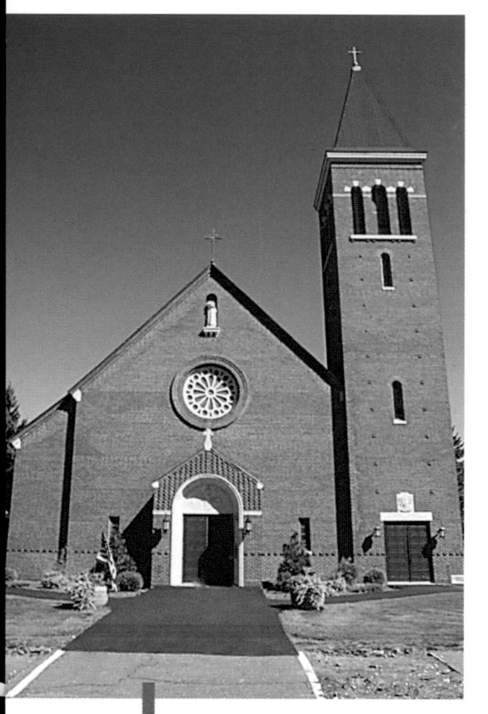

St. Bruno/St. Remi, Van Buren

VAN BUREN

1. **St. Bruno**, known as the mother of the churches in its region, had been a mission of St. Basil in New Brunswick, Canada, before it was established as a parish in 1838 under Antoine Gosselin, a priest from the Diocese of Quebec, as its pastor (1838-52). Then, in 1884, after American Madawaska came under the jurisdiction of the Diocese of Portland in 1870, the Marists took over responsibility for the parish and continued operating the parish attracting at least twenty-five parishioners who became Marist priests. In 1986, the American Legion Post, N. 49, dedicated a monument in the town in memory of at least forty from this parish who lost their lives in defense of the nation (thirty in World War II alone). Since 1991, St. Remi in Keegan has been merged with this parish which also cares for St. Rose Mission Chapel on Long Lake during the summer. The church, now known as St. Bruno/ St. Remi, was renovated and restored in 2002.

2. **St. Mary's College**, founded by the Marists in 1887, was the first Catholic College in Maine. When the college was forced to close in the next century, it served as St. Mary's High School for a few years (1926-32) before the Marists assumed responsibility for the teaching in the town's high school for boys (1942-70).

3. Acadian Village, which was listed on the National Register for Historic Sites in 1977, is located on U. S. One and has a replica of Our Lady of Assumption, an eighteenth century church.

WALLAGRASS

St. Joseph's was founded in 1890 under Father Joseph S. Marcoux (d. 1918) as its first pastor (1890-1918). Starting with 225 families and 1100 parishioners, it had grown to 260 families and 1200 parishioners by 1955.

St. Francis de Sales, Waterville

WATERVILLE

1. **Holy Spirit** was formed as a parish, on July 1, 1996, out of the three city parishes under the Diocese of Portland: St. Francis de Sales, Sacred Heart, and Notre Dame du Perpétuel Secours.

2. Although the First Mass was offered in the home of Jean-Baptiste and Sarah (Dostie) Matthieu in July of 1841 by Father Moise Fortier (d. 1845), it was John Bapst who had built the first church, **St. John's**, there in 1851. It became the center of the first parish in the city, when, on the instructions of Bishop Bacon, Bapst installed Father Jean B. Nicolyn (d. 1869) as its first pastor in 1855. By that time, the French Canadians were increasing the population of the town because of employment at the C. P. Hathaway Company which manufactured shirts until 2002.

3. **St. Francis de Sales** was established in 1874 to replace St. John's with David J. Halde (1834-91) as its first pastor. Narcisse R. Charland was perhaps its most famous pastor (1880-1923). The Ursulines once ran a school for girls here (1888-1969) and the Brothers of Christian Instruction ran one for boys (1928-69) until the Catholic Consolidated School came into existence (1969-74). Though the Catholic cemetery is named for St. Francis de Sales and dates from the late 1890s, there is also the older Halde Cemetery, dating from the first pastor, and used between 1873 and 1959. Since its recent restoration was launched by Father Gerard C. Doyon (d. 1990), it has been dedicated in his memory.

4. **Sacred Heart** was established mainly for 1,200 French and 265 Irish parishioners out of part of St. Francis Parish in 1906 with John E. Kealy (d. 1934) as its founding pastor (1906-18). Its school (1953-69) became part of the short-lived consolidated one in 1969. The parish church, once famous for its four choirs (adult, child, male, and youth) had 3,000 members in 1981.

5. **Notre Dame du Perpétuel Secours** was established in 1910 under Henri Gory (d. 1921), as its founding pastor, to care for the influx of more French Canadians. The first church was destroyed by fire in 1913 and its second church was replaced by the present one which, in 1971 during the pastorate (1966-85) of Albert J. Berard, became the first church in Maine constructed in an octagonal shape. By 1985, the parish was ministering to 3,266 parishioners.

6. **St. Joseph** (Maronite) was established in 1927 for Syrian Catholics under Joseph A. Awad as its founding pastor (1927-33). Today, as a parish of the Maronite Rite of the Catholic Church, it belongs to the Maronite Diocese of Brooklyn. Joseph E. Awad, distant relative of the first pastor, was the pastor (1942-55) who founded the school in 1945 (it lasted until 1972) and had Eugene Cardinal Tisserant, on October 4, 1950, bless the cornerstone of the present church which was entirely renovated in 1988. From at least fifty families at its birth, the parish grew to some 200 families by its golden jubilee.

Sacred Heart, Waterville

7. **Ursulines** became famous as educators in this city after a band of six led by Mother Marie du Sacré Coeur came in 1888 from Three Rivers in Quebec to undertake the education of the children in the Parish of St. Francis de Sales. Having quickly established themselves as leaders in education, they were responsible for Mt. Merici Academy in 1911, not to mention the contributions they have made throughout the diocese in primary and secondary education.

Blessed Sacrament Sisters Convent, Waterville

8. **Servants of the Blessed Sacrament** have been providing for the spiritual enrichment of the Catholics at this center for more than a half century since their arrival in the spring of 1947.

9. **Mt. St. Joseph Holistic Care** Community is sponsored by the Sisters of St. Joseph.

10. **Seton Village**, Inc. is a charitable enterprise of the Diocese of Portland providing housing on Carver street for the elderly.

Seton Village, Waterville

Notre Dame, Waterville

pastor (1916-69), the parish saw the construction of its modernized Gothic stone church by F. W. Cunningham & Son of Portland which drew on the quarries in Milton, New Hampshire. The parish is the mother church of St. Mary's, St. Edmund's, and of the Catholic churches in Gorham, Standish, and Windham. Among those whose remains are buried in the parish cemetery is the famous entertainer Rudy Vallée (1901-86).

2. **St. Mary's** was established under William J. Culbert (d. 1943) as its first pastor (1916-32) by taking the English-speaking Catholics of St. Hyacinth's in 1916. Patrick J. Barrett (d. 2002), an army chaplain from 1944 to 1965, was pastor (1965-84) and opened the present church in 1973. From seventy-five families at its birth, the parish grew to 650 by 1991. Its school, which opened in 1929 under the Franciscan Sisters, came under the Sisters of Mercy in 1945 before it was forced to close in 1969.

WELLS

St. Mary's Church, Wells

St. Mary's was established in 1970 under William J. Kelly (d. 1986), described as "a priestly man and manly priest," as its first pastor (1970-77). Previously, it had been a summer mission of St. Martha's in Kennebunk. The present church was opened in 1980 after the old church had served from 1920 to 1980. This is the town from which Esther Wheelwright (1696-1780), who became the first English-speaking superior of the Ursulines in 1760, was taken captive in 1703 from her father's (John Wheelwright) garrison house (at "Town's End"). The parish, which began with 250 families, numbered 1,200 in 2002 and also includes All Saints Mission in Ogunquit.

St. Hyacinth, Westbrook (St. Hyacinth Historical Society photograph)

WESTBROOK

St. Mary, Westbrook

1. **St. Hyacinth's** was established in 1879 by under Alexis D. DeCelles (d. 1901) who, as pastor (1879-1901), named it for a Polish saint, the patron of his home Diocese of St. Hyacinth in Canada. Originally a mission of the Cathedral, the parish had about 175 families at its birth and grew to number 650 before St. Mary's was created out of it in 1916. Under Msgr. Philippe E. Desjardins (1876-1969) as its

Junior High Youth Ministry, St. Mary's Parish, Westbrook (Larry Guertin Photograph)

St. Edmund, Westbrook

3. **St. Edmund's** was established as a parish in 1975 under Roger D. Labrecque (d. 1978) as its first pastor (1975-78) with at least 1000 parishioners, more than half under the age of twenty.

WHITEFIELD

1. Founded in 1818 by Dennis Ryan (1786-1852), **St. Dennis** had a number of pastors who left a memorable legacy, including Edward Warren Putnam from 1820 to 1863, Anthony Sinischalchi (also known as John DeAnthony) from 1875 to 1887, and Benedict J. Reilly (1915-84), a native of the parish, from 1977 to 1984. With St. Ann's on Indian Island and St. Patrick's in Newcastle, the church is one of the three oldest in the diocese. Next to the present brick church, which was dedicated by Bishop Fenwick in 1833 and placed on the National Register of Historic Places in 1976, is the historic cemetery of the original pioneers of the parish. From about a handful of families at its birth, the parish grew to at least 225 households when it celebrated its 175th in 1993.

2. **Whitefield Academy** was established under the Sisters of Mercy as a convent school for girls in 1871. In 1873, the sisters were employed in the town's Public School No. 13. This was not surprising since Father Ryan had been a selectman of the town in 1826 and headed the school committee for about a decade even though two-thirds of its citizens were non-Catholic.

WILTON

St. Mary was established here as a parish in 1928. A new church was constructed in 1951 but it was closed in 1995 when the parish was merged with St. Joseph's in Farmington.

Interior, St. Dennis, Whitefield

WINDHAM

Formerly a mission of St. Mary's in Westbrook and St. Anne's in Gorham, **Our Lady of Perpetual Help** was established in 1974 under Robert G. Lavoie (b. 1928) as its founding pastor (1974-86). The church was built in 1970 and the parish, which once grew at the rate of 100 families a year, had 980 of them registered by 1980. The parish also embraces St. Raymond, a mission on Crescent Lake in East Raymond.

WINN

Though now a mission of St. Mary's in Lincoln, **Sacred Heart** had been established as a parish in 1881. Centered northeast of Bangor on the Penobscot River, its boundaries then included an area larger than the State of Rhode Island.

Youth Ministry, Our Lady of Perpetual Help Parish, Windham

Our Lady of Perpetual Help, Windham

St. John The Baptist, Winslow

St. Francis Xavier, Winthrop

St. Joseph the Baptist School, Winslow

Sisters of St. Joseph Living Waters Spiritual Center, Winslow

St. Gabriel, Winterport

WINSLOW

St. John the Baptist was established for French Canadians in 1926 under John W. Frawley (d. 1962) as pastor (1926-53). The present church was dedicated in 1957 under Msgr. Emmanuel R. Grondin (d. 1973) as pastor (1953-72). The parish school, which opened under the Ursulines in 1928 and continued under the Sisters of St. Joseph, was still in operation in 2002. From 378 families at its birth, the parish grew to 1400 by 1982. The parish is noteworthy for the number of those who died in the service of the nation (twenty-two in World War II alone) and for the grotto dedicated to Our Lady of Lourdes on the church grounds. The famous scriptural scholar, Eugene A. La Verdiere (b. 1936), a Blessed Sacrament Father, is from this parish.

WINTERPORT

Although **St. Gabriel's** dates from the time of Father John Bapst, S. J., in the 1850s, it was not established as a parish until 1877. The copy of Raphael's "Madonna of the Chair," which hangs over the main altar is a gift of the Jesuit who obtained it in a visit to Rome.

WINTHROP

St. Francis Xavier, a parish established Lakes Region of the central part of the state in 1913, was under Edward B. Henry (d. 1919), its first pastor (1913-16) who left it to serve as a chaplain in the United States Navy in World War I. In 1855, before the French Canadian influx, the town had only two Catholic families, a number which increased to 250 families by 1945. Today the parish extends to the St. Stanislaus Mission in Monmouth and to the St. Leo Mission in Litchfield.

YARMOUTH

Sacred Heart, which was set up as a mission back in 1876, did not become a parish until 1900 with James A. Flynn (d. 1939) as its first pastor (1900-07). The first Catholics into the area were the Irish who came with the building of the Grand Trunk Railroad and the First Mass was said in the home of Patrick Dorin by Father Thomas Kenney, on November 12, 1856. The present stone church, dedicated in 1928, has an historic organ purchased from a church in New York and installed in 1985. Also, the parish cares for the chapel (1964), dedicated to St. Jude (originally, St. Joseph) in the flourishing town of Freeport.

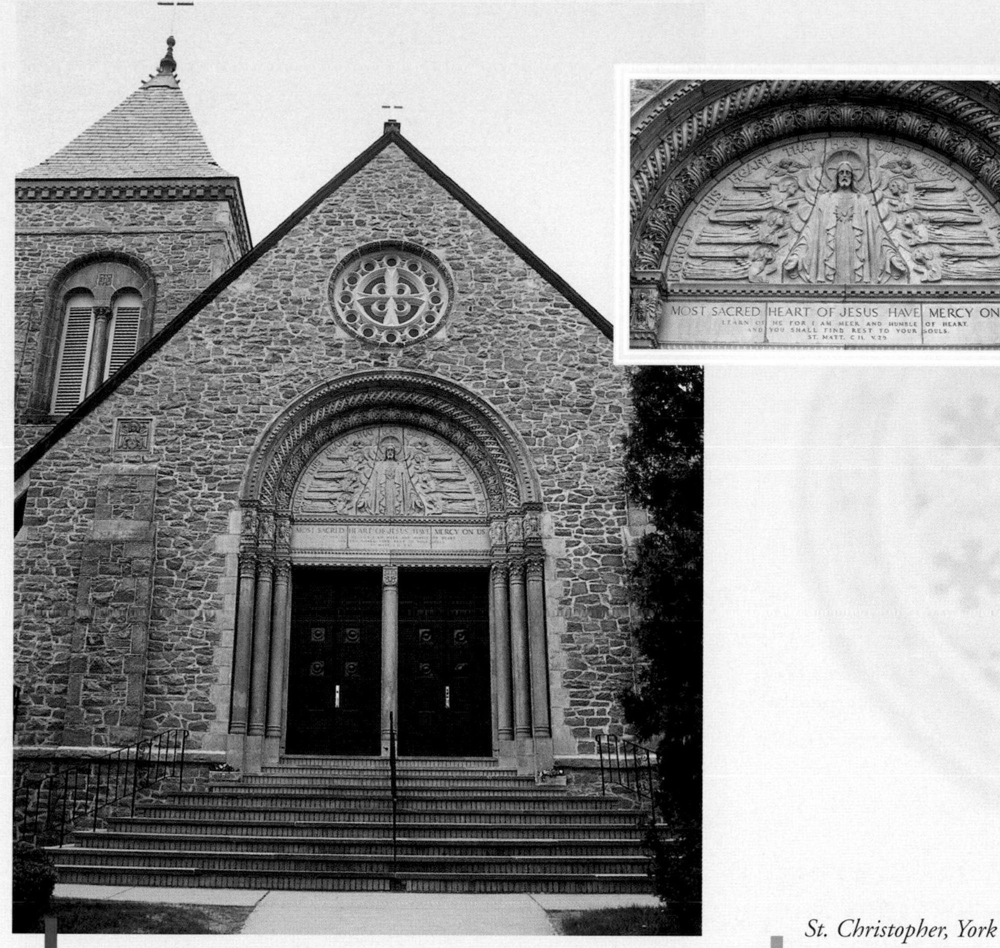

Sacred Heart, Yarmouth

St. Christopher, York

YORK

At York Harbor, **St. Christopher-by the sea** (formerly known as St. Christopher's) was established in 1946. The present church dates from 1970.

YORK BEACH

The summer mission, which began in 1901 with twenty families under the name of **St. Mary, Star of the Sea** in York Beach, was established as a parish in 1961. Then it was separated from Limerick and took care of the workers in the Kittery Navy Yard. However, in 1997, it reverted to the status of a mission. The Cavanaugh Family has been associated with the care of this church for a hundred years.

Star of the Sea, York Beach

PARISHES IN THE DIOCESE OF PORTLAND

A. BEFORE ITS ESTABLISHMENT (1604-1853)

YEAR	PLACE
1604	Holy Cross (Ste. Croix Island)
1613	Saint Sauveur (Mount Desert Island)
1635	Pentagoet (St. Peter's, Castine)
1646	Narantsouak (Assumption, Kennebec River)
1648	Our Lady of Holy Hope (Castine)
1694	Panawamské (St. Ann's, Penobscot River)
1694	Anmesokkanti (Sandy River)
1696	Pégouaki (Saco River)
1698	Naurakamig (Androscoggin River)
1798	St. Mary's (now St. Patrick's, Newcastle)
1804	St. Ann's (Pleasant Point, Perry)
1818	St. Dennis (North Whitefield)
1828	St. Joseph (Eastport)
1828	Holy Name of Jesus (Machias)
1830	St. Dominic's (Portland)
1832	St. Michael's (now St. John's, Bangor)
1834	St. Mary of Assumption (Augusta)
1834	St. Benedict's (Benedicta)
1838	St. Bruno's (Van Buren)
1839	St. Mary of the Visitation (Houlton)
1843	St. Luce's (Frenchville)
1849	Immaculate Conception (now St. Mary's, Bath)

B. AFTER ITS ESTABLISHMENT (1853-2003)

[Under Bishop John Bernard Fitzpatrick (1853-1854)]

Under Bishop David William Bacon (1854-1874)

1855 St. John's (now St. Francis de Sales, Waterville)
1856 Cathedral Immaculate Conception (Portland)
1857 St. David's (now St. Bernard's, Rockland)
1857 St. Joseph's (Lewiston)
1858 St. Mary of the Assumption (Biddeford)
1862 St. Joseph's (Ellsworth)
1862 St. Joseph's (Old Town)
1863 St. Joseph's (Gardiner)
1864 Immaculate Conception (Calais)
1870 St. Peter (now SS Peter & Paul, Lewiston)
1870 St. Joseph's (Biddeford)
1870 St. Louis (Fort Kent)
1871 St. David's (Madawaska)
1872 St. Mary's (Bangor)

Under Bishop James Augustine Healy (1875-1900)

1877 St. Gabriel's (Winterport)
1877 St. John the Baptist (Brunswick)
1879 St. Hyacinth's (Westbrook)
1881 O.L. of the Sacred Heart (now Sacred Heart, Caribou)
1881 Notre Dame de Lourdes (Skowhegan)
1881 Sacred Heart (Winn)
1883 St. Sylvia's (now Holy Redeemer, Bar Harbor)
1885 St. Joseph's (Farmington)
1885 St. Ann's (Lisbon)
1886 St. Michael's (South Berwick)
1887 St. Patrick's (Lewiston)
1887 Notre Dame de Lourdes (Springvale)
1887 St. Augustine's (Augusta)
1888 St. Mary of the Assumption (Orono)
1889 St. Agatha's (St. Agatha)
1889 Sacred Heart (Hallowell)
1889 St. Ambrose's (Richmond)
1890 St. Joseph's (Wallagrass)
1890 St. Vincent de Paul (Bucksport)
1891 Immaculate Heart of Mary (Fairfield)
1891 St. Francis of Assisi (Belfast)
1892 St. Ignatius Martyr (Sanford)
1892 St. Mary's (Eagle Lake)
1892 St. Anthony's (Jackman)
1893 St. Anne's (Dexter)
1893 Nativity of the B.V.M. (now St. Mary's, Presque Isle)
1894 St. Charles Borromeo (St. Francis)
1894 St. Rose of Lima (Jay)
1894 St. Denis (Fort Fairfield)
1896 Holy Rosary (Caribou)
1896 St. Teresa's (Brewer)
1896 Sacred Heart (Portland)
1898 St. Thomas Aquinas (Dover-Foxcroft)
1899 St. Martin of Tours (Millinocket)
1899 St. André's (Biddeford)
1900 Sacred Heart (Yarmouth)

Under Bishop William Henry O'Connell (1901-1906)

1902 St. Mark's (Ashland)
1902 St. Louis (Auburn)
1902 St. Mary of Lourdes (Lincoln)
1902 St. Athanasius (Rumford)
1905 St. John the Baptist (Rumford)
1905 St. James the Greater (Baileyville / Woodland)

Under Bishop Louis Sebastian Walsh (1906-1924)

1906 Holy Family (Daigle)
1906 Sacred Heart (Waterville)
1907 St. Ann's (Pleasant Point, Perry)
1907 St. Sebastian's (Madison)
1907 St. Mary's (Lewiston)
1907 St. James (Kingman)
1909 St. Martha's (Kennebunkport)

1909 St. Joseph's (Portland)
1910 Notre Dame du Perpetuel Secours (Waterville)
1911 Holy Cross (South Portland)
1911 St. Peter's (Portland)
1911 St. Bridget's (North Vassalboro)
1912 St. Peter's (East Millinocket)
1912 Holy Family (Greenville)
1913 St. Francis Xavier (Winthrop)
1913 Sacred Heart (Lubec)
1914 Holy Family (Lisbon Falls)
1914 St. Catherine of Siena (Norway)
1915 St. Louis (Portland)
1916 St. Raphael's (Kittery)
1916 Most Holy Trinity (Saco)
1916 St. Mary's (Westbrook)
1919 St. Louis (Limestone)
1920 St. Agnes (Island Falls)
1920 St. Peter's (Bingham)
1920 St. Joseph's (Hamlin)
1921 St. Matthew's (Limerick)
1922 St. Patrick's (Portland)
1923 Sacred Heart (Auburn)
1923 St. Remy's (Keegan)
1923 Holy Family (Sanford)
1923 St. Christopher's (Peaks Island)
1923 Holy Family (Lewiston)
1923 Holy Cross (Lewiston)
1923 Saints Cyril and Methodius (Lisbon Falls)

Under Bishop John Gregory Murray (1925-1931)

1926 St. Ann's (Indian Island, Old Town)
1926 Mt. Calvary (now St. John's, South Portland)
1926 St. Joseph's (Brewer)
1926 St. Margaret's (Old Orchard Beach)
1926 St. Theresa of the Infant Jesus (Mexico)
1926 St. John the Baptist (Winslow)
1927 Our Lady of Peace (Berwick)
1927 St. Joseph Maronite Church (Waterville)
1927 St. Agnes (Pittsfield)
1927 St. Joseph's (Mars Hill)
1927 Our Lady of the Lakes (Oquossoc)
1928 St. Mary's (Old Town)
1928 Our Lady Queen of Peace (Boothbay Harbor)
1928 St. Mary's (Wilton)
1928 St. Theresa's (Stockholm)
1929 St. Francis Xavier (Brownville Junction)
1929 Christ the King (Hebron)
1929 St. Thomas Aquinas (Madawaska)
1929 St. Ann's (Peter Dana Point, Princeton)
1929 St. Ignatius (Northeast Harbor)
1929 Notre Dame de Lourdes (Saco)
1929 St. Leo the Great (Howland)
1930 St. Charles Borromeo (Brunswick)
1930 St. Gerard's (Grand Isle)
1930 St. John the Baptist (St. John)

Under Bishop Joseph Edward McCarthy (1932-1955)

1933 St. Ann's (Danforth)
1934 St. Ann's (Bradley)
1934 Star of the Sea (Stonington)
1936 St. Joseph's (Sinclair)
1946 St. Christopher's (York Harbor)

Under Bishop Daniel Joseph Feeney (1955-1969)

1961 St. Mary, Star of the Sea (York Beach)
1962 Our Lady of Ransom (Mechanic Falls)
1962 St. Pius X (Portland)
1963 St. Theresa's (Oakland)
1967 Our Lady of Good Hope (Camden)
1967 Our Lady of Wisdom (Orono)
1967 St. Ann's (Gorham)
1967 St. Gregory's (Gray)
1968 Holy Martyrs of North America (Falmouth)
1968 St. Andrew's (Augusta)
1968 St. Bartholomew's (Cape Elizabeth)
1968 St. Matthew's (Hampden)
1968 St. Philip's (Auburn)

Under Bishop Peter Leo Gerety (1969-1974)

1970 St. Mary's (Wells)
1970 Saints Athanasius & John (Rumford)
1971 St. Joseph's (Bridgton)
1974 Our Lady of Perpetual Help (Windham)

Under Bishop Edward Cornelius O'Leary (1974-1988)

1975 Our Lady of the Rosary (Sabattus)
1975 St. Edmund's (Westbrook)
1981 St. Philip (Lyman)
1988 St. Maximilian Kolbe (Scarborough)

Under Bishop Joseph John Gerry (1988-2003)

1991 St. Bruno (Van Buren) & St. Remy (Keegan)
1992 Holy Family (Old Town)
1995 Holy Trinity (Lisbon Falls)
1996 Holy Spirit (Waterville)
1997 Sacred Heart & St. Dominic (Portland)
2002 St. Charles (St. Francis) & St. John (St. John)

SCHOOLS IN THE DIOCESE OF PORTLAND

A. BEFORE ITS ESTABLISHMENT (1604-1853)

YEAR	PLACE
1694	Narantsouak (Mission, Kennebec River)
1696	Anmesokanti (Mission, Androscoggin River)
1696	Pégouaki (Mission, Saco River)
1698	Naurakamig (Mission, Androscoggin River)
1804	St. Ann's (Pleasant Point, Perry)
1828	St. Ann's (Indian Island, Old Town)

B. AFTER ITS ESTABLISHMENT (1853-2003)

[Under Bishop John Bernard Fitzpatrick (1853-1854)]

1854 St. Joseph's (Ellsworth)

Under Bishop David William Bacon (1854-1874)

1864 St. Aloysius (Portland)
1865 St. Dominic's (Portland)
1865 Notre Dame Academy (Portland)
1865 St. John's (Bangor)
1871 Academy at St. Dennis (North Whitefield)
1873 St. Elizabeth's (Portland)
1873 Public School No. 13 (North Whitefield)

Under Bishop James Augustine Healy (1875-1900)

1877 Kavanagh School (Portland)
1878 Notre Dame de Lourdes (Lewiston)
1878 Indian School (Indian Island, Old Town)
1879 Indian School (Pleasant Point, Perry)
1879 Indian School (Peter Dana Point, Princeton)
1881 St. Joseph's (Lewiston)
1881 St. Joseph's Academy (Portland)
1882 St. Joseph's (Biddeford)
1883 Dominican Block (Lewiston)
1884 St. Patrick's (Lewiston)
1885 Immaculate Conception (Calais)
1885 St. Joseph's (Old Town)
1887 St. Paul's (Lewiston)
1887 St. Mary's College (Van Buren)
1888 St. Francis de Sales (Waterville)
1891 Sacred Heart (Van Buren)
1892 St. Louis (Auburn)
1892 St. Augustine's (Augusta)
1892 St. Mary's (Biddeford)
1893 Sacred Heart (Portland)
1893 Healy Asylum (Lewiston)
1894 St. John the Baptist (Brunswick)
1894 St. Hyacinth's (Westbrook)
1896 St. Mary's (Bangor)
1898 St. Joseph's (Wallagrass)
1899 The Bailey School (Frenchville)

Under Bishop William Henry O'Connell (1901-1906)

1901 St. André's (Biddeford)
1903 St. Ignatius (Sanford)
1904 Notre Dame de la Sagesse (St. Agatha)
1905 Our Lady of Mount Carmel (Lille)
1906 St. Louis (Fort Kent)
1906 St. Remy (Keegan)
1906 Sacred Heart Convent (Jackman)

Under Bishop Louis Sebastian Walsh (1906-1924)

1907 Holy Innocents' Home (Portland)
1909 Cathedral High (Portland)
1909 Our Lady of Mercy (Bath)
1909 The Catholic Institute (Portland)
1909 St. Michael (South Berwick)
1911 St. Mary's Academy (Houlton)
1911 St. Michael's Home (Bangor)
1911 Immaculate Heart of Mary (Fairfield)
1911 Mount Merici (Waterville)
1912 St. Joseph's College (Portland, now Standish)
1912 St. Anthony's (Jackman)
1913 St. Edward's (Bar Harbor)
1913 Notre Dame de Lourdes (Skowhegan)
1914 St. Mary's (Augusta)
1914 St. John the Baptist (Rumford)
1915 St. Joseph's (Portland)
1916 Holy Family (Daigle)
1916 St. Mary's Girls High School (Bangor)
1916 St. Mary's (Eagle Lake)
1916 St. Mary's (Lewiston)
1916 St. Mary's Catholic High School (Orono)
1917 Catholic Institute High School (Portland)

1919 Notre Dame (Springvale)
1919 King's Academy (Portland)
1920 St. Louis Home (Scarborough)
1920 The Champlain School (Van Buren)
1920 Notre Dame (Waterville)
1922 St. Benedict's High School (Benedicta)
1922 Holy Cross (South Portland)
1922 St. Teresa's (Brewer)
1923 St. Rose of Lima (Jay)
1923 St. Patrick's (Portland)
1923 Holy Family (Sanford)
1923 St. Ignatius High School (Sanford)

Under Bishop John Gregory Murray (1925-1931)

1926 Holy Family (Lewiston)
1926 St. Mary's High School (Van Buren)
1926 St. Theresa's (Mexico)
1926 Cheverus High School (Portland)
1927 Holy Cross School (Lewiston)
1928 St. Joseph's Orphanage (Lewiston)
1928 John Bapst High School (Bangor)
1928 St. Francis Boys Jr. High (Waterville)
1928 St. John the Baptist (Winslow)
1928 Ave Maria Academy (Sabattus)
1929 St. Mary's (Westbrook)
1929 St. Louis High School (Biddeford)
1929 Holy Rosary (Caribou)
1929 Notre Dame de Lourdes (Saco)
1929 St. Athanasius (Rumford)
1930 St. Thomas Aquinas (Madawaska)
1930 The Keegan School (Van Buren)
1931 Notre Dame Institute (Alfred)
1931 Stella Maris Academy (Biddeford)
1931 St. Bernadette School (Lisbon)

Under Bishop Joseph Edward McCarthy (1932-1955)

1933 Saint-Gerard (Grand Isle)
1936 St. Joseph Academy (South Berwick)
1937 St. André Girls High School (Biddeford)
1938 The Lincoln Public (Grand Isle)
1939 Collège Séraphique, St. Francis (Biddeford Pool)
1939 St. Martin of Tours (Millinocket)
1940 Sacred Heart Academy (Jackman)
1941 Oblate Preparatory Seminary (Bucksport)
1941 St. Dominic High for Boys (Lewiston)
1944 St. Mary's Public School (Caswell Plantation)
1944 Oblate Junior College (Bar Harbor)
1944 The Hill School (Connor Plantation)
1944 St. Joseph's Public School (Hamlin)
1945 The Dewey School (Frenchville)
1945 St. Joseph's (Waterville)
1945 Sacred Heart Juniorate (Winthrop)
1946 St. Dominic High for Girls (Lewiston)
1946 Sacred Heart (North Caribou)
1947 St. Joseph's (Farmington)
1947 St. Mary's (Old Town)
1947 The Harding Public School (St. John Plantation)
1947 The Roosevelt Public School (St. John Plantation)
1948 Marie Joseph Academy (Biddeford Pool)
1948 St. Anthony High School (Kennebunkport)
1948 The Montfort School (St. Agatha)
1949 St. Matthew's (Limerick)
1949 The Acadia School (Madawaska)
1949 The Evangeline School (Madawaska)
1949 Oblate Seminary (Bar Harbor)
1950 La Mennais College (Alfred)
1950 The Market Street School (Fort Kent)
1952 Sacred Heart (Auburn)
1952 Madawaska Public High School (Madawaska)
1953 St. Francis College (Biddeford Pool)
1953 Sacred Heart (Waterville)

Under Bishop Daniel Joseph Feeney (1955-1969)

[No Schools]

Under Bishop Peter Leo Gerety (1969-1974)

1969 St. Dominic Regional High School (Lewiston)
1969 Catholic Consolidated School (Waterville)
1969 Catherine McAuley High School (Portland)
1970 St. Athanasius & St. John (Rumford)
1972 St. Thomas Consolidated School (Sanford)

Under Bishop Edward Cornelius O'Leary (1974-1988)

[No Schools]

Under Bishop Joseph John Gerry (1988-2003)

1992 St. James (Biddeford)
1993 St. Agnes (Pittsfield)
2000 All Saints School (Bangor)
2001 (New) St. Dominic Regional H. S. (Auburn)

The Diocese of Portland is grateful to the following organizations, support from which helped make this publication possible.

COMMUNITY COUNSELLING SERVICE
461 Fifth Avenue
New York NY 10017
888-553-9693 www.ccsfundraising.com

Community Counselling Service (CCS) is proud to have been a part of the rich tradition of the Church in Maine. We are please to have served Holy Cross Parish, South Portland; St. Bartholomew Parish, Cape Elizabeth; St. Joseph Parish, Portland; and St. Anne Parish, Gorham, in their successful fund-raising efforts. CCS is the most widely recommended fund-raising firm to Catholic institutions worldwide. For more than 55 years, CCS has designed successful campaigns and feasibility/planning studies for arch/dioceses, parishes, secondary schools, colleges and universities, healthcare institutions, and religious communities.

MARSH, INC.
2 Portland Square
Portland M 04101
207-774-5911 - www.marsh.com

Marsh Inc. is the world's leading risk and insurance services firm. Our mission is to create and deliver risk solutions and services that make our clients more successful. Since our formation in 1871, we have grown into an enterprise with 410 owned-and-operated offices and 38,000 colleagues, who serve clients in more than 100 countries. We are pleased to provide the Roman Catholic Diocese of Portland with risk management, insurance-brokering and program-management services, as well as reinsurance-brokering, risk and financial modeling and associated advisory services.

MERCY HOSPITAL
144 State Street
Portland ME 04101
207-879-3000 - www.mercyme.com

Mercy Hospital is a radiant example of the many commitments of the Sisters of Mercy, who have served the people of Maine since 1865. In 1918 the Diocese of Portland opened Queens Hospital, with 25 beds and four Sisters of Mercy as staff. When a new 150-bed hospital opened in 1943, sponsorship was transferred to the Sisters of Mercy, and as Mercy Hospital it carried on the healing work of Christ for the people of the Diocese of Portland. A member of Catholic Health East, Mercy as "the heart of healing" provides clinically excellent, compassionate healthcare for all, with special concern for the poor and disadvantaged. Currently licensed for 230 beds, Mercy Hospital also offers many other programs, including treatment for Eating Disorders and for Substance Abuse, and a school for radiologic technicians.

ROBINSON, KRIGER & MCCALLUM
Attorneys at Law
12 Portland Pier
P.O. Box 568
Portland ME 04112-0568
207-772-6565 - www.rkmlegal.com

Robinson, Kriger & McCallum (RK&M) is a professional team of attorneys, paralegals and staff providing legal services to businesses, insurers and individuals in the areas of litigation and workers' compensation law, business and corporate law, general practice, estate planning, family law, (environmental, land use) administrative law, municipal law, and appellate practice. We are proud to provide legal counsel to the Roman Catholic Diocese of Portland.

It is our privilege to lend support for this magnificent work in recognition of those men and women whose sacrifices and dedication have contributed to the success of the Diocese of Portland.

ST. JOSEPH COLLEGE
278 White's Bridge Road
Standish ME 04084-5263
207-892-6766 - www.sjcme.edu

St. Joseph's College is a Roman Catholic liberal arts college for men and women of all faiths, offering academic excellence in a magnificent yet friendly residential campus setting on the shore of Sebago Lake — "330 acres of possibilities." Founded in 1912 by the Portland Regional Community of the Sisters of Mercy, St. Joseph's College offers students a sense of belonging and personal attention in value-centered environment rooted in the Catholic liberal arts tradition. In addition to residential undergraduate programs, St. Joseph's is known nationally and internationally for its Distance Education Programs. In a special service to the Church in Maine, the College coordinates specialized training for lay people who desire to dedicate their gifts of time and talent to Church ministry.

SISTERS OF CHARITY HEALTH SYSTEM
Campus Avenue
P.O. Box 7291
Lewiston ME 04243-7291
207-777-8100 - www.stmarysmaine.com

The Sisters of Charity Health System, a member of the Covenant Health Systems, provides comprehensive medical and social services to Androscoggin County and beyond, including: St. Mary's Regional Medical Center; St. Marguerite d'Youville Pavilion, Maine's largest nursing home; Community Clinical Services, providing primary care and specialized medical services; Maison Marcotte, an independent living center for the elderly and disabled; WorkMed Occupational Health Services, providing worksite services to businesses; Good Shepherd Food Pantry; the Neighborhood Housing Initiative, creating affordable housing in downtown Lewiston; the Haiti Mission, which sends medical teams and supplies to aid the poor and medically underserved; and the Bates Street Family Health Center, which brings needed medical services to the heart of downtown Lewiston.

THE SOCIETY OF JESUS OF NEW ENGLAND
85 School Street
Watertown, MA 02472
www.nenjesuits.org

Ever since the first recorded Mass in Maine was offered at the mouth of the Kennebec River in 1611, the Jesuits have been a part of the history of the Diocese of Portland. They founded and cared for the missions on the rivers of Maine in colonial times. They were active in the nineteenth century in forwarding the frontiers of the Catholic faith in the state under the leadership of Rev. John Bapst S.J. Their legacy is evident today in Cheverus High School, a distinguished private co-educational college preparatory school, and in their service to parishes such as Sacred Heart/ St. Dominic, Portland, St. Joseph, Gardiner, and St. Pius X, Portland.